Downtown 4

English for Work and Life

EDWARD J. MCBRIDE

THOMSON

HEINLE

Australia • Canada • Mexico • Singapore • Spain • United Kingdom • United States

THOMSON

HEINLE

Downtown 4
English for Work and Life
Edward J. McBride

Publisher, Academic ESL: James W. Brown
Executive Editor, Dictionaries & Adult ESL: Sherrise Roehr
Director of Content Development: Anita Raducanu
Director of Product Marketing: Amy Mabley
Senior Field Marketing Manager: Donna Lee Kennedy
Product Marketing Manager: Laura Needham
Editorial Assistant: Katherine Reilly
Senior Production Editor: Maryellen E. Killeen

Development Editor: Kasia McNabb
Development Editor: Amy Lawler
Project Manager: Tünde Dewey
Senior Print Buyer: Mary Beth Hennebury
Photo Researcher: Christina Micek
Indexer: Alexandra Nickerson
Proofreader: Maria Hetu
Design and Composition: Jan Fisher/Publication Services
Cover Design: Lori Stuart
Cover Art: Jean-François Allaux
Interior Art: Jean-François Allaux, Mona Mark, Scott MacNeill
Printer: Courier Corporation/Kendallville

Printed in the United States of America
1 2 3 4 5 6 7 8 9 10   09 08 07 06

For more information contact Thomson Heinle, 25 Thomson Place, Boston, MA 02210 USA, or you can visit our Internet site at elt.thomson.com

For permission to use material from this text or product, submit a request online at http://www.thomsonrights.com

Any additional questions about permissions can be submitted by email to thomsonrights@thomson.com

ISBN 10: 0-8384-4381-8
ISBN 13: 978-0-8384-4381-1

ISBN 10 ISE: 1-4130-1544-1
ISBN 13 ISE: 978-1-4130-1544-7

Library of Congress Cataloging-in-Publication Data
McBride, Edward J., 1950–
  Downtown : English for work and life / Edward J. McBride.
    p. cm.
  "Book 4."
  ISBN: 0-8384-4381-8 (alk. paper)
   1. English language--Textbooks for foreign speakers. 2. English language--Business English--Problems, exercises, etc. 3. Life skills--Problems, exercises, etc. I. Title.

PE1128.M225 2004
428.2'4'02465--dc22   2004047869

Dedication

To all the wonderful students who have given me, over the years, at least as much as I have given them.

Acknowledgments

The author and publisher would like the thank the following reviewers for the valuable input:

Elizabeth Aderman
New York City Board of Education
New York, NY

Jolie Bechet
Fairfax Community Adult School
Los Angeles, CA

Cheryl Benz
Georgia Perimeter College
Clarkston, GA

Chan Bostwick
Los Angeles Unified School District
Los Angeles, CA

Patricia Brenner
University of Washington
Seattle, WA

Clif de Córdoba
Roosevelt Community Adult School
Los Angeles, CA

Marti Estrin
Santa Rosa Junior College
Santa Rosa, CA

Judith Finkelstein
Reseda Community Adult School
Reseda, CA

Lawrence Fish
Shorefront YM-YWHA
   English Language Program
Brooklyn, NY

Giang Hoang
Evans Community Adult School
Los Angeles, CA

Arther Hui
Mount San Antonio College
Walnut, CA

Renee Klosz
Lindsey Hopkins Technical
   Education Center
Miami, FL

Carol Lowther
Palomar College
San Marcos, CA

Barbara Oles
Literacy Volunteers of
   Greater Hartford
Hartford, CT

Pamela Rogers
Phoenix College
Phoenix, AZ

Eric Rosenbaum
BEGIN Managed Programs
New York, NY

Stan Yarbro
La Alianza Hispana
Roxbury, MA

Contents

Contents

Contents

Contents

Contents

Contents

Contents

Contents

Contents

EFF	CASAS	LAUSD Intermediate High	Florida LCP-D	Texas LCP-D
Many EFF skills are practiced in this chapter, with a particular focus on: • Reading with understanding • Speaking so others can understand • Cooperating with others • Making decisions • Taking responsibility for learning • Learning through research • Using information and communications technology	• **Lesson 1:** 4.4.3, 4.5.1, 4.6.1, 4.6.2, 4.6.3, 4.6.5, 4.7.4, 4.8.1, 4.8.3, 4.9.1, 7.2.1, 7.4.2 • **Lesson 2:** 0.1.2, 0.1.6, 4.4.3, 4.6.1, 4.7.4, 4.8.1, 4.8.3, 4.8.4, 7.2.1 • **Lesson 3:** 1.1.3, 4.2.4, 4.4.3, 4.4.4, 4.4.8, 4.5.6, 4.6.2, 4.6.3, 4.7.4, 4.8.1, 4.8.6, 6.7.2, 6.7.4, 7.2.1, 7.2.4, 7.3.1, 7.3.2, 7.5.1	**Competencies:** 4, 13, 15, 38a, 38b, 38c, 39a, 39b, 39c, 40c, 41, 43 **Grammar:** 8a, 19b, 19c, 25, 1, 20	• **Lesson 1:** 53.01, 55.01, 56.01, 56.02, 57.01, 59.01, 66.01, 66.02, 66.06, 67.02 • **Lesson 2:** 53.01, 55.01, 56.01, 56.02, 57.01, 59.01, 66.01, 66.02, 67.02, 67.06 • **Lesson 3:** 53.01, 54.02, 55.01, 56.01, 56.02, 57.01, 66.02, 66.06, 67.02, 67.06, 68.03	• **Lesson 1:** 53.01, 55.01, 56.01, 56.02, 57.01, 57.02, 59.01, 62.02, 66.01, 66.02, 66.03, 66.06, 66.07, 66.08, 67.02 • **Lesson 2:** 53.01, 55.01, 56.01, 56.02, 57.01, 59.01, 60.01, 66.01, 66.02, 66.07, 66.08, 66.10, 66.15, 67.02 • **Lesson 3:** 53.01, 53.02, 53.03, 53.04, 54.02, 55.01, 56.01, 56.02, 57.01, 66.02, 66.03, 66.06, 66.07, 66.08, 66.09, 66.10, 66.15, 66.16, 66.18, 67.02, 68.03
Many EFF skills are practiced in this chapter, with a particular focus on: • Reading with understanding • Guiding others • Taking responsibility for learning • Learning through research • Using math to solve problems	• **Lesson 1:** 0.1.2, 0.1.3, 1.9.1, 2.2.2, 5.1.6, 5.3.1, 5.3.3, 5.3.5, 5.3.7, 5.6.1 • **Lesson 2:** 0.1.2, 0.1.3, 1.9.2, 4.2.1, 4.4.3, 4.6.5, 4.7.4, 4.8.1, 4.8.2, 4.8.3, 5.4.1, 5.4.3, 5.4.4, 5.6.3, 6.1.1, 6.1.2 • **Lesson 3:** 4.8.1, 5.2.1, 5.2.2, 5.3.6, 7.2.1, 7.2.3, 7.4.2, 7.4.3, 7.4.4	**Competencies:** 3, 25a, 25b, 25c, 25d, 44 • Citizenship: **Grammar:** 24, 18,	• **Lesson 1:** 56.01, 56.02, 56.03, 60.04, 60.06, 66.01, 66.02, 66.06, 67.02, 67.06 • **Lesson 2:** 56.01, 60.04, 67.02, 68.03 • **Lesson 3:** 55.01, 56.01, 63.02, 63.04, 66.01, 66.02, 66.06, 67.01, 67.06, 68.03	• **Lesson 1:** 56.01, 56.02, 56.03, 60.04, 60.06, 62.05, 66.01, 66.02, 66.04, 66.06, 66.07, 66.08, 66.09, 66.15, 67.02 • **Lesson 2:** 52.06, 56.01, 60.04, 66.04, 66.08, 66.10, 67.02, 68.03 • **Lesson 3:** 55.01, 56.01, 63.02, 63.04, 66.01, 66.02, 66.04, 66.06, 66.07, 66.08, 66.09, 66.10, 66.15, 67.01, 68.03

To the Teacher

Attempting to learn a new language can often be challenging and even frustrating. But learning English should also be fun. That's the idea I was given by the wonderful administrator who hired me twelve years ago to teach my first ESL class. She took me aside as I was about to walk nervously into class for the first time. "Make your students comfortable," she said. "Make the class fun. And teach them what they really need to know."

Twelve years of teaching and about ten thousand students later, these simple, yet essential, ideas have become guiding pedagogical principles for me. In each of my classes, I have striven to teach students what they need to know, in a way that is both comfortable and enjoyable. Ultimately, that's the philosophy behind *Downtown*, too. The simplicity of the layout of each page, along with the logical, slow-paced progression of the material makes it a comfortable text for both teachers and students to use. I've included a wide variety of activities, as well as playful features like "Game Time" to make *Downtown 4* an enjoyable text to use. And, by developing the text with a focus on standards-based competencies, I've sought to teach students the information they most need to know.

This four-level, competency-based series is built around the language skills students need to function in both their everyday lives and in the workplace, while giving a good deal of attention to grammar. It is a general ESL text that pays more attention to work-related language needs than is typical. The goal of the text is to facilitate student-centered learning in order to lead students to real communicative competence.

The first page of each chapter of *Downtown 4* presents an overview of the material of the chapter in context, using a picture-dictionary format. This is followed by three lessons, with the third lesson focusing on work-related English. Many of the structures and key concepts are recycled throughout the lessons, with the goal of maximizing student practice. Each lesson is carefully scaffolded to progress from guided practice to more communicative activities in which students begin to take more control of their own learning.

Each chapter concludes with a Chapter Review, which provides material that practices and synthesizes the skills that students have been introduced to in the previous three lessons. The review culminates in a "Teamwork Task" activity. This activity gives students the opportunity to work together to apply the skills they have learned to complete a real world type of task. At the end of each chapter, you will find *Downtown Journal*, which reviews instructional content and introduces critical thinking and problem solving.

Each chapter presents a variety of activities that practice grammar, as well as reading, writing, listening, and speaking skills. Problem-solving activities are also included in many lessons, and are particularly emphasized at the higher levels.

The material in **Downtown 4** is presented in real-life contexts. Students are introduced to vocabulary, grammar, and real-world skills through the interactions of a cast of realistic, multiethnic characters who function as parents, workers, and community members in their own "downtown" world.

My intention in developing **Downtown 4** was to provide an easy-to-use text, brimming with essential and enjoyable language learning material. I hope **Downtown 4** succeeds in this and that it helps to cultivate an effective and motivating learning atmosphere in your classroom. Please feel free to send me your comments and suggestions at the Thomson Heinle Internet site: elt.thomson.com. Ancillary material includes Teacher's Editions, workbooks, audio cassettes/CDs, transparencies, and an *ExamView® Pro* assessment CD-Rom containing a customizable test bank for each level.

Downtown: English for Work and Life

Downtown **offers a well-balanced approach that combines both a standards-based and a grammar-based syllabus. This gives English learners the comprehensive language skills they need to succeed in their daily lives, both at home and at work.**

A highly-visual chapter opener introduces unit vocabulary in the context of a reading and outlines chapter goals.

Audio Tapes and CDs enhance learning through dialogues, listening practice, readings, and pronunciation exercises.

Theme-based chapters include three lessons. The third lessons focuses on the skills and vocabulary necessary for the workplace.

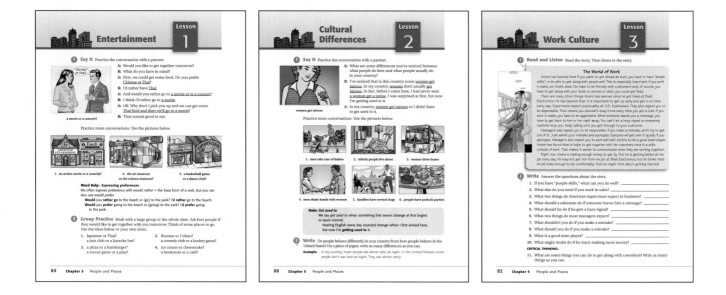

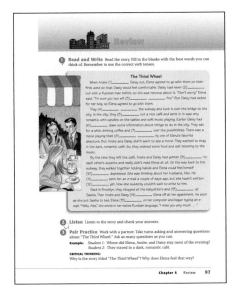

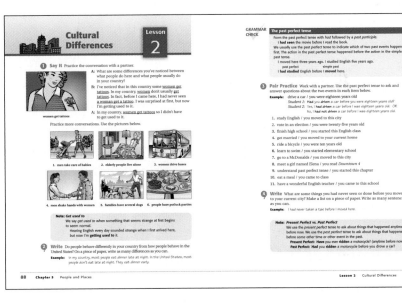

The strong grammar syllabus supports the integrated language learning focus.

Pair Practice and **Teamwork Task** sections increase student communication while engaging critical thinking skills.

A variety of fun, practical features such as *Say It, Problem Solving,* and *Game Time* use the grammar from the unit in semi-controlled and open-ended activities.

Review pages practices all skills learned in the chapter and let students synthesize what they have learned.

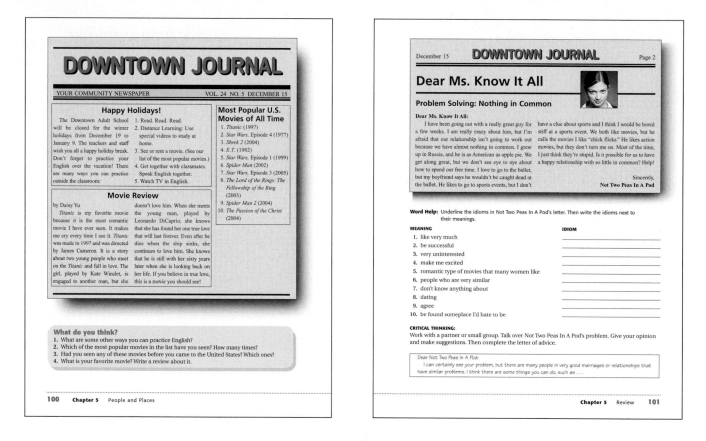

The "**Downtown Journal**" at the end of each chapter reviews instructional content and introduces critical thinking and problem solving activities.

Downtown **Components**

Audio Tapes and CDs enhance learning through dialogues, listening practice, readings, and pronunciation exercises.

Workbooks reinforce lessons and maximize student practice of key reading, writing, listening, speaking and grammar.

Transparencies can be used to introduce lessons, develop vocabulary, and stimulate expansion activities for Student Books 1 and 2.

Assessment CD-ROM with *ExamView® Pro* allows teachers to create, customize, and correct tests and quizzes quickly and easily.

Teacher's Editions with ArtBank CD-ROM provide student book answers and teaching suggestions.

Alignment with the CASAS, SCANS, EFF Competencies and state standards supports classroom and program goals.

Photo Credits

Chapter 1
Page 4, Counter clockwise: © Kayte M. Deioma / PhotoEdit, © David Young-Wolff / PhotoEdit, © Royalty-Free/Corbis, © Royalty-Free/Corbis, © Royalty-Free/Corbis, © Image Source/ Getty Images
Page 5   © Royalty-Free/Corbis
Page 13 © Blend Images / Alamy

Chapter 2
Page 31, T: © Michael Newman / PhotoEdit,
Page 31, M: © Mark Harmel / Alamy
Page 31, B: © Royalty-Free/Corbis
Page 33 © Tony Freeman / PhotoEdit

Chapter 3
Page 55 © Nicholas Eveleigh / SuperStock

Chapter 4
Page 66, T: © Steve Skjold / Alamy
Page 66, BL: © A. Ramey / PhotoEdit
Page 66, BM: © ACE STOCK LIMITED / Alamy
Page 66, BR: © Lauree Feldman/Index Stock Images

Chapter 6
Page 106, L:© Elizabeth Whiting & Associates/CORBIS
Page 106, M: © Bruce Miller / Alamy
Page 106, R: © Peter Gridley/Getty Images
Page 115, T: © image100 / SuperStock
Page 115, M: © Art Vandalay/Getty Images
Page 115, B: © George Shelley/CORBIS

Chapter 7
Page 124, TL: © Robert Brenner / PhotoEdit
Page 124, TR: © David Woods/CORBIS
Page 124, BL: © Dennis Wilson/CORBIS
Page 124, BR: © Susan Van Etten / PhotoEdit
Page 129, L: © Masterfile Royalty Free (RF)
Page 129, R: © age fotostock / SuperStock

Chapter 9
Pg. 167, © Marc Romanelli/Getty Images

Chapter 10
Page 194, L: © Francis G. Mayer/CORBIS
Page 194, M: © Bettmann/CORBIS
Page 194, R: © Mary Evans Picture Library / Alamy

Nice to Meet You

GOALS

✓ Talk about important life events

✓ Use short answers correctly

✓ Communicate with school personnel

✓ Understand rules and regulations

✓ Fill out a school registration form

✓ Write a note to a teacher

✓ Make logical conclusions

✓ Use capital letters appropriately

✓ Write a chronological paragraph

What is happening in the pictures?

1 **Read and Listen** Read the story. Then listen to it.

Hello, New York

Elena and her son, Sasha, recently moved from Russia to New York. They have been living in New York for about a month, but Elena still feels like a visitor. New York is the third city Elena has lived in. She thinks it is the most difficult to get to know, but also the most interesting. Every day she walks around the streets with her eyes wide like a tourist. Sometimes she visits tourist attractions like the Statue of Liberty and the Empire State Building.

Elena grew up in a small city in Russia. After she got married, she moved to Moscow for three years. Then she came to the United States with her parents and Sasha. They are all living in a section, or borough, of New York called Brooklyn.

In Brooklyn, Elena likes to see all the different ethnic shops when she walks around her neighborhood. Right now she is carrying a bag of groceries from a Russian market and a pretty shirt from a Chinese clothing store. She enjoys meeting people from all over the world. She has already met some interesting neighbors in her own building. One is a Chinese woman whose name is Daisy.

Tomorrow Elena is going to register her son for school. The elementary school has classes for adults too, so she is also going to register herself for an English class. She hopes that when her English is better, she will be able to find a good job in her new city.

 Write Find these verb tenses in the story. Write an example of each.

1. a simple past tense verb _____

2. a simple present tense verb _____

3. a present continuous verb _____

4. a present perfect continuous verb _____

5. a present perfect tense verb _____

6. a future tense verb _____

New Friends and Neighbors

1 Say It Practice the conversation with a partner.

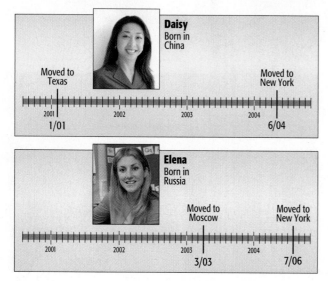

Daisy
Born in China

Moved to Texas
2001   2002   2003   2004
1/01   6/04
Moved to New York

Elena
Born in Russia

Moved to Moscow   Moved to New York
2001   2002   2003   2004
          3/03   7/06

A: Where are you from, <u>Elena</u>?

B: I was born in <u>Russia</u>. I moved to the U.S. in <u>July of 2006</u>. How about you, <u>Daisy</u>? When did you move here?

A: I came from <u>China in 2001</u>. The first place I lived was <u>Texas</u>.

B: How long did you live there?

A: I lived <u>in Texas for about three and a half years</u>.

B: How long have you been living here?

A: I've been living here since <u>June of 2004</u>.

B: How do you like living here?

A: I love it. It's a really exciting city.

Practice more conversations. Use the time lines below.

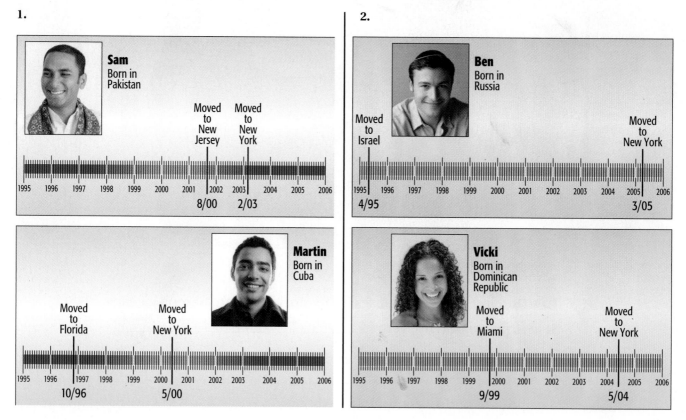

1.

Sam
Born in Pakistan

Moved to New Jersey   Moved to New York
1995 1996 1997 1998 1999 2000 2001 2002 2003 2004 2005 2006
                    8/00   2/03

Martin
Born in Cuba

Moved to Florida   Moved to New York
1995 1996 1997 1998 1999 2000 2001 2002 2003 2004 2005 2006
     10/96   5/00

2.

Ben
Born in Russia

Moved to Israel   Moved to New York
1995 1996 1997 1998 1999 2000 2001 2002 2003 2004 2005 2006
4/95   3/05

Vicki
Born in Dominican Republic

Moved to Miami   Moved to New York
1995 1996 1997 1998 1999 2000 2001 2002 2003 2004 2005 2006
               9/99   5/04

Pair Practice Practice the conversation with a different partner. Use real information.

 Write Create a time line of the places you have lived. Include where you were born, any other places you have lived, and the dates.

Born	Present

4 **Group Practice** Walk around your classroom and speak to at least five classmates. Introduce yourself and tell where you are from. Ask your classmates where they are from, what other places they have lived, and how long they lived in each place. Make a list of all the different places your classmates have lived.

Culture Tip

On the move
The average American moves nine times during his or her lifetime. How many times have you moved?

5 **Write** Use the time line to answer the questions about Andre. Answer in complete sentences.

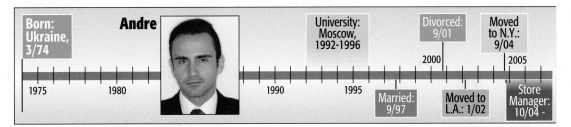

1. How old is Andre? _____
2. How long was he married? _____
3. How many times has he been married? _____
4. How many different places has he lived? _____
5. Where does he live now? _____
6. How long did he live in L.A.? _____
7. How long has he been living in New York? _____
8. When did he get divorced? _____
9. How long has he been a store manager? _____
10. Where was he living when he got divorced? _____

6 **Pair Practice** Work with a partner. Ask and answer the questions in Activity 5.

Write Think about the most important events in your life. They can be good or bad, but they should be events that changed your life. Make a list of these events and write when they happened.

EVENTS   WHEN

_____   _____

_____   _____

_____   _____

_____   _____

_____   _____

_____   _____

 Pair Practice Work with a partner. Tell your partner about the important events in your life. Your partner will ask questions, take notes, and then fill in the time line below about your life.

Born

 Group Practice Work in groups of four or five. Tell the group about your partner. The other students will ask more questions.

Example: *Student 1:* My partner got married for the first time in 1992.
                Student 2: How many times has he been married?
                Student 1: He's been married twice. He moved to the U.S. in 2002.
                Student 3: Where was the first place he lived in the U.S.?

GRAMMAR CHECK

> ## Short answers: *do, have, be*
>
> We often use short answers to respond to *yes/no* questions.
> A short answer consists of a **subject** and an **auxiliary**, or **helping verb.**
> Make sure the auxiliary verb in the answer matches the one in the question.
>   A: **Do** you **have** a car?
>   B: Yes, **I do.**
>   A: **Have** you **eaten** dinner yet?
>   B: No, I **haven't.**
>
> ***Check Point:***
>   ✓ It is not correct to use a main verb in a short answer.
>   **Do** you **play** the piano? Yes, I *do.* (NOT: Yes, I *play.*)

Write Write a short answer to each question.

1. Do you play any musical instruments? _____

2. Are you interested in sports? _____

3. Does your father live in the United States? _____

4. Have you seen any good movies recently? _____

5. Are you working now? _____

6. Do you have any children? _____

7. Is this your first English class? _____

8. Have you ever seen the Statue of Liberty? _____

9. Did you come to the United States by plane? _____

10. Were you in class yesterday? _____

11. Do you have any relatives in this city? _____

12. Have you spoken to the teacher outside of class? _____

13. Does it rain a lot in your native country? _____

14. Did you have a job in your native country? _____

15. Were you working last summer? _____

11 **Pair Practice** Work with a partner. Ask and answer the questions in Activity 10.

Culture Tip

Small talk
Small talk refers to topics of conversation that aren't very serious, such as the weather or a local sports team. It is often polite to make small talk in social situations with new neighbors, classmates, or coworkers.

 Teamwork Task Work in teams of three or four.
1. **Brainstorm:** Work together to create a list of important events in a person's life. List as many events as you can.
2. **Rank:** Work together to rank the four most important events in a person's life. There are no right or wrong answers—just your opinion. You must agree on four things. If a teammate doesn't agree, try to change his or her mind.

1. _____   3. _____

2. _____   4. _____

Homework

Create a time line of the life history of someone you know. It could be a friend or relative, or a famous person if you know the important events of his or her life.

New Schools

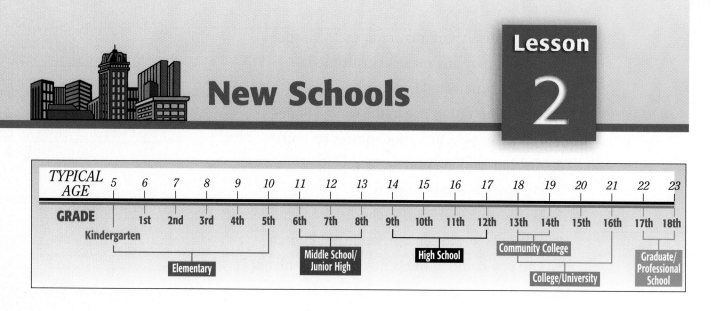

1 **Say It** Practice the conversation with a partner. Use the chart above.

Son

5

PS 291 Elementary

have proof of immunization

A: <u>PS 291 Elementary</u>. Can I help you?

B: Yes. My <u>son is five</u> years old. I'd like to register <u>him</u> for <u>kindergarten</u>. Can you tell me when the next school year starts?

A: It starts on September 5.

B: What do I have to do to register?

A: First, your <u>son</u> must <u>have proof of immunization</u>. All children must <u>have proof of immunization</u> in order to register.

B: Do you have classes for adults, too?

A: Yes, we do. We have some excellent adult education classes here.

B: Do adults have to <u>have proof of immunization</u>, too?

A: No. That isn't necessary for adults.

Practice more conversations. Use the pictures below.

Daughter, 12

Lefferts Junior High

1. have proof of address

Daughter, 15

Midwood High School

2. have a birth certificate or passport

Grandson, 8

St. Martin's Academy

3. pass an entrance exam

Necessity, permission, or obligation

Use *must* for legal or formal necessity.
Use *have to, need to,* or *have got to* for personal, or informal, necessity.
Use *not have to* to show that something is not necessary.

> Students **must** pass an entrance exam. (formal necessity)
> I **have to** pick up my son. (personal necessity)
> You **don't have to** buy a car. (It's not necessary; you have a choice.)

Use *may* or *be allowed to* for permission.
Use *may not* or *be not allowed to* to show that something is not permitted.
Use *be supposed to* to show obligation.

> You **may / are allowed to** leave early. (You have permission.)
> Students **may not** talk in class. They **aren't allowed to** talk. (Talking isn't permitted in class.)
> Students **are supposed to** do their homework. (obligation)

Check Points:
✓ *May* can also be used to express possibility.
✓ *Must* can also be used to express a logical conclusion and, in the negative, prohibition.

2 **Read and Write** Read the story. Circle the best words to complete the story.

Registration Information

ESL Literacy	ESL Intermediate Low	ESL Conversation
ESL Beginning Low	ESL Intermediate High	Distance Learning
ESL Beginning High	ESL Advanced	English for Work

All ESL students (**1.** must / need) take an assessment test before registering. However, students (**2.** must not / don't have to) register for the level indicated on their assessment result form. Students (**3.** may / have to) register for one level higher or one level lower that the test result indicates. For example, if test results show a Beginning High level, students are (**4.** allowed / supposed) to register for a Beginning Low or an Intermediate Low class. All students (**5.** have to / are allowed to) complete a registration form before the first day of class.

Students (**6.** may / must) register for as many as three classes, but (**7.** may not / don't have to) register for two classes given during the same time period. Students (**8.** have / are supposed) to attend all class sessions. Students (**9.** must / may) bring a note of explanation after each absence.

Please note: Students who want to register for only distance learning (**10.** must not / don't have to) take the assessment test. It isn't required.

Students (**11.** are not allowed to / don't have to) smoke on campus. Smoking is prohibited.

Listen Listen and check your answers to Activity 2.

Write Do the following sets of sentences have the same or different meanings? If different, explain why.

1. Students must not smoke on campus. Students may not smoke on campus.

   _____

2. Students don't have to arrive early. Students may not arrive early.

   _____

3. I need to take an assessment test. I've got to take an assessment test.

   _____

4. Students are allowed to do their homework. Students are supposed to do their homework.

   _____

5. Students may eat in the cafeteria. Students are allowed to eat in the cafeteria.

   _____

Listen Listen to the conversation between Elena and the office clerk. Fill out the registration form for Elena with the information you hear.

School Registration Form

		/ /
LAST NAME	FIRST NAME	DATE

ADDRESS

TELEPHONE	E-MAIL

/ /	
DATE OF BIRTH	PLACE OF BIRTH

☐ EMPLOYED   ☐ UNEMPLOYED   ☐ SEEKING WORK

HIGHEST GRADE COMPLETED	DEGREE

NATIVE LANGUAGE	OTHER LANGUAGES

PRIMARY REASONS FOR STUDYING ENGLISH

Pair Practice Work with a partner. Ask and answer questions about Elena. Use the information from the registration form.

7 **Read and Write** Read the story. Then help Elena write her letter.

At PS 291 Elementary, children are not allowed to arrive late. If a child is late three times, his parent must write a note of explanation to the child's teacher before the child can return to class. When a child is absent, he also must have a note when he returns to school. Sasha was late three times last week. Help Elena write a note to Sasha's teacher by filling in the blanks below. Use the words in the box.

sorry	supposed to	late	responsible	has to
allow	allowed	be able	has to	have to

Dear Ms. Martin:

I'm (1)_____ that Sasha was (2)_____ for class

three times last week. I know he is (3)_____ arrive before 8:00 A.M.,

but sometimes there are things he (4)_____ do in the morning that

he does very slowly. He (5)_____ dress himself, for example, and brush

his teeth. I know a lot of kids in first grade don't (6)_____ dress

themselves. But I want Sasha to be a (7)_____ person, so I

(8)_____ him to take care of himself as much as possible. I hope

Sasha will be (9)_____ back in class today. And I'm sure he will

(10)_____ to arrive earlier in the future.

Sincerely,
Elena Petrova

8 **Teamwork Task** Work in teams of four or five.
1. Work together to make a list of *acceptable* reasons why a student might be absent or late for school. Then make a list of *unacceptable* reasons. Write as many reasons as you can.
2. Make a list of rules for your class and school. Work together to list things students **must do**, things students are **not allowed to do**, and things that students **don't have to do.** When you are finished, read your list to the class.

Homework

Write a note to your teacher. Explain why you were late or absent from class, or why you broke some other class rule. Apologize for the problem.

A New Job

1 Read and Listen Read the story. Then listen to the story.

A New Job

Elena graduated from college with a degree in accounting. She worked as an accountant for three years in Russia before she came to the United States. But she hasn't worked as an accountant in the United States. Accounting in the U.S. is very different from accounting in Russia, so now she has to retrain herself. She has to start by learning English.

Elena studied English in high school, but she didn't take it very seriously and, unfortunately, she didn't learn very much. She also took English classes for a year when she lived in Moscow, but she still doesn't speak English well enough to get the kind of job she wants. So, she is going to register for some more English classes in New York.

Other than English, Elena isn't sure yet what classes she is going to take. She could take an accounting class, but she thinks she isn't ready for that yet. She could take a banking class, or a tax preparation class, because those classes train you to get a job right away. But she hasn't made a decision yet.

2 Write Answer the questions with information from the story.

1. How long did Elena work as an accountant in Russia?

   _____

2. How long has she worked as an accountant in the United States?

   _____

3. How much English did Elena learn in high school? _____

4. How many English classes has she taken in New York? _____

5. Why does she have to retrain herself? _____

6. How is her English now? _____

7. What kind of class is she definitely going to take? _____

8. What other classes might she take? Why? _____

CRITICAL THINKING:

9. What is the most difficult thing about moving to a new country? Why?

   _____

10. Is it better to take a job as quickly as possible when you arrive in a new place, or is it better to take some classes before you get a job? Why?

    _____

Note: Simple past, simple present, or present perfect?

Use the *simple past* for an action completed at a specific time in the past or when an action is final.

    I **went** to the park yesterday.

    Hemingway **wrote** five novels. (He's dead, so he won't write any more.)

Use the *simple present* to tell what is happening now, but not for how long.

    She works at Macy's. (<u>NOT</u>: She works at Macy's **for 3 months**.)

Use the *present perfect*

- when the time of an action is not stated or important:

    He**'s been** to Las Vegas. (When he went is not important.)

- to tell how long something has continued, from the past to the present:

    I**'ve been** a teacher for ten years. (I'm still a teacher.)

- when the time period is not finished (today, this year, etc.), or the action isn't final:

    She **has seen** five movies this month. (She might see another one. The month is not finished.)

---

3 **Write** Use the time line to answer the questions. Write complete sentences.

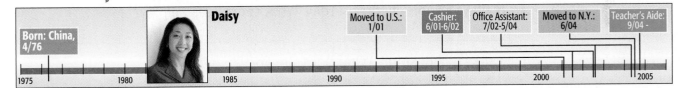

1. When did Daisy come to the United States? _____

2. How long did Daisy work as a cashier? _____

3. Where does Daisy work now? _____

4. How many jobs has Daisy had in the U.S.? _____

5. How long has Daisy been a teacher's aide? _____

6. How old is Daisy now? _____

7. How old was Daisy when she came to the U.S.? _____

4 **Listen** Listen and take notes. Then create a time line for Freddy with the information you hear.

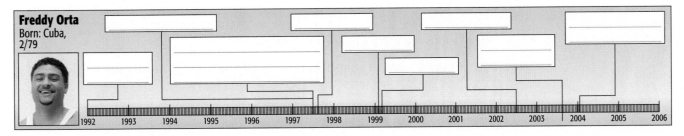

5 **Pair Practice** Work with a partner. Ask and answer questions about Freddy's life and work history. Ask as many questions as you can.

Could for possibility; Must for logical conclusion

Another use of *could* is to indicate that something is possible, but not certain. Another use of *must* is to indicate probability—there is enough information to say something is probably true, though it still is not certain.

Elena is from Europe. She **could be** from France, or she **could be** from Denmark. But if we know that she speaks Russian, we can say that she **must be** from Russia.

Note: Hobbies

Hobbies are activities that people do regularly because they enjoy them. Sometimes they are like jobs, but a job you don't get paid for is a hobby. For example, playing music can be a hobby, or it can be a job if it is how you support yourself.

 6 Write Elena's friends all have jobs and hobbies. Use *could* to write several possibilities about each of Elena's friends. Write complete sentences.

1. Vicki plays a musical instrument. What does she play?

   She could play the guitar, or she could play the piano, or she could play...

2. Freddy plays a sport every Saturday. What sport does he play?

   _____

3. Alice works in a hospital. What does she do?

   _____

4. Ana drives for a living. What does she drive?

   _____

5. Ben is a salesperson. What does he sell? _____

6. Eric works at a school. What does he do? _____

7. Hamid works with his hands. What does he do?

   _____

 7 Write Use the information below to make logical conclusions about the people in Activity 6. Write complete sentences.

1. Vicki's musical instrument is very big and heavy. *It must be a piano.*

2. Freddy runs a lot and uses his head to score goals. _____

3. Alice helps doctors in the emergency room. _____

4. Ana wears a tuxedo and transports her clients in a long, luxurious vehicle.

   _____

5. Ben knows everything about computers. _____

6. Eric works every day in an ESL classroom. _____

7. Hamid knows how to build houses. _____

 Teamwork Task Work in teams of three or four. Look at the picture of Elena's party. What logical conclusions can you make about the people? Write as many sentences as you can.

<u>Andre must speak Russian. He has an English-Russian dictionary.</u>

_____

_____

_____

_____

_____

_____

_____

> **Note: Capitalization**
> Use capital letters for the first letter of the first word in a sentence and the names of people, places, streets, and other geographic names. Capitalize the first letter of nationalities, languages, days of the week and months of the year, and the names of holidays and names of organizations (the Republican Party, the University of California). Also, use capital letters for important words in a title: *The Old Man and the Sea.*

9 **Read** Read the story. Circle any mistakes in capitalization. How many mistakes can you find?

> Hamid has lived in the united states for six years. He is from egypt. He arrived on the thanksgiving holiday six years ago. he lived in texas for a year before he moved to New york. Now He has been living here for almost five years.
>
> Hamid has had four different jobs since he moved to New York. First he got a job installing windows for a window company in brooklyn. His boss, a man named hossain from pakistan, didn't treat him very well, so he quit after a few Months. then he got a better job for a large Company as a window installer. He works six days a week from monday to saturday because he is saving money for his Wedding.
>
> Last year hamid met his girlfriend, giang. giang is from china and speaks chinese in addition to english. She speaks both Languages very well. Now he and Giang are engaged and they are planning to get married in central park in april.

 10 **Write** Write a chronological paragraph about your life. Tell about the places you have lived and when you lived there. Tell about any jobs you have had in the U.S. and the jobs you had before you arrived in the U.S. Include where you live and work now. Don't forget to use capital letters when necessary.

Game Time

Guess the word
Your teacher will divide the class into small groups. Then your teacher will write one word on the board for each group. He or she will write only the first letter of the word with blank spaces where the other letters should be. Your group must guess letters to fill in the blanks. The group that guesses the complete word first wins.

1 Read and Listen Read the story. Then listen to the story.

A Difficult Decision

Elena has been a single parent since she moved to the United States. Sasha's father, Alex, is still in Russia. He is waiting for permission to join his wife and child in the U.S. Nobody knows how long that will take. It could be a short time or it could take many years. In the meantime, Elena is determined to be strong and to do the best she can for her son and herself. But she has already learned that being a single parent is not easy.

Before she got married, Elena made a decision to apply, along with her parents and brother, for a visa to immigrate to the United States. Her aunt and uncle were willing to sponsor her, but it still took several years for her application to be approved. When it was approved, she had to make a very difficult decision.

She decided to come to the U.S. with the rest of her family, but without her husband.

In New York, Elena has her parents and her aunt and uncle to help her. Her Aunt Sonia and Uncle Morris have lived in the U.S. for ten years. They have a small but successful business. Her aunt is her sponsor, so she is supposed to help Elena get started in her new country. Aunt Sonia found her an apartment before she arrived. She also gave Elena a part-time job in her business. But Elena understands that the job is temporary and that she has to find a "real" job and a new career as soon as she can.

It was a very difficult decision for Elena to move to a new country with her little boy and without her husband. She hopes she made the right decision.

2 Write Answer the questions about the story.

1. How long has Elena been a single parent? _____

2. Why does Sasha's father want a visa? _____

3. How long will it take for Sasha's father to get a visa? _____

4. When did Elena apply for a visa? _____

5. Who was Elena's sponsor? _____

6. What is a sponsor supposed to do? _____

7. How long have Elena's aunt and uncle been in the U.S.? _____

CRITICAL THINKING:

8. Do you think Elena made the right decision? Why or why not?

_____

9. What do you think could happen to Elena and her family in the future. Write some possibilities. Use *could*. _____

_____

Write Correct the mistakes. Rewrite the incorrect sentences. If there are no mistakes, write *correct*.

1. How long ago have you moved here?

   _____

2. She has lived in several different places.

   _____

3. Do you live in New York? Yes, I live.

   _____

4. Children must to have immunizations before they start school.

   _____

5. You may pay your taxes. It's the law.

   _____

6. He speaks with a strong foreign accent. He should be an immigrant.

   _____

7. Is this your first English class? Yes, it does.

   _____

8. The last job she had was in florida.

   _____

9. Does she have any children? Yes, she has.

   _____

10. She has been worked there for two years.

   _____

 Write Ask a classmate about his or her job, education, family, and the different places he or she has lived. Write three past tense, three present perfect, and three future tense questions.

1. _____
2. _____
3. _____
4. _____
5. _____
6. _____
7. _____
8. _____
9. _____

5 **Pair Practice** Work with a partner. Ask and answer the questions in Activity 4. Write the answers on a sheet of paper.

Teamwork Task Work in teams of four or five.

1. Choose one student volunteer. Ask the volunteer questions about his or her life. Use the information to fill in the time line below. Ask about the places he or she has lived, jobs, marriages, children, and any other important events in his or her life.

Born

2. Work together to write a chronological paragraph about your volunteer's life. One student should write the sentences, and the other teammates should edit them. Look for mistakes in grammar, spelling, and capitalization.

Pronunciation Lost /h/ sound

A. The /h/ sound of *he* is usually lost when we ask *yes/no* questions. Listen and repeat the linked sounds.

1. Is he . . . (izzy)	*Izzy* from Mexico?	Yes, he is.
2. Does he . . . (duzzy)	*Duzzy* have a car?	No, he doesn't.
3. Has he . . . (hazzy)	*Hazzy* had lunch yet?	Yes, he has.
4. Was he . . . (wuzzy)	*Wuzzy* in class yesterday?	No, he wasn't.
5. Did he . . . (diddy)	*Diddy* pass the test?	Yes, he did.

B. Work with a partner. Point at male students in your class and ask your partner the *yes/no* questions above. Use the fast, linked pronunciation.

I can . . .			
• talk about important life events.	1	2	3
• use short answers correctly.	1	2	3
• communicate with school personnel.	1	2	3
• understand rules and regulations.	1	2	3
• fill out a school registration form.	1	2	3
• write a note to a teacher.	1	2	3
• make logical conclusions.	1	2	3
• use capital letters appropriately.	1	2	3
• write a chronological paragraph.	1	2	3

1 = not well   2 = OK   3 = very well

DOWNTOWN JOURNAL

YOUR COMMUNITY NEWSPAPER   VOL. 24 NO. 1 AUGUST 15

Downtown Adult School
Total student population: 1200 students

Number of students with 0 children	600
Number of students with 1 child	400
Number of students with 2 children	120
Number of students with 3 or more children	80

Child care is a problem for many of our adult students.

The Midwood Child-Care Center . . .

. . . has openings for children from 3 to 5 years of age. The center is open from 7:30 A.M. to 4:30 P.M., Monday to Friday. Children must be enrolled in the program at least two days a week. Enrollment forms are available in the school office. Cost of full-time child care is on a sliding scale as follows:

Monthly Salary	Cost Per Week For One Child
$5,000 +	$125
$4,000–4,999	$100
$3,000–3,999	$75
$2,500–2,999	$50
Less than $2,500	$40

CHILD CARE NEEDED

New student, Elena Petrova, needs help with occasional child care. She has one child—a 5-year-old boy. She can't pay much, but will exchange babysitting with you. Let's try to help Elena! Leave your name in the office if you can help.

What do you think?

1. Read the bar graph above. Figure out the percentages. What percentage of students have no children? One child? Two children? Three or more children?
2. Create a bar graph for your class. Ask how many students have no children, one child, two children, or more than two. Then draw the graph and find the percentages.
3. If Elena earns $400 a week from her part-time job, how much will she have to pay for child care? If she earned $800 a week, how much would she have to pay per month?

Dear Ms. Know It All

Problem Solving: Child Care

Dear Ms. Know It All:

I am a single parent with a three-year-old toddler to bring up. I recently moved back to the Big Apple because my father is sick and my mother can't make ends meet by herself. Unfortunately, I don't have very much money either, so I need to look for a job ASAP. But I can't look for a job if I have my son with me all day. My mom already has her hands full working part-time and taking care of my dad, so she can't lend me a hand with my son. In September, he'll be off to kindergarten, but for now my head is spinning about what to do. Can you steer me in the right direction?

Sincerely,

Up the Creek Without a Paddle

Note: Idioms

An *idiom* is a word or group of words that has a special meaning different from the usual or literal meaning of the words.

My boss **hit the ceiling** when I came in late. (The boss got upset. He didn't really hit the ceiling.)

Word Help: Match the idioms with their meanings.

1. _____ the Big Apple
2. _____ ASAP
3. _____ be off
4. _____ bring up (someone)
5. _____ toddler
6. _____ make ends meet
7. _____ have (your) hands full
8. _____ lend someone a hand
9. _____ my head is spinning
10. _____ steer me in the right direction

a. raise from childhood
b. New York City
c. give me advice
d. a small child
e. pay your bills
f. help someone
g. as soon as possible
h. I'm confused
i. be very busy
j. go someplace

CRITICAL THINKING:

Work with a partner or small group. Talk about Up the Creek's problem. Make a list of ideas that might help. Then complete the letter of advice. Remember to use *could* for possibilities. Share your letter with the class.

Dear Up the Creek Without a Paddle:
    I can't take care of your son for you, but I can suggest some things you could do. For example, . . .

Love and Marriage

Then

Now

1 Read and Listen Read the story. Then listen to it.

Changes

Elena sometimes thinks about how different her life has become since she and Sasha moved to the United States. In some ways, their lives are better. New York is an interesting place to live. There are more job opportunities for Elena and more educational opportunities for both her and Sasha. But, in some ways, their lives are more difficult now.

In Russia, Elena used to live with her husband. She had someone who could help her with all the household chores. Her husband used to cook some of their meals, and he used to help take care of Sasha. She used to have time to relax and read a magazine after dinner. Now the only thing she reads is children's books with Sasha to help him learn English. In Russia, Elena didn't have to take care of everything by herself.

When she thinks about her life in Russia, Elena feels homesick. She misses her husband, of course. But it isn't just him. She misses everything about her old life. In Russia, Elena had a good job in an accounting office. In Russia, she didn't need a resume to find a job. She got her jobs by networking with her friends and former classmates. Now Elena needs a resume and more education in order to get a good job. Tomorrow she is going to get started writing her resume. Then maybe she'll get a good job and stop feeling homesick!

Then

E. PETROVA

Now

RESUME

Culture Tip

Single-parent families

According to the U.S. Census Bureau, 26 percent of all households with children have only one parent living in the home.

 Write Make a list of things that used to be true for Elena and Sasha, but aren't true anymore. Write on a piece of paper.

In Russia, Elena used to live with her husband.

Parenting

1 **Say It** Practice the conversation with a partner.

live with my family / have a
driver's license

A: Where did you use to live before you came to the United States?

B: I used to live in <u>China</u>.

A: How was your life different in <u>China</u>?

B: Well, I used to <u>live with my family</u>, but now I don't.

A: I don't <u>live with my family</u>, either.

B: Also, I never used to <u>have a driver's license in China</u>, but now I do.

A: <u>Having a driver's license</u> is really important here.

B: Yes, it is.

Practice more conversations. Use the pictures below.

1. **smoke cigarettes / speak English**

2. **go dancing a lot / have a full-time job**

3. **walk to work / ride on the subway**

GRAMMAR CHECK

Used to

Used to refers to the habitual past. We use it to talk about things that occurred many times in the past, but don't occur anymore. Use *used to* with the base form of a verb.

We **used to work** together. (But we don't anymore.)

Check Point:

✓ It is common to say *never used to* for negative statements.

I **never used to cook** when I was younger, but now I cook every day.

2 **Pair Practice** Practice the conversation in Activity 1 again. This time use information from your life. Tell your partner where you used to live, something you used to do, but don't do anymore. Mention something you never used to do, but do now.

3 Write On a piece of paper, list the things you used to do when you were younger, but don't do anymore. Then make another list of things you *never* used to do when you were younger, but do now. Write as many things as you can.

4 Pair Practice Work with a partner. Tell your partner about things you used to do. Ask each other questions to continue the conversation.

Example: *Student 1:* I used to have a job, but now I don't.
Student 2: Really? What kind of job did you have?

Student 1: I used to play sports when I was younger.
Student 2: What sports did you play?

5 Pair Practice If possible, find a partner from a different country or culture. Ask your partner questions about parenting when he or she was growing up.

1. parents / help children with their homework?

   Did parents use to help children with their homework when you were growing up?

2. fathers / spend a lot of time with their children?

3. parents / give teenagers an allowance?

4. parents / take their children to school?

5. parents / spank their children?

6. parents / find husbands or wives for their sons and daughters?

7. children / watch a lot of TV?

8. children / play outside in the neighborhood without an adult?

9. teenagers / go to parties or dances without an adult?

10. teenagers / do housework at home?

6 Group Practice *Find someone who . . .* Work in a large group or with the whole class. Ask your classmates "Did you use to . . ." questions for the sentences below. Find a person who says "Yes" for each statement. When a person says "Yes," write his or her name on the line. Keep asking questions until you have a different name on each line.

1. _____ used to go dancing a lot. (but doesn't anymore)

2. _____ used to dislike studying English.

3. _____ used to have a lot of chores to do at home.

4. _____ used to stay out late on weekends.

5. _____ used to disagree a lot with his or her parents.

6. _____ used to dislike doing homework.

7. _____ used to think his or her parents knew everything.

8. _____ used to have a favorite pet.

Gerunds as subjects

A *gerund* is the *-ing* form of a verb used as a noun. Sometimes gerunds are used as the subject of a sentence.

Cooking is fun. (*Cooking* is the subject.)

Learning English takes a long time. (*Learning English* is the subject. This is a gerund phrase.)

Check Point:

✓ Use *not* in front of a gerund to make it negative.

Not speaking English is a big problem in the United States.

7 **Read and Write** Read the story. Underline the gerund subjects.

Raising a Happy, Healthy Child

Raising a happy, healthy child is difficult in today's world. But there are some things you can do to make the job a little easier. First of all, don't let your child have too much soda or junk food. Eating too much junk food will cause weight and health problems for your child. Fat children are usually unhealthy children. Teaching children to exercise every day is an important part of keeping them healthy.

Making children play with other children at an early age is important because it teaches them valuable social skills. Making children do household chores every day is a good idea because it teaches responsibility. Reading to children is important because it teaches them to love books and learning. Letting them watch a lot of TV is a good idea because it teaches them about their culture and about the world. Also, speaking to children about family problems is a good idea. It teaches them that everyone has problems they have to solve.

Children need to be independent at an early age these days. So, allowing children to choose their own friends is a good idea. Telling teenagers not to do something will only make them want to do it more. So, letting teens make their own decisions is the best idea. Allowing teenagers to go to parties alone and stay out as late as they want will make them more independent and happier. Being a good parent is one of the most important things a person can do in life. So, spend a lot of time with your children when they are young. Spending time with them is the best way to make sure they become happy, healthy people.

CRITICAL THINKING:

Do you agree with all of the statements in the story? Check (✓) the parts of the story you agree with. Make an *X* next to the parts you don't agree with. Then write sentences with gerund subjects that tell your opinions about raising a child.

Example: Raising a happy, healthy child is/isn't difficult in today's world.

8 Write Complete each sentence with a gerund phrase. Give your own opinions.

1. _____ is the most important thing a father can do for his children.

2. _____ is the most important responsibility of a mother.

3. _____ is the most important thing for a child to learn.

4. _____ is a serious problem many teenagers have.

5. _____ is a mistake some parents make with their children.

9 Listen Listen and write the positive or negative gerund phrases you hear. Then check (✓) whether you agree or disagree with each statement.

1. _____ children right and wrong is a problem in many American families.

Agree _____ *Disagree* _____

2. _____ too much TV causes anxiety for children and makes their behavior worse.

Agree _____ *Disagree* _____

3. _____ children with their homework makes them better students.

Agree _____ *Disagree* _____

4. _____ teenagers to date in high school makes them better students.

Agree _____ *Disagree* _____

5. _____ children too much freedom makes them confused and anxious.

Agree _____ *Disagree* _____

10 Teamwork Task Work in teams of three or four.

1. **Brainstorm:** Work together to list things that are important for being a good parent. Use gerund phrases. Write as many as you can. Report your list to the class.

Example: *Teaching a child right from wrong is very important.*

2. **Rank:** Your teacher or a volunteer will write on the board all the things your class reported. Work with your team to choose the three most important things that make someone a good parent. Compare your ranking with the other teams.

Dating

1 **Teamwork Task** Work in teams of three or four. Look at the picture of Elena's party. Looking at the picture, make a list of as many nouns, adjectives, and verbs as you can.

> **Note: Parts of speech**
> A *noun* is the name of a person, a place, a thing, or an idea.
> An *adjective* is a word that describes a noun.
> A *verb* is a word that tells the action of a sentence.

2 **Say It** Practice the conversation with a partner.

Vicki / honest / tells you exactly what she thinks

A: So, who was at Elena's party?

B: Some very interesting people.

A: Anybody I know?

B: Maybe. Do you know <u>Vicki</u>?

A: I'm not sure. What does <u>she</u> look like?

B: <u>She's pretty. She has long, curly brown hair.</u>

A: Is <u>she</u> the one who <u>wears a lot of jewelry</u>?

B: Yes, that's <u>her</u>.

A: I don't know <u>her</u> very well. What is <u>she</u> like?

B: <u>She's very honest. She's the kind of person who tells you exactly what she thinks.</u>

A: I like people like that.

Practice more conversations. Use the pictures below.

1. **Al / entertaining / makes you smile**

2. **Andre / smart / always has something interesting to say**

3. **Freddy / strong / makes you feel safe**

> **Note: Adjectives**
> Some adjectives describe physical appearance—how someone looks.
> Other adjectives describe personality or character—how someone behaves.

3 **Listen** Listen and write the adjectives in the correct box. Then add a few more of your own.

PHYSICAL APPEARANCE ADJECTIVES	PERSONALITY ADJECTIVES
tall	quiet

Adjective clauses

An *adjective clause* is a group of words that describes a noun. The clause includes a subject and a verb. Adjective clauses that describe a person usually begin with *who*.

She is a woman **who enjoys helping people.**

There is the man **who lives next door to me.**

4 **Write** Complete the sentences with an adjective clause.

1. A good father is a man who _____ .

2. A good mother is a woman who _____ .

3. A wonderful husband is a man who _____ .

4. In my country, women like men who _____ .

5. In my country, men like women who _____ .

6. In the U.S., women like men who _____ .

7. In the U.S., men like women who _____ .

8. My best friend is someone who _____ .

9. My parents are people who _____ .

10. My teacher is someone who _____ .

5 **Write** Describe three people you know: a classmate, a friend or family member, and a famous person. Don't write their names. Use physical adjectives, personality adjectives, and an adjective clause for each person. See if your classmates can guess the famous person you describe.

Example: He's tall and very handsome. He's smart and funny. He's the kind of person who makes you laugh when you're with him.

1. _____

2. _____

3. _____

6 **Write** Describe yourself. Use physical adjectives, personality adjectives, and four adjective clauses. See if your classmates agree with your description.

7 **Teamwork Task** Work in teams of three or four. Discuss and decide on the three most important adjectives that describe a good friend. Then decide which three adjectives are most important to describe a good boss. Report your adjectives to the class.

A good friend	A good boss
_____	_____
_____	_____
_____	_____

8 **Listen** Listen to the three dating service profiles. Complete the profiles by filling in the missing gerunds.

---

1. Mr. ROMANTIC   32, 5'7", 155 pounds

I think of myself as a lover, not a fighter. I try to get along with everybody. I am the kind of guy who will bring you flowers every time we go out. I believe in (1.)_____ doors for women and in (2.)_____ a woman feel like a queen. I dream about (3.)_____ "I love you" every morning. If you want to wake up with a kiss every day and always be surrounded by flowers, I might be the guy for you. I look forward to (4.)_____ from you soon. Thank you for (5.)_____ my profile.

---

2. STRONG AND SILENT   34, 6'2", 210 pounds

I am not good at (1.)_____ about myself. I am the kind of man who lets his actions speak for him. I am quiet and serious. I am a man who works hard and plays hard. I believe in (2.)_____ my best at everything I do. I believe in (3.)_____ the truth all the time and I insist on (4.)_____ the truth from you. If you want a man who will never lie to you and will always be there when you need someone to take care of you, I am the man for you. I look forward to (5.)_____ from you soon.

---

3. THE GOOD LIFE   40, 5'10", 190 pounds

I am very successful and generous. I believe in (1.)_____ high goals and in (2.)_____ hard to achieve them. I have always succeeded in (3.)_____ everything I wanted to do except in (4.)_____ my perfect mate. Could it be you? I have a good job, a high income, and a nice home. (5.)_____ is my love and I want to see as many different countries as possible. (6.)_____ in good restaurants is one of my hobbies. I am looking forward to someday (7.)_____ a soul mate to travel around the world with me.

---

 9 **Group Practice** Work in groups of three or four. Read and discuss the profiles of the three men above. Talk about what you like and don't like about them. Which man would you recommend for Daisy? Daisy is thirty years old and would like to meet a nice man. List the reasons for your choice.

GRAMMAR CHECK ✓

Gerunds after verb + preposition combinations

Verb + preposition combinations are often followed by gerunds. Here are some common verb + preposition combinations that are followed by gerunds:

care about	believe in	look forward to
complain about	succeed in	apologize for
dream about	plan on	thank (*someone*) for
talk about	insist on	forgive (*someone*) for
think about	feel like	

10 **Read** Read the personal ads in Activity 8 again. Circle the gerunds that follow prepositions. How many can you find?

11 **Write** Complete the sentences with gerund phrases.

1. Sometimes I dream about _____ .

2. Right now I am thinking about _____ .

3. I am looking forward to _____ someday.

4. I sometimes complain about _____ .

5. Someday I plan on _____ .

6. Right now I feel like _____ .

7. I thanked _____ for _____ .

8. I believe in _____ .

12 **Pair Practice** Work with a partner. Read your sentences from Activity 11 to each other. Tell your partner if you have the same feelings or not.

Example: *Student 1:* Sometimes I dream about having a really big house.

Student 2: I dream about having a really big house, too. OR
I don't. I never dream about having a big house.

Homework

Pretend you are single. Create a personal ad for yourself. It doesn't have to be true or too personal. Use at least one adjective clause and at least one gerund after a verb+preposition combination.

Game Time

How many nouns?

Work in small groups. Your teacher will give each group a picture. Together make a list of nouns and/or verbs you think of looking at the picture. The group with the most words wins.

1 Read and Listen Read the story. Then listen to the story.

Writing a Resume

Elena has been thinking about writing a resume for several days, but she hasn't been able to do it yet. The main problem is that she needs to write an objective. The objective should be the job she is looking for right now. But she doesn't know what job she wants right now. She just wants a full-time job with a good paycheck that will teach her something new and help her to pay her bills. Unfortunately, she can't write that as her resume objective.

Elena is grateful to her aunt for giving her a job, but she would like to get a more interesting job. She is good at working with numbers and she likes working with people. She wants to practice her English on her job, if possible. She is capable of doing most office work except maybe answering telephones and taking messages. She is excited about finding and starting a new job.

Daisy has offered to help Elena write her resume. Daisy has written and rewritten her own resume many times. And she has been successful at creating good professional resumes for several of her friends. She is looking forward to sitting down with her new friend, Elena, and helping her write a nice, clear, professional resume. She has no doubt that Elena will find a job soon.

2 Write Fill in the blanks below with words from the story. Try to write the words without looking at the story.

1. Elena has been thinking about _____ .

2. Elena's _____ should be the job she is looking for now.

3. Elena is grateful to her aunt for _____ .

4. Elena is good at _____ .

5. Elena is capable of _____ .

6. Elena is excited about _____ .

7. Daisy has been successful at _____ for some of her friends.

8. Daisy has no doubt that Elena _____ .

CRITICAL THINKING:

What are some ways that Elena could look for a job? Make a list on a piece of paper.

Gerunds after adjective + preposition combinations

Gerunds also follow adjective + preposition combinations. Here are some common adjective + preposition combinations that are followed by a gerund:

good at	excited about	responsible for
tired of	worried about	interested in
capable of	concerned about	successful at/in
afraid of	famous for	grateful (to someone) for

3 **Write** Complete the sentences with a gerund or gerund phrase.

1. I am good at _____ .

2. My teacher is interested in _____ .

3. I am not afraid of _____ .

4. _____ is famous for _____ .

5. I am tired of _____ .

6. I am grateful to _____ for _____ .

7. _____ is worried about _____ .

8. I am capable of _____ .

4 **Listen** Listen to the conversations between Elena and her friends. Write sentences about Elena's friends using adjective + preposition combinations.

1. Vicki   *Vicki is worried about* _____ .

2. Daisy   _____

3. Andre   _____

4. Freddy   _____

5. Alice   _____

6. Al   _____

> **Note: A resume**
>
> A *resume* is like a job application that you create for yourself. The format is flexible, but all resumes should contain four parts: *Personal Information, Work History* or *Experience, Education,* and *Skills.* If you have strong skills, for example, but not much experience or education, you can start with the *Skills* section. On the other hand, if you have a good education but not much experience, you can start your resume with the *Education* section. Most resumes also include an *objective.* The objective is the job you are looking for right now.

Write Where on a resume would you write each piece of information below? Answer with *Personal Information, Work History, Education, Skills,* or *Objective.*

1. can type 55 words per minute   _____

2. 718-555-2211   _____

3. six months experience as a cashier   _____

4. seeking an entry-level cashier position   _____

5. B.A. in English—West Valley University   _____

6. EDMC7@aol.com   _____

7. know how to drive large 18-wheelers   _____

8. computer literacy and computer application classes   _____

9. a teacher's aide position at a small preschool   _____

10. duties included cutting and styling men's and women's hair   _____

> **Note:** *Resume objectives* vs. *long-term goals*
> A *resume objective* should be the job you are looking for, and are qualified for, right now. Your *long-term goal* is a job you might want in the future, but that you are not likely to get right now. For example, your long-term goal might be to manage a small business, but your objective now might be a cashier job in a small business. Later you might apply for a manager or assistant manager job.

 Listen Listen and write the objective you hear for each person. Don't write the person's long-term goal.

1. Daisy   _____

2. Freddy   _____

3. Alice   _____

4. Hamid   _____

5. Elena   _____

Write Use Elena's resume on the next page to answer the questions.

1. What job does she want now? _____

2. How many different jobs has she had? _____

3. Where does she work now? _____

4. What job skills does she have? _____

5. What was her highest level of education? _____

6. How long did she work as a junior accountant? _____

Pair Practice Work with a partner. Ask your partner questions about Elena's resume. Ask as many questions as you can.

Elena Petrova
1950 Ocean Avenue
Brooklyn, New York 11230

(718) 555-5868   EllaPet@coldmail.com

OBJECTIVE: To obtain an entry-level position in a bank or accounting office

WORK EXPERIENCE: July 2006 – Present. Office Assistant
ABC Imports, Inc. 3345 Kings Highway, Brooklyn, NY 11230
Duties include: typing, filing, helping customers with orders,
tracking customer's online orders.

June 2004 – May 2006. Junior Accountant
Accurate Accounting. Moscow, Russia
Was responsible for monthly payroll of 500+ employees.
Duties included authorizing and tracking paychecks
and resolving employee payroll problems.

EDUCATION: September 1999 – June 2003
Kaluga Technical College
BA Degree in Accounting

SKILLS: COMPUTER SKILLS: Familiar with many software programs;
expert with accounting programs.

Excellent math skills
Bilingual Russian/English

9 Teamwork Task Work in teams of three or four. On a piece of paper, write a list of questions that you can answer from Elena's resume. Use as many different verb tenses as you can.

Example: What kind of job is Elena looking for?

Homework
Create a resume for yourself. Bring it to class to show to your teacher and classmates. They will help you make it even better.

1 **Read and Listen** Read the story. Then listen to the story.

A Big Mistake?

Daisy is thirty years old and has never been married. She has had two boyfriends. She used to have a boyfriend when she was in college in China. Then she dated a man in New York for about six months. The man who she dated in New York was Chinese-American. The man who she dated in China was Chinese. Now Daisy is interested in dating men who are not Chinese. She sometimes thinks about finding a nice, handsome man who speaks English perfectly and who can teach her everything about English and the United States that she doesn't know. But then she thinks about her parents and she gets nervous. Her parents think that marrying, or even dating, outside her culture is a big mistake. Accepting a non-Chinese husband would be very difficult for them.

Daisy used to agree with her parents. Living in New York, however, has changed her attitude. In New York, she has met people from different countries and cultures, and they all seem interesting and nice. The truth is that Daisy is excited about getting to know people who are not Chinese. She is grateful to her parents for raising her so well and for giving her love and an education, and she is worried about hurting them. But now she is a thirty-year-old adult. She is responsible for making her own decisions about her life. So, she plans on opening her heart, meeting different kinds of people, and letting her heart decide what is best for her. She hopes that isn't a big mistake.

2 **Write** Find the gerunds in the story and circle them. How many can you find?

3 **Write** Answer the questions about the story.

1. What nationality of men has Daisy dated? _____

2. Who is she interested in dating? _____

3. What do Daisy's parents think about dating outside her culture?

   _____

4. What is Daisy excited about? _____

5. What is Daisy grateful to her parents for? _____

6. What is she worried about? _____

7. What does she plan to do? _____

CRITICAL THINKING:

8. What do you think? Do you agree with Daisy's parents that dating outside your culture is a big mistake? Why or why not?

Write Correct the sentences. If there are no mistakes, write *correct* on the line.

1. Daisy use to live in China.

   _____

2. Raise a child in New York is difficult.

   _____

3. Meeting a man in New York is easy.

   _____

4. Elena never used to pay her rent in Russia.

   _____

5. Daisy wants to meet someone is tall.

   _____

6. *Big* is a noun.

   _____

7. She used to be married, but she doesn't anymore.

   _____

8. He's dreaming about get a new car.

   _____

9. Now she's responsible for pay all the bills.

   _____

10. Elena is grateful her parents helping her.

    _____

5 **Pair Practice** Work with a partner. Take turns asking and answering questions about household chores (shopping for groceries, cooking, washing dishes, etc.). Answer with an adjective clause.

Example: Student 1: Who is the person who pays the bills in your home?
Student 2: I am the one who pays the bills in my home.
Student 1: Who washes the dishes in your home?

6 **Write** Write at least ten sentences about how your life is different now from how it used to be when you lived in a different place. Write some things that you used to do, but don't do anymore. Write some things that you never used to do, but do now.

7 **Teamwork Task** Work in teams of four. Work together to create a resume for the volunteer. Ask questions to complete each section of the resume. **Student 1** is the volunteer. He or she completes the personal information. **Student 2** completes the work experience section. **Student 3** completes the education section. **Student 4** completes the skills section.

Help each other to make each section the best you can.

Pronunciation Linking

We often link the consonant sound at the end of a word with a vowel sound at the beginning of the following word. Listen and repeat the linked two-word combinations.

1.	dream about	*drea – mabout*	I **dream about** taking a vacation.
2.	talk about	*tal – kabout*	Let's **talk about** the job.
3.	think about	*thin – kabout*	Let's **think about** going to the beach.
4.	plan on	*pla – non*	I **plan on** moving soon.
5.	insist on	*insis – ton*	I **insist on** paying the bill.
6.	afraid of	*afrai – dof*	She's **afraid of** dogs.
7.	good at	*goo – dat*	He's **good at** math.
8.	succeed in	*succee – din*	She'll **succeed in** finding a job.

I can . . .			
• use *used to* to talk about past habits.	1	2	3
• compare past and present living situations.	1	2	3
• discuss cultural differences in parenting.	1	2	3
• describe people using physical and character adjectives.	1	2	3
• interpret and create a personal ad.	1	2	3
• interpret a resume.	1	2	3
• understand a resume objective.	1	2	3
• create a resume.	1	2	3
• discuss cultural differences in dating.	1	2	3
• distinguish parts of speech.	1	2	3
• use gerunds appropriately.	1	2	3

1 = not well   2 = OK   3 = very well

DOWNTOWN JOURNAL

YOUR COMMUNITY NEWSPAPER   VOL. 24 NO. 2 SEPTEMBER 15

Have Coffee; Meet People; Learn about Other Cultures . . .

Downtown Café

Monday through Friday,
3:00 P.M.–5:00 P.M.

Come meet and mingle at the ESL Downtown Café. You will be introduced to a student from a different culture. Practice your English together by teaching your partner about your culture. Talk about the important ideas, customs, and rituals of your native culture. Learn how similar or different other people's ideas are.

STUDENT SURVEY: The Perfect Man/Woman

Of course there isn't really any perfect man or perfect woman. We all have our flaws. What qualities do you think would be the most important in a perfect man and a perfect woman? Complete the sentences below with your opinion. Then give the paper to your teacher. Your teacher will tell you the results of your class survey.

A perfect man is someone who _____

A perfect woman is someone who _____

What We Fight About

According to the American Psychological Association, nearly all arguments between married couples are about the same four things: money, time, children, and other people. Below are the results of last month's married-student survey of our own Downtown Adult School population.

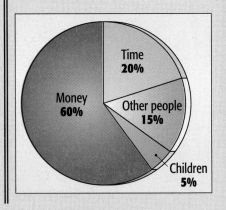

What do you think?

1. Think about relationships between men and women in your country and between men and women in the United States. In what ways are relationships between men and women different here? In what ways are they the same?
2. What do you think are the three things that couples argue or disagree about most in your country?

Dear Ms. Know It All

Problem Solving: Dating

Dear Ms. Know It All:

I am an eighteen-year-old immigrant and have been living with my parents in New York for about two years. My problem is about dating. Dating in New York is very different from dating in my country. In my culture, eighteen-year-old girls don't go out alone on dates with men. They can date, but they usually go to dances or school events. And they always go on dates in groups with other girls or with responsible adults.

My problem is that I met this guy who might be my soul mate. He is a real dreamboat and I am crazy about him. He says that I am the girl of his dreams. But he is twenty-six years old, and he doesn't want to go on dates with groups of girls. He wants to be alone with me! Until now, I have avoided that because it makes me very nervous. But I am afraid I'm going to lose the love of my life because of this fear. What should I do? I don't want to lose my honey.

Sincerely,
Home Alone

What do you think?

Find the idioms in the letter that describe someone who you are dating or are attracted to. Underline them. Do you know any other idioms that have the same meaning?

CRITICAL THINKING:

Work with a partner or small group. Talk about Home Alone's problem. Make a list of things that you think she should do. Then complete the letter of advice. Use gerunds in your letter.

> Dear Home Alone:
>
> There are some suggestions I can make to help you keep your sweetheart without losing your reputation. First of all, meeting him in a public place . . .

GOALS

- ✓ Describe ways to save money
- ✓ Use adjective clauses to describe products
- ✓ Interpret consumer advertising
- ✓ Interpret banking information
- ✓ Understand a credit card statement
- ✓ Read and interpret a spreadsheet
- ✓ Create a monthly budget
- ✓ Make returns or exchanges
- ✓ Identify misleading ads
- ✓ Write a letter of complaint
- ✓ Use verbs that take gerunds

What is happening in the picture?

1 🎧 **Read and Listen** Read the story. Then listen to it.

Bills

Elena is sitting in her dining room looking at her bills and trying to plan a monthly budget. She has been sitting there for an hour, but she has only paid two bills so far. She hasn't finished planning her budget, either. Mostly, she has been looking at coupons and ads and thinking about how to save money.

Elena has to make a budget now because the $3,000 she brought with her from Russia, her life savings, is shrinking fast. She doesn't make enough money to buy and do all the things she wants to every month. She has monthly bills for rent, gas, and electricity. She has bills for her English class, for Sasha's gym class, and for clothes. And, of course, she spends money on groceries, transportation, and restaurants. So, she needs to either make more or spend less money.

She has been considering applying for a credit card or a personal loan from a bank to help her pay her bills until she finds a better job. Of course, she wants to avoid borrowing too much money, but there are some things she can't help spending money on. Her gas and electric bills are high. English class costs $150 a month and Sasha's gym class costs $40 a week. Maybe she spends too much money on clothes, but she wants to look nice. Also, she likes to take Sasha to a restaurant once a week.

Hopefully, she will get a better job soon. But, in the meantime, she is thinking about the best way to budget the little money she has.

2 **Write** How can Elena save money? List things that she could do on a piece of paper.

CRITICAL THINKING:

Should Elena get a credit card or a personal loan? Why or why not?

1 **Say It** Practice the conversation with a partner.

laptop computer

A: What are you doing?

B: I'm looking at <u>computers</u>. I've been looking at them for about an hour.

A: How many have you looked at?

B: I've looked at a lot. I've been thinking about getting a <u>laptop computer</u>. What do you think about that?

A: I think you ought to get a <u>laptop computer</u> if you really want one. You only live once, you know.

B: OK. Maybe I will. Thanks for your advice.

A: No problem.

Practice more conversations. Use the pictures below.

1. **black ski jacket**

2. **three-piece suit with a vest**

3. **small color tattoo**

GRAMMAR CHECK

Present perfect continuous

Use the *present perfect continuous* to talk about actions that started in the past and continue in the present.

She **has been baking** cookies for three hours.

We also use the present perfect continuous for actions that have recently finished but still have some connection to the present.

Your hair is wet. I guess **you've been swimming.**

Check Point:

✓ We don't usually use a continuous form with nonaction verbs. For nonaction verbs, use the present perfect instead of the present perfect continuous.

I **have known** her for three years. (NOT: I **have been knowing** her for three years.)

Common nonaction verbs

Feelings	Possession	Senses	Mental States	Other Verbs
want	have	see	know	cost
need	own	hear	understand	mean
like	belong	taste	remember	
love		smell	forget	
hate		look	believe	
prefer			think (opinion)	
feel				

Check Points:

✓ Some verbs can be either action or nonaction, depending on their use.

    I **am tasting** the soup. (action) It **tastes** good. (nonaction)

    I **am smelling** the flowers. (action) They **smell** good. (nonaction)

✓ *See* and *feel* can also have action meanings.

✓ *Look* with a preposition is an action verb: *look at, look for*

✓ *Think* with a preposition is an action verb: *think about*

✓ *Have* for possession is a nonaction verb, but *have* also has many action meanings: *have lunch, have fun, have a baby,* etc.

Write Circle the correct verb in each sentence.

1. Vicki (looks / is looking) very sad. I wonder what happened.

2. I (hear / am hearing) a beautiful songbird right outside the window.

3. It isn't so difficult. I (understand / am understanding) it.

4. Elena's mother (thinks / is thinking) that credit cards are very dangerous.

5. Alice (looks / is looking) for a new, inexpensive computer.

6. Daisy is at a party. She (has / is having) a good time.

Write Write sentences using either the present perfect continuous or the present perfect tense.

1. Vicki is shopping. (since 5:00)   *Vicki has been shopping since 5:00.*

2. Freddy wants to buy a new car. (since June) _____

3. Daisy is saving money. (for a year) _____

4. Daisy works at a school. (for a while) _____

5. Al sings at a nightclub. (for two years) _____

6. Hamid owns his own business. (for five years) _____

7. Elena is looking for a new sofa. (since August) _____

8. Vicki has a credit card. (for a long time) _____

4 Pair Practice Work with a partner. Ask and answer *How long . . .* questions about Activity 3.

Example: *Student 1:* How long has Vicki been shopping?
Student 2: She has been shopping since 5:00.

5 Say It Practice the conversation with a partner.

A: Can I help you?

B: Yes. I'm looking for <u>a cell phone</u>.

A: Then you've come to the right place. We have lots of <u>cell phones</u> here. What kind of <u>phone</u> are you interested in?

B: I want <u>a phone</u> that <u>has a camera</u>.

A: This one <u>has a camera and it's only $149</u>.

B: Is there anything else I ought to know about it?

A: Well, you should know that it <u>requires a one-year service contract</u>.

B: Hmm. I'll have to think about that. Thank you for telling me.

has a camera

Practice more conversations. Use the pictures below.

1. **has a zipper instead of buttons**

2. **is easy to understand**

3. **is friendly and easy to train**

Culture Tip

The fine print

Do you read the small (or fine) print when you read an ad? Advertisements often contain negative information, or things they are required by law to tell you, in smaller print that you might not notice when you first read an ad. Reread ads and pay attention to the fine print! It's there to inform and protect you.

Adjective clauses with *that*

Adjective clauses that describe a thing usually start with *that* or *which*. *That* is more common and less formal. Do not use *what* in adjective clauses.

I want a car *that* **gets good gas mileage**. (NOT: I want a car *what* **gets good gas mileage**.)

Check Point:

✓ Adjective clauses that tell about people can begin with *that* or *who*.
   She's the girl **that/who** I told you about.

6 **Write** Pretend you are shopping for each of the following things. Use an adjective clause to describe more exactly what you are looking for.

Example: an English book   I want an English book that explains grammar well.

1. an apartment   I want an apartment that . . . _____
2. a movie   _____
3. a credit card   _____
4. a computer   _____
5. a new jacket   _____
6. a television   _____
7. shoes   _____
8. a restaurant   _____
9. a dog   _____
10. an English class _____

7 **Teamwork Task** Work in teams of three or four. Pretend you are going to buy a car, a wallet, and an English book. Work together to write three adjective clauses for each item that describe exactly what you want. Write your clauses on a piece of paper.

Game Time

Game Time: What is it?

1. Write eight common objects on a piece of paper, such as a pen, a key, a cat, a stove, etc. Your teacher will take your lists and mix them up.

2. Find a partner. Your teacher will give you one of the lists of objects. Use adjective clauses to describe the objects to your partner. Your partner has to guess what each thing is.

Example: *Student 1:* It's something that opens a door.
             Student 2: Is it a key?

You get a point if your guess is correct. The pair with the most points wins.

Money

Word Help: Banking terms

interest = the amount of money you pay a bank for borrowing their money, or the amount of money the bank pays you for holding your money

balance = the amount of money you have in an account

minimum balance = the least amount of money you must keep in an account to avoid paying a penalty

service charge = the amount a bank charges for holding your account

per-check charge = the amount you have to pay for each check you write

bounced check = a check written without enough money in the account, or *insufficient funds*, to cover the check

1 **Say It** Practice the conversation with a partner.

BIG BUCKS CHECKING ACCOUNT

Bank *of* Brooklyn **2.75%** *current interest rate*

No service charge. No per-check charge with minimum balance.
Required minimum balance: $1,500

$39 charge for checks written with insufficient funds

A: I've been thinking about opening a checking account. Could you give me some information about them?

B: Yes, of course. Do you want an account that pays interest?

A: I'm not sure. What is the current interest rate?

B: Our interest rate right now is <u>2.75%</u>.

A: Is there a minimum balance required for this account?

B: <u>Yes. This is an account that requires a $1,500 minimum balance</u>.

A: Is there a service charge or a per-check charge?

B: <u>No, there is no service charge or per-check charge as long as you keep the minimum balance.</u>

A: Is there a charge for checks written with insufficient funds?

B: There is a <u>$39</u> charge for bounced checks. Would you like to fill out an application?

A: I'm going to have to think about it. Thank you.

Practice more conversations. Use the information below.

PREMIUM CHECKING ACCOUNT
2% Interest Rate
Minimum Balance: $1,000
$5 per month service charge
No per-check charge
$35 fee for returned checks

1.

NO MINIMUM BALANCE
NO INTEREST
ZERO-BALANCE CHECKING
$0.50 PER CHECK
$10 PER MONTH SERVICE CHARGE
$29 fee for checks written with insufficient funds

2.

Word Help: Banking terms
total credit line = how much you are allowed to borrow
APR = the interest rate you have to pay
average daily balance = the average amount you owe during the month
finance charges = how much you have to pay for interest this month

Bank of Brooklyn
Golden Vista Card

Statement Date:.................10-24-06
PAYMENT DUE DATE:.........11/21/06
Minimum Payment Due:. **$54.00**

Account Number:....123-456-789-1011
Customer Service:.......1-800-555-3353

Transactions

Date	Description	Amount
10/22	Late Fee	$39.00
10/24	**Payment – *Thank You***	–$200.00
10/15	Healthy Woman Fitness Club	$39.00
10/16	Chevon Gas	$32.50
10/20	New York Fish Company	$36.40
10/27	Rocks Restaurant	$46.80
	TOTAL PURCHASES	**$154.70**

Previous Balance:.................$2,876.95
Payments Credits:.................–$200.00
Purchases, Debits:................+$193.70
Finance Charges:....................+$29.95
New Balance:.................. **$2,900.60**

Total Credit Line:.................$5,000.00
Available Credits:................$2,100.00
Cash Access Line:.................$1,000.00

Finance Charges

Category	APR	Average Daily Balance	Finance Charge
Purchases	12.24%	$2,872.11	$29.95
Cash Advances	22.24%	0	0
		Total Finance Charges:.......	**$29.95**

2 Write Use Daisy's credit card statement above to answer the questions.

1. How much does Daisy have to pay this month? _____

2. What is the due date on the bill? _____

3. When did the bank receive her last payment? _____

4. How much did she have to pay for being late? _____

5. How much does she owe to the Bank of Brooklyn now? _____

6. How much more is she allowed to charge on this card? _____

7. How much were her finance charges for this month? _____

8. What interest rate is she paying for her purchases? _____

9. What is the interest rate for a cash advance? _____

10. How much did Daisy charge this month? _____

3 **Group Practice** *Find someone who . . .* Work with a large group or the whole class. Ask your classmates questions until you find someone who says "Yes" to each of the statements below. When someone says "Yes," write his or her name on the corresponding line and ask the follow-up question in parentheses. Keep asking questions until you have a different name on each line below.

1. _____ has more than one credit card. (How many?)

2. _____ has never had a credit card. (Wants one?)

3. _____ knows what his or her credit card interest rate is. (What?)

4. _____ knows what his or her credit limit is. (What?)

5. _____ has gone over the limit on a credit card. (When?)

6. _____ has made a late payment on a credit card. (How much / late fee?)

7. _____ thinks credit cards are wonderful. (Why?)

8. _____ thinks credit cards are terrible. (Why?)

4 **Listen** Listen to the conversation. Complete the bank account application for Elena.

PERSONAL INFORMATION
*(*Required Information)*

First Name* _____ MI ___ Last Name* _____

Social Security Number* ___ / ___ / ___ Phone Number ( ) Date of Birth* ___ / ___ / ___

Address (No P.O. Boxes)* _____ Apt. # ___

City* _____ State* _____ Zip* _____

E-mail Address _____ ☐ Own ☐ Rent ☐ Parents/Relative ☐ Other Monthly Payment _____

EMPLOYMENT OR SOURCE OF INCOME

Name of Current Employer or Business _____

Annual Gross Household Income _____ Work Phone ( )

☐ Retired ☐ Disabled ☐ Small Business Owner ☐ Other

BANKING RELATIONSHIP

Do you have a relationship with the Bank of Brooklyn? _____

If yes, what is your Account Number? _____

5 **Pair Practice** Work with a partner. Ask and answer questions about Elena's application information.

Word Help: Spreadsheets

Spreadsheets are grids of **rows** and **columns** that contain **labels** and **values**.
- **Rows** run across the spreadsheet from left to right and are named by numbers.
- **Columns** run up and down the spreadsheet and are named by letters.
- **Cells** are the boxes where the rows and columns meet. They are named by numbers and letters. For example: Cell 4B = "85"; Cell 10A = "Total Spent"
- **Labels** are words or names that explain the information in a spreadsheet.
- **Values** are numeric information or numbers.

	A	B	C	D	E
1	Month	August	September	October	
2	Rent	$800	$800		
3	Utilities	$110	$100		
4	Telephone	$85	$70		
5	Transportation	$95	$90		
6	Groceries	$360	$340		
7	Restaurants/ Cafés	$230	$210		
8	Clothes	$225	$105		
9	Medical/ Dental/Other	$110	$60		
10	Total Spent	$2,015	$1,775		

 Pair Practice Work with a partner. Ask and answer the questions with the information from the spreadsheet.

1. How much did Elena spend on groceries in August? _____

2. How much did she spend on utilities in August? _____

3. Which row tells how much she spent on clothes? _____

4. Which column contains information about September? _____

5. How much total did she spend in September? _____

6. How much more did she spend in August? _____

Now ask and answer more questions about Elena's spreadsheet.

7 Teamwork Task Work in teams of three or four. Elena's take-home pay is $1,800 a month. She doesn't want to spend more money than she makes. Create a budget for Elena. Write your budget in the spreadsheet above in Column D. Explain what Elena is going to do to save money.

Homework

Make a list of financial institutions in your neighborhood. Call two of them and ask what the interest rate is on their basic savings accounts. Look up two other financial institutions on the Internet. Can you find interest rates on their Web sites?

Customer Service

Lesson 3

1 Read and Listen Read the story. Then listen to the story.

Customer Service

Vicki works in the customer service department of the *Downtown Department Store*. That means that part of her job is to listen to customers' complaints. She doesn't mind hearing complaints as long as the customers are honest and the complaints are legitimate. But she can't help feeling annoyed with people who come to her with bogus complaints and tell her things that are not true.

Yesterday a woman came in to return an expensive dress. It was a yellow dress and it had a brown stain that looked like a coffee stain. "Did you wear the dress?" Vicki asked.

The woman denied wearing it. "The stain was there when I bought it," she said. Vicki knew that the woman had worn the dress. She knows that the *Downtown Department Store* doesn't sell dresses with big brown stains on them. But Vicki is supposed to avoid arguing with customers, so she just continued to smile.

Some people enjoy taking advantage of the store policy by returning things even after they've worn or used them. Vicki always recommends exchanging a stained or broken product for a new one. But sometimes the customer wants a refund rather than an exchange. The store doesn't like to return cash to people for broken or stained products unless there is a manufacturer's warranty that permits returning a damaged product for a full refund. But the *Downtown Department Store* doesn't mind giving store credit to customers who have a legitimate complaint.

When Vicki encounters people who tell her bogus stories, she sometimes imagines arguing with them about it. But, of course, she never does because she would probably get fired. Her job is to listen to customers' complaints and report exactly what they say. So, she just listens and smiles and tries not to get upset.

Word Help: Meaning from context

Find these words in the story. Try to guess their meanings from the words around them. Don't use a dictionary. Then match each word with its meaning.

1. _____ legitimate
2. _____ bogus
3. _____ deny
4. _____ admit
5. _____ refund
6. _____ encounter
7. _____ recommend

a. return money
b. true or real
c. advise, give your opinion
d. say "no" to or about something
e. meet
f. false, not real
g. confess, say that you did something

Write Complete the sentences with information from the story.

1. If customers are honest, their complaints are probably _____ .

2. If customers are dishonest, their complaints are probably _____ .

3. Some people enjoy _____ of the system.

4. Customers rarely admit _____ .

5. Vicki is supposed to avoid _____ .

6. Vicki always recommends _____ .

7. The *Downtown Department Store* doesn't mind _____ .

Culture Tip

Receipts

Always keep your receipts! Most businesses in the U.S. will take back or exchange something you recently bought as long as you have a receipt. Is it easy to return or exchange things in your country?

GRAMMAR CHECK

Verbs that take gerunds

Some verbs are followed by a gerund (the *-ing* verb form used as a noun), but they cannot be followed by an infinitive.

Vicki **avoids arguing** with customers. (NOT: Vicki avoids **to argue** with customers.)

 Write Read the story again. Find all of the gerunds and underline them. If a gerund follows a verb, circle the verb. List the verbs that take gerunds.

_____

_____

_____

 Write Complete the sentences in the chart with a gerund.

CUSTOMER SERVICE RULES
Avoid _____ with customers. It will only make you upset.
Keep _____ even when you know what they are going to say.
Practice _____ even when you don't feel happy.
Insist on _____ a receipt before authorizing a refund or exchange.
Always recommend _____ a defective product for a new one.
Try to enjoy _____ to people even when they are difficult.
Never stop _____ the nice, friendly person you are.

Common verbs that take gerunds

admit	delay	finish	imagine	recommend
appreciate	deny	stop	mind	suggest
avoid	discuss	quit	miss	
can't help	dislike	keep (on)	permit	
consider	enjoy	practice		

Check Point:

✓ Some verbs can be followed by either a gerund or an infinitive and keep the same meaning. Examples include *like, love, hate, begin, start, continue,* and *prefer.*

 Write Complete the sentences with the verb in parentheses and a gerund or gerund phrase.

1. Customer: "Well, I did wear the dress once." (admit)

   <u>The customer admitted wearing the dress</u>

2. Customer: "No, I never wore the blouse." (deny)

   _____

3. Vicki: "Why don't you exchange the pants for a bigger size." (suggest)

   _____

4. Salesperson: "In my opinion, you should get a large screen TV." (recommend)

   _____

5. Alice walked away because she didn't want to talk to the manager. (avoid)

   _____

6. Elena wants to find a better job sometime soon. (imagine)

   _____

 Pair Practice Work with a partner. Use the cues below to ask and answer questions. Use gerunds in your answers.

Example: avoid doing?
Student 1: What is something you avoid doing?
Student 2: I avoid taking the subway late at night.

1. dislike doing?
2. can't help doing?
3. quit doing?
4. really enjoy doing?
5. imagine doing in the future?
6. like practicing?
7. miss doing?
8. admitted or denied recently?
9. recommend doing this weekend?
10. look forward to doing this weekend?

Say It Practice the conversation with a partner.

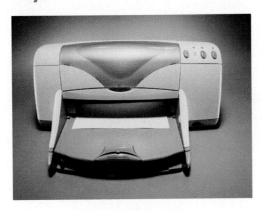

the paper jams a lot

A: Good morning. May I help you?

B: Yes, please. I bought this <u>printer</u> here yesterday, and I'd like to return it.

A: Can you tell me the problem with it?

B: Yes. <u>The paper jams a lot</u>.

A: Do you have your receipt?

B: Yes, I do.

A: Would you consider exchanging it for another one?

B: No, I'd like a refund.

A: Is store credit OK?

B: No. I'd prefer getting my money back. Is that possible?

A: Yes. Just fill out this refund request form and the manager will return your money.

Practice more conversations. Think about things that you have bought and would like to return. Give a reason why you want to return each thing.

Read and Write A misleading ad is an advertisement that contains information that is not completely true. If something looks "too good to be true," then it probably isn't true. For example, an ad that says "Free Puppies" is misleading if you have to pay for a license and shots before you can take the puppy. Although the puppy is free, you can't have it for free. Read the ads below. Underline the parts of the ads that are true. Circle the parts that are misleading.

1.

2.

3.
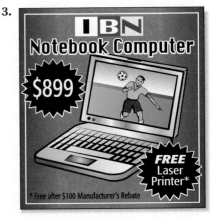

CRITICAL THINKING:

Which ad is the most misleading? Which is the least misleading? Why?

9 Read Read the letter of complaint.

> 2255 Ocean Avenue
> Brooklyn, New York 11238
> October 2, 2006
>
> Mr. Robert Williams—Manager
> R.W. Electronics
> 2255 Flatbush Avenue
> Brooklyn, N.Y. 11230
>
> Dear Mr. Williams:
>
>   I bought a Suny CD player at your store on September 28. I still have the receipt. When I brought it home and tried to use it, I found that the sound wasn't loud enough. That's a big problem for me because I plan to use the CD player for parties, and I need a CD player with louder sound.
>
>   Your assistant manager recommended exchanging the CD player for another one. He said that store policy doesn't permit returning the item for cash. I believe I should get a refund because I wasn't able to try out the CD player before I bought it.
>
>   The cost of the CD player, including tax, was $75.75. Please let me know if you will be able to refund my money.
>
> Sincerely,
> *Daisy Yu*

10 Write Answer the questions about the letter of complaint.

1. Who wrote the letter? _____

2. Who did she write to? _____

3. What did she buy and when did she buy it? _____

4. What is her problem with the product? _____

5. What doesn't she want to do? _____

6. What is her request? _____

CRITICAL THINKING:

7. Do you think the manager should return Daisy's money? Why or why not?

11 Teamwork Task Work in teams of three or four. Write a letter of complaint about a product you bought and were not happy with. Include when you bought it, how much it cost, and why you are unhappy with it. Request a refund, following the business letter format of Daisy's letter.

Game Time

Two truths and a lie

Write three sentences using the verbs *enjoy*, *avoid*, and *dislike*, and a gerund. Two of your sentences should be true and one not true. Read them to the class. If your classmates don't guess which one is the lie on the first try, then you win.

 Read and Listen Read the story. Then listen to the story.

Making Ends Meet

Ever since she arrived in New York, Elena has been spending (1) <u>several hundred dollars a month more than she earns</u>. That means that she has been "living over her head." When she arrived from Russia, she had (2) <u>almost $3,000</u>, but now she has (3) <u>less than $1,000</u> left. So, it's time for her to make some changes.

Now Elena is trying to spend less money. She is avoiding buying (4) <u>unnecessary things</u>. She has stopped buying (5) <u>silly toys for Sasha</u>. And the last time she bought new clothes was (6) <u>about a month ago</u>. She has also delayed buying some furniture she would like to get for her apartment. In fact, Elena hasn't bought anything new for her apartment in about a month.

But there are some things she hasn't stopped doing. She still has to pay her rent and utility bills. She hasn't stopped taking (7) <u>English classes</u>, and she hasn't stopped paying for Sasha's gym class (8) <u>because she thinks it's important for him to exercise every day</u>. And she wants him to be in a class with kids his own age who speak Russian. There are several Russian children in the class. She is still spending money on subway passes, but she isn't taking the bus to the beach anymore because she can walk there in about fifteen minutes, and she needs the exercise, too. She hasn't been exercising as much as she used to in Russia. She isn't taking Sasha (9) <u>to eat in nice restaurants</u> anymore. But sometimes she can't help buying (10) <u>a slice of pizza</u> when she gets off the subway after work. The pizza shop at the subway station has the best pizza in New York. When she buys pizza for herself, she sometimes brings home some for Sasha, too, and then she doesn't have to cook dinner. So, that is another way of making ends meet.

2 **Write** On a piece of paper, make a list of things that Elena has been doing since she came to New York and is still doing. Then make a list of things she has recently stopped doing.

CRITICAL THINKING:

"Making ends meet" is an idiom. From the story, what do you think it means?

_____

_____

_____

3 **Write** Write a question for each underlined part of the story. Use the question words given. Then ask and answer the questions with a partner.

1. How much? <u>How much money has Elena been spending since she</u>
   <u>arrived in New York?</u>

2. How much? _____

3. How much? _____

4. What? _____

5. What? _____

6. When? _____

7. What? _____

8. Why? _____

9. Where? _____

10. What? _____

4 **Write** Correct the mistakes in the following sentences. If there are no mistakes, write *correct*.

1. The woman denied to wear the dress. <u>The woman denied wearing the dress.</u>

2. She needs a job what pays at least ten dollars an hour.

   _____

3. Your hair is wet. I guess you have swum. _____

4. "His check bounced" means that he had insufficient funds in his account to pay the check. _____

5. I don't want a refund or store credit. I want my money back. _____

6. The customer service representative suggested exchange the camera.

   _____

7. I have been having a headache all day. _____

8. Nobody enjoys to return clothing. _____

9. A misleading ad means nothing in the ad is true. _____

10. She was really happy with the new computer so she wrote a letter of complaint. _____

5 **Write** Read the story on page 57 again. Circle the gerunds. How many can you find? What verbs do the gerunds follow? Make a list.

VERB	GERUND
_____	_____
_____	_____
_____	_____
_____	_____
_____	_____

6 **Teamwork Task** Work in teams of three or four. Pretend that you are a family and that your family's take-home pay is $3,000 a month. Create a monthly budget. You can use the labels in Elena's spreadsheet on page 51, or you can choose to spend money on different things.

INTERNET IDEA
Go online to a bank or financial services Web site. Write down the current interest rates for home mortgages, car loans, and any other loans you can find. Report your information to the class.

Pronunciation Rising intonation
Yes/No questions and clarification questions usually end with rising intonation.

A. Listen and repeat the following questions. Practice making your voice rise at the end of the sentences.

1. May I help you?

2. Do you work here?

3. You want a house that has a what?

4. Is store credit OK?

5. Would you like to talk to the manager?

6. Do you have your receipt?

B. Now ask a partner more *yes/no* and clarification questions. Practice using rising intonation.

I can . . .			
• describe ways to save money.	1	2	3
• use adjective clauses to describe products.	1	2	3
• interpret consumer advertising.	1	2	3
• interpret banking information.	1	2	3
• understand a credit card statement.	1	2	3
• read and interpret a spreadsheet.	1	2	3
• create a monthly budget.	1	2	3
• make returns or exchanges.	1	2	3
• identify misleading ads.	1	2	3
• write a letter of complaint.	1	2	3
• use verbs that take gerunds.	1	2	3

1 = not well   2 = OK   3 = very well

DOWNTOWN JOURNAL

YOUR COMMUNITY NEWSPAPER   VOL. 24 NO. 3 OCTOBER 15

What's Your Credit Score?

Your FICO score, or credit score, is a number that banks and other financial institutions use to evaluate how good or bad your credit history is. It is important because your FICO score will often determine how high an interest rate you will pay if you borrow money. The best rates go to people who have FICO scores of 700 or higher. If your score is below 620, you probably won't get the best interest rates, and you might even have trouble getting a loan.

If you have not borrowed any money, then you probably have a low FICO score or no FICO score at all. There are some things you can do to raise or improve your credit score. Financial professionals recommend never making late payments on a loan or other credit account. Making late payments will lower your credit score. Making late payments on a home or car loan will lower your score a lot.

FICO Scores

| Poor | Fair | Good | Excellent |

300   350   400   450   500   550   600   650   Average 700   750   800   850

If you cosign for someone else's loan, you are responsible for it. If he or she makes late payments, they will go on your record, too. Defaulting on a loan will damage your score a lot. Declaring bankruptcy will destroy your score for seven years. How much your score is lowered by a late payment depends on how much you owed, how recently it happened, and how many late payments you have.

It is possible to raise your credit score. Consider opening more credit accounts as long as you can make your payments on time. Having a longer history of credit will raise your score, so it is better to delay closing accounts you have had for a long time even if you don't use them anymore. Consider asking banks to raise your credit

limit on credit cards. Higher credit limits will raise your score because your score is partly determined by the amount of credit you have available compared to the amount you owe. So, the key to higher scores is to have high credit limits on your cards, but not use them very much.

Words you should know about credit:

cosigner: someone who uses his name and credit to help someone else get a loan

default: when you don't pay back money you have borrowed

bankruptcy: a legal process that asks a court to take away your debts because you can't pay them

What do you think?

List ways you can improve your credit score. Then make a list of things you should avoid doing if you want a higher credit score.

Dear Ms. Know It All

Problem Solving: Money

Dear Ms. Know It All:

    I am a thirty-year-old single mother who has gone back to school at a community college. The problem is that I am working only part-time right now, and I don't make enough money to pay all my monthly bills. I spend in the ballpark of $400 a month more than I make. I am sure I will be able to get a better job and make more money when I finish school. But, in the meantime, I need a boost to get over the hump. So, I am thinking about getting a loan or a couple of credit cards to save my neck. My first idea is to use lots of plastic to get me through this school year. But I am afraid that I might get in over my head with credit card interest and dig a hole I won't be able to easily climb out of. What should I do?

Sincerely,
Drowning Slowly In My Bills

Word Help:

Underline the idioms in Drowning Slowly's letter. Then write the idioms next to their meanings.

MEANING	IDIOM
1. approximately, not exactly	*in the ballpark*
2. get past a temporary problem	
3. credit cards	
4. have a problem I can't handle	
5. some help	
6. between now and another event	
7. cause a problem	
8. get out of a difficult situation	

CRITICAL THINKING:

Work with a partner or small group. Talk about Drowning Slowly's problem. Make a list of things you think she could or should do. Then complete the letter of advice.

> Dear Drowning Slowly:
>   I think there are some things you can do to keep from "getting in over your head."

The Community

GOALS

✓ Identify and talk about places in the community

✓ Use infinitives to describe purpose

✓ Use prepositions to describe location and direction

✓ Ask and answer questions about my community

✓ Work together to create a community information page

✓ Use a street map to find and describe locations

✓ Identify community resources for various problems

✓ Write a formal letter of concern about a community issue

✓ Distinguish fact from opinion

✓ Use infinitives in different kinds of sentences

How does Elena's neighborhood compare to yours? What is similar? What is different?

1 Read and Listen Read the story. Then listen to it.

Diversity

Elena loves the diversity of her Brooklyn neighborhood. She likes to walk down the street and look into all the stores and shops. There is a pizza shop right next to the subway. She often stops there on her way home from work. She usually orders a slice of pizza and then stands for a few minutes in front of the store to eat it. It's interesting to watch all the people hurrying home from work.

There is a Chinese discount store where everything is always on sale. She likes to go in there to see what kind of bargains she can find. Sometimes she finds really nice things for very low prices. Across the street there is a Russian pharmacy where she goes to pick up medications and to get special Russian cosmetics that she likes. Around the corner there is a post office where she goes to buy stamps and to mail letters.

There are also several ethnic restaurants in the neighborhood. There is a Russian café that has good coffee and pastries. There is a Chinese seafood restaurant that she intends to visit for a nice shrimp dinner when she gets a new job. And there is a Japanese restaurant that has delicious sushi. Elena plans to try all the neighborhood restaurants when she gets a new job and has more money. But right now she is happy just to know that there are so many interesting places nearby.

TONY'S PIZZA

F G

 Write What places are in Elena's neighborhood? Write the places and the reasons Elena might go to each one.

PLACE	REASONS
_____	_____
_____	_____
_____	_____
_____	_____
_____	_____
_____	_____

The Neighborhood

1 **Say It** Practice the conversation with a partner.

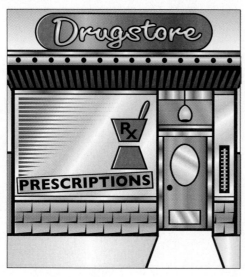

cosmetics

A: What do you like about this neighborhood?

B: There are a lot of things I like about it. For example, I like being able to go to the <u>drugstore</u> when I want to.

A: What do you go to the <u>drugstore</u> for?

B: I go there to <u>pick up my prescriptions</u>. And I also go there in order to get <u>cosmetics</u>. You can't get good <u>cosmetics</u> in some places.

A: Yes, I guess that's true.

Practice more conversations. Use the pictures below.

1. educational toys

2. mangoes

3. fish stew

GRAMMAR CHECK

Infinitives of purpose

We often use an infinitive to show a purpose or reason for something. You may use *in order to* as the complete form or just *to* as the shortened form.

She went to the donut shop (**in order**) **to get** coffee and a donut.

2 **Write** Look at the picture of Elena's neighborhood on pages 62–63. Pretend you live there. On a piece of paper, list the places in the neighborhood that you would go to and why. Write as many sentences as you can.

Example: I would go to the newspaper stand to buy a newspaper.

Word Help: Prepositions of place and direction

Prepositions of place tell the location of a person, place, or thing.
   The belt is **around** his waist. (a place)

Prepositions of direction describe movement.
   He drove **around** the block. (a direction)

These prepositions can describe either location or movement:

above	behind	in	through
across	below	into	throughout
against	beneath	in front of	to
along	beside	near	toward(s)
among	between	off	under
around	beyond	on	up
at	down	out of	within
away from	from	over	

 Read and Write Read the story on page 62 again. Underline all the prepositions of place or direction in the story. Write the prepositions below along with their objects.

PREPOSITION	OBJECT
down	the street

 Write Look at the picture of Elena's neighborhood on pages 62 and 63. Write sentences about the picture using prepositions of place or direction from the list above. Use each preposition only once. Write as many sentences as possible.

5 **Pair Practice** Work with a partner. Ask and answer questions about Elena's neighborhood. Ask as many questions as you can.

Say It Practice the conversation with a partner.

borrow a book / use the Internet

A: Do you ever go to the <u>library</u> in your community?

B: Yes, I go to the <u>library</u> once in a while.

A: What do you go there for?

B: I usually go there to <u>borrow a book</u>.

A: I guess that's a good reason.

B: How about you? Do you ever go to the <u>library</u>?

A: Yes, I do. Sometimes I go there to <u>use the Internet</u>.

B: That's a good reason, too.

Practice more conversations. Use the pictures below. Give your own reason for going to each place.

1. mail a package / ?   2. fill a prescription / ?   3. buy roses for Valentine's Day / ?

7 **Pair Practice** Work with a partner and continue the conversation in Activity 6. Ask about other places in your community. Answer with true information.

Example: *Student 1:* Do you ever go to a gas station in your community?
Student 2: Yes, I do. I go there to get gas for my motorcycle. How about you?
Student 1: I go there to put air in my bicycle's tires.

GRAMMAR CHECK

Verbs that take infinitives

Here are some common verbs that take (or can be followed by) infinitives:

agree	expect	mean	promise	would like
appear	forget	need	offer	would love
attempt	hope	plan	refuse	like*
(can) afford	intend	prefer	remember	love*
decide	learn (how)	pretend	want	hate*
begin*	start*	continue*		

Check Point:
  ✓ The verbs with an asterisk (*) can take either a gerund or an infinitive.
    She likes **shopping**. She likes **to shop**.

8 **Pair Practice** Work with a partner. Ask and answer the questions using a verb followed by an infinitive.

Example: . . . something you agreed to do with someone recently?
Student 1: What is something you agreed to do with someone recently?
Student 2: I agreed to go to a movie with my friend last week.

1. . . . a place you expect to go next weekend?
2. . . . something you need to buy for your home?
3. . . . a local restaurant you intend to eat at?
4. . . . a place in your neighborhood where you refuse to go?
5. . . . a place you promised to take someone?
6. . . . something expensive you plan to buy in the future?
7. . . . something you forgot to do recently?
8. . . . a place you decided not to go anymore?
9. . . . something you would love to buy, but can't afford to buy right now?

9 **Teamwork Task** Work in teams of three or four.

1. Make a list of places in your community to do each of the following things:
   - a good place to eat lunch
   - a cheap place to buy groceries
   - a place to see a doctor
   - a good Italian or Chinese restaurant to have dinner
   - a nice place to take a child
   - a good place to rent a video
   - a place to see a movie

2. Now write sentences about the places you listed. Write seven sentences using seven different verbs from Word Help on page 65.

Example: *The Lobster is a good place to eat lunch. I promise to take you there on your next birthday.*

Game Time

Two truths and a lie

Write three sentences on a piece of paper describing things that you plan or expect to do this week. Two of them should be true and one a lie. Put a ✓ next to the true things and an X next to the lie. Give the paper to your teacher. Your teacher will read your sentences out loud. If the class doesn't guess which one is a lie on the first guess, then you win.

Problems and Services

Soho Area - NYC

1 **Listen** Listen to the conversations. Write the numbers of the community service agencies below in the circles on the map.

1. Employment Development Office

2. Post Office

3. Housing Authority Office

4. Sanitation Bureau

5. Animal Control Agency

6. Community Health Center

7. Senior Citizen Center

8. Public Library

9. Neighborhood Legal Services

10. Police Station

Say It Practice the conversation with a partner. Use the map on page 68 to give directions.

find a job

A: I'm trying to <u>find a job</u>. Is there some community agency that can help me <u>find a job</u>?

B: Yes, I'm sure there is. Have you tried calling the <u>Employment Development Office</u>?

A: No, I haven't. Do they help you <u>find a job</u>?

B: That's one of the things they do. Why don't you go there in person and talk to them.

A: Do you know where it is?

B: Yes, it's <u>on Broadway just south of Houston Street</u>.

A: OK. I'll go there tomorrow. Thanks for the suggestion.

B: No problem.

Practice more conversations. Use the pictures below.

1. **get back a security deposit**

2. **complain about a landlord**

3. **get a stray dog off the street**

Think about three or four more problems. What community agency could help? Practice the conversation again with the new problems.

Write Read the list of community service agencies on page 68. Write the name of the agency you would contact for each of the following problems.

1. You need to find some information in an encyclopedia.

_____

2. Your grandmother wants to meet some other retired people.

_____

3. Your former employer won't pay you money he owes you.

_____

4. There's a man with a knife shouting at someone on your street.

_____

5. Your child needs immunizations in order to register for school.

_____

6. You want to get a recycling bin.

_____

Group Practice Work in groups of three or four. Choose three of the community service agencies on page 68. Brainstorm a list of reasons you might go to those agencies. Then share your reasons with the class.

GRAMMAR CHECK

Infinitives after *it*

When infinitives are the subject of a sentence, we usually start the sentence with *it*.
It is important **to learn** English.
The infinitive often follows an adjective, such as *good, bad, dangerous, easy, difficult, interesting, important, necessary, convenient,* and *polite*.

Check Point:
✓ It is also possible to start a sentence with an infinitive, but the sentence sounds very formal.
    To shout isn't polite. (formal)
    It isn't polite **to shout.** (more common)

 Write Rewrite the following sentences. Change the gerund to an infinitive and write what is true about your neighborhood or community.

1. In some neighborhoods waiting for a bus at night is dangerous.

    In my neighborhood it isn't dangerous to wait for a bus at night.

2. In some cities using public transportation is convenient.

    _____

3. In some neighborhoods speaking English isn't necessary.

    _____

4. In some neighborhoods renting an apartment is very expensive.

    _____

5. In some neighborhoods having police on the street is important.

    _____

6. In some communities making friends with neighbors is easy.

    _____

6 **Pair Practice** Work with a partner who doesn't live close to you. Change the statements in Activity 5 to questions and ask your partner about his or her community. Use *Is it* + an infinitive.

Example: *Student 1:* Is it dangerous to wait for a bus at night in your neighborhood?
              Student 2: No, it isn't.   *OR*   Yes, it is.

Write Use an infinitive phrase to complete the sentences about your neighborhood or community.

1. In my neighborhood it is easy _____ .

2. In my city it is illegal _____ .

3. In my neighborhood it is normal _____ .

4. In my community some people are afraid _____ .

5. In my community it isn't polite _____ .

6. In my neighborhood it is dangerous _____ .

8 **Pair Practice** Work with a partner. Ask your partner his or her opinion about what is important to make a good community. Check the appropriate column.

IS IT IMPORTANT TO . . .	VERY IMPORTANT	IMPORTANT	NOT VERY IMPORTANT
have friendly neighbors?			
have clean streets?			
have a park nearby?			
have a lot of parking spaces?			
be close to a supermarket?			
be close to a school?			
not be overcrowded?			
feel safe on the street at night?			
be near a bus or train stop?			
have a lot of trees?			
not have a lot of dogs nearby?			
be near a church?			
live near family or relatives?			

9 **Teamwork Task** Work in teams of three or four. Think about the things that make a community a good place to live. Choose and rank the five most important things.

1. The most important thing is to . . . _____

2. The second most important thing is to . . . _____

3. _____

4. _____

5. _____

Homework

Write a paragraph comparing and contrasting your neighborhood with Elena's neighborhood. Tell how they are alike. (Her neighborhood has a pizza shop and mine does, too.) Tell how they are different. (Her neighborhood has a subway, but mine only has a bus stop.)

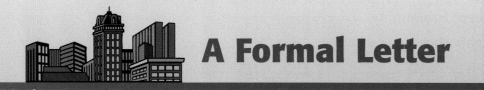

1 🎧 **Read and Listen** Read the story. Then listen to the story. Underline the infinitives.

A Letter of Concern

Elena thought there was a problem in her neighborhood, so she invited several of her neighbors to come to her apartment to talk about it. After they discussed the problem, Elena asked her neighbors to help her do something about it. Vicki advised Elena to call the local police station and to talk to the police about the problem. But Elena wanted to do something more serious than just talk to someone. Finally, they decided to write a letter of concern. It took a little while, but Elena finally persuaded Daisy to write the letter because she had the best writing skills of their group. The others agreed to help. This is what they wrote:

Concerned Women of Ocean Avenue
1950 Ocean Avenue
Brooklyn, N.Y. 11238
November 4, 2006

Captain Neil Tasso
75th Precinct
2305 Avenue X
Brooklyn, N.Y. 11230

Dear Captain Tasso:

We are a group of women who live in the neighborhood near your police station. We are writing to ask you to help us with a problem. The problem is that the area around our subway station isn't safe for women coming home alone at night. There are no bright lights outside the subway station and no police officers stationed there late at night. The street outside the station is so dark that you can't see if a dangerous person is standing in a doorway waiting to grab you as you walk past.

We would like you to put a police officer at this location from about 10:00 P.M. to about 3:00 in the morning. Also, we'd like you to please replace the broken streetlights and put even more lights on the street around the subway station for our safety.

Thank you for listening to our concern.

Sincerely,

Elena Petrova, *Daisy Yu, Vicki Martinez,* Alice Charles

2 **Write** Answer the questions about the reading and the letter.

1. What did Elena invite her neighbors to do? _____

2. What did Elena ask her neighbors to do? _____

3. What did Vicki advise Elena to do? _____

4. What did they finally decide to do? _____

5. What did Elena persuade Daisy to do? _____

6. Who are the Concerned Women of Ocean Avenue? _____

7. Who did the Concerned Women write to? _____

8. What is the problem they are concerned about? _____

9. Why is it a problem? _____

10. What two solutions did they suggest to solve the problem? _____

_____

Note: Fact or Opinion?
A *fact* is something that you can prove to be true.
   There are two schools in my neighborhood.
An *opinion* is something you think or feel that cannot be proven. It is a personal belief or view.
   The schools in my community aren't very good.

---

3 **Read and Write** Read the letter to Captain Tasso again. Underline two facts in the letter. Circle two opinions.

4 **Group Practice** Work in a group of three or four people who live in the same community as you do. On a piece of paper, make a list of facts about your community. Then make a list of opinions about your community. Try to write ten facts and ten opinions that you can all agree on.

FACTS

There are four banks in
   our neighborhood.

OPINIONS

The Chinese restaurant on Ocean Avenue
   has very good food.

GRAMMAR CHECK

Verb + object + infinitive

Some verbs are usually followed by an object and an infinitive.

   verb   *object*   *infinitive*
   She **asked**   **us**   **to write** a letter.

These verbs are often followed by a noun or object pronoun and an infinitive:

advise	encourage	order	teach
allow	expect	permit	tell
ask	invite	persuade	want
convince	need	remind	would like

5 **Write** Complete the sentences with an object and an infinitive.

1. Our teacher doesn't allow _____.

2. My father/mother taught _____.

3. My parents didn't expect _____.

4. _____ would like _____.

5. When I was a teenager, my parents didn't permit _____.

6. Someone once invited _____.

7. _____ asked _____.

8. In the future I will remind _____.

9. _____ told _____.

Word Help: *so, such*

So or *such* can be used to introduce a result clause.

So is used with an adjective before the result clause.
   The street was **so dark** (that) I couldn't see anything.

Such is used with a noun before the result clause.
   It was **such a dark street** (that) I couldn't see anything.

6 **Write** Match each problem with a result to make a complete sentence.

1. ____ My street is so crowded with cars . . .

2. ____ My neighbors are so unfriendly . . .

3. ____ My street is so noisy . . .

4. ____ My neighborhood is so boring . . .

5. ____ My street is so dirty . . .

6. ____ My street is so dark at night . . .

a. that there is always garbage on the street.

b. that I can't find anything to do at night.

c. that no one ever says hello to me.

d. that it is difficult to sleep at night.

e. that I can't see who is on the street.

f. that I can never find a place to park.

7 **Pair Practice** Work with a partner. Tell your partner each of the problems in Activity 6. Your partner will suggest a solution to the problem.

Example: *Student 1:* My street is so crowded with cars that I can never find a place to park.
   Student 2: Why don't you rent a garage? That would solve your problem.

Write Match each statement with a result to make a complete sentence.

1. _____ I live in such a friendly neighborhood . . .
2. _____ I live in such a convenient neighborhood . . .
3. _____ I live in such an interesting community . . .
4. _____ I live in such a diverse neighborhood . . .
5. _____ I live in such wonderful neighborhood . . .

a. that I do all my shopping nearby.
b. that I often get together with my neighbors.
c. that people speak many different languages.
d. that there is always something to do.
e. that there are never any vacant apartments.

 Pair Practice Work with a partner. Tell your partner each of the sentences above about your neighborhood or community. Your partner will ask a follow-up question. Continue each conversation as long as you can.

Example: Student 1: I live in such a friendly neighborhood that I often get together with my neighbors.
Student 2: Really? What do you do with them?
Student 1: Sometimes we have parties at each other's homes.
Student 2: That's great. How often do you have parties with them?

> **Note: Infinitives after *too* and *enough***
> We also use infinitives after *too* and *enough* to complete the idea of a sentence.
> It is **too dangerous to walk** alone at night in this neighborhood.
> It isn't safe **enough to walk** alone at night in this neighborhood.

Write Combine the sentences. Use *too* or *enough* and an infinitive.

1. The train station is far from my home. I can't walk there.

   The train station is too far from my home to walk there. OR The train station isn't close enough to my home to walk there.

2. The police captain doesn't have much time. He won't listen to our problems.

   _____

3. Elena doesn't make a lot of money. She can't buy a new car.

   _____

4. The streetlights aren't very bright. You can't see very well at night.

   _____

5. The library closes early. You can't go there after work.

   _____

6. Sasha is very young. He can't walk to school by himself.

   _____

Listen Listen and help these concerned citizens write their letter by filling in the missing words.

Concerned Citizens of Downtown
222 Broadway
New York, NY 10025
November 2, 2006

Ms. Lisa Bernstein
Director—Animal Control Agency
2705 Spring St.
New York, NY 10036

Dear Ms. Bernstein:

We are writing to you today (1)_____ in our neighborhood.

Every night there are stray dogs (2)_____ without their owners

and without any leashes. We believe that (3)_____ to our kids.

Our children are (4)_____ when these dogs are nearby. We

believe that our children (5)_____ on the street when there are

stray dogs around.

These dogs also knock over our garbage cans and cause our street

(6)_____. The dogs (7)_____ and

(8)_____ for us to catch them. So, we are asking you

(9)_____ for them. Or, if they already have homes,

(10)_____ their owners (11)_____ of their yards

at night.

Thank you for your help with this problem.

Sincerely,

The Concerned Citizens of Downtown

Teamwork Task Work in teams of four or five.

1. Choose a problem from this chapter or a real problem in your community. Decide which agency on page 68 (or in your community) can help you with this problem.

2. Work together to write a letter of concern about the problem to the agency you chose. Make sure that you state the problem, tell at least two reasons why it is a problem, and suggest at least two possible solutions.

Review

1 **Read and Listen** Read the story. Then listen to the story.

The Ocean Avenue Child-Care Co-op

Elena has learned that it is difficult to find good and inexpensive child care in her community. It is very important for a single parent to have a reliable child-care provider. There is a professional child-care center in her neighborhood, but it is too expensive for Elena to use. So, she has decided to start a child-care cooperative, or "co-op," in her neighborhood. Being part of a child-care co-op means that Elena will agree to take care of other people's children one night a week or a few hours on the weekend. In exchange, other parents will watch Sasha at another time of the week if Elena needs someone to watch him.

Elena put an ad in her school newsletter to advertise her idea. In the ad, she asked other parents with children between the ages of three and nine to call her for information about the new Ocean Avenue Child-Care Co-op. Four other parents called to say they were interested in her idea. Now Elena is planning to have a meeting to meet the parents and to set up a schedule. She thinks it is important for everyone to be comfortable with each other before they agree to leave their children in each other's care. Later on, they will organize a playdate at the park so the children can meet each other and all the parents.

Elena hopes that these parents are as nice as they sounded on the phone and that the co-op will work. It would be a good solution to her child-care problem. Of course, she would prefer to have her husband with her in New York. But at the moment that isn't possible. So, she is trying to do the best she can.

2 **Write** Underline all the infinitives you can find in the story. Write the infinitives in the correct columns.

Infinitive after *It*	Infinitive of purpose	Infinitive after verb	Infinitive after verb and object
_____	_____	_____	_____
_____	_____	_____	_____
_____	_____	_____	_____
_____	_____	_____	_____
_____	_____	_____	_____
_____	_____	_____	_____
_____	_____	_____	_____
_____	_____	_____	_____

Write Answer the questions about the story on page 77.

1. What has Elena learned? _____

2. What is a reliable child-care provider? _____

3. How expensive is the child-care center in Elena's neighborhood? _____

_____

4. What will Elena agree to do for other parents? _____

5. What did Elena say in her ad? _____

6. What is the purpose of the meeting at Elena's house? _____

_____

7. What does Elena hope to do? _____

8. What would be the best solution for Elena's child-care problem?

_____

Write Correct any mistakes in the sentences. If there are no mistakes, write *correct*.

1. Elena goes to the pharmacy for to fill her prescriptions.

_____

2. Elena expects go to the Chinese restaurant someday.

_____

3. He threw the football throughout the window.

_____

4. I can't afford to shop at that store. It's expensive enough.

_____

5. I live in such a nice neighborhood why I never want to move.

_____

6. Continue walking along Ocean Avenue and you'll see it on the right.

_____

7. It isn't necessary taking a taxi.

_____

8. Our teacher allows to come late to class.

_____

9. She invited me to be in her child-care co-op.

_____

10. The store was too expensive that I walked out without buying anything.

_____

5 Teamwork Task Work in teams of three or four. Together, build your ideal community. Choose ten things you would like to have in your community. Choose from the list below or use your own ideas. When you are finished, read your ten choices to the class. See if the other teams agree or disagree with you.

clean streets
quiet neighbors
friendly neighbors
a nice park
a supermarket
a library
a good school
a Laundromat
a post office

lots of parking spaces
a bus or train nearby
a fast-food restaurant
a high-quality restaurant
a hospital or clinic
a cheap child-care center
people from your native country
a church or other religious
   center

inexpensive apartments
cheap stores to shop
convenient to your job
a café or a bookstore
safe, well-lit streets
a public swimming pool

Pronunciation Rising and falling intonation

Yes/No questions and clarification questions usually end with rising intonation. Information questions usually end with falling intonation.

Listen to the following questions and draw an up arrow ↑ for rising intonation and a down arrow ↓ for falling intonation. Then listen again and repeat with correct intonation.

1. Is he your son?
2. Where is the gas station?
3. Is it on the corner?

4. Where do you live?
5. Did you say the second floor?
6. Are you from Russia?

I can. . .			
• identify and talk about places in the community.	1	2	3
• use infinitives to describe purpose.	1	2	3
• use prepositions to describe location and direction.	1	2	3
• ask and answer questions about my community.	1	2	3
• work together to create a community information page.	1	2	3
• use a street map to find and describe locations.	1	2	3
• identify community resources for various problems.	1	2	3
• write a formal letter of concern about a community issue.	1	2	3
• distinguish fact from opinion.	1	2	3
• use infinitives in different kinds of sentences.	1	2	3

1 = not well   2 = OK   3 = very well

DOWNTOWN JOURNAL

YOUR COMMUNITY NEWSPAPER   VOL. 24 NO. 4 NOVEMBER 15

Child-Care Cooperative?

I would like to start a child-care cooperative group with other parents from our school or community. My idea is to exchange babysitting with other parents who know and trust each other. Members must agree to provide free child care for several hours a week. In return they will receive free child care from other members of the group when they need or want it.

If you have a child between 3 and 9 years old and you are interested in a child-care group, please call Elena at 718-555-5868.

Who Do Children Live With

Live with two parents 70%

Live with mother only 23%

Live with father only 3%

Live with neither parent 4%

Child-Care for Children Under 6 Whose Mothers Work Full-Time

At child-care or day-care center	39%
With a relative	33%
With a non-relative	32%
Parents only	12%

Numbers add up to more than 100% because some children participated in more than one type of non-parental arrangement

Don't Trash It— Recycle

Recycling makes sense. In fact, it makes dollars and cents. Recycling saves money for everyone. It saves our natural resources, saves space in our landfills, and helps protect our environment for our children's future. And it can earn money for our school at the same time!

Starting this month, Downtown Adult School will have recycling bins available at the north end of the parking lot. The bins will be for paper, plastic, and metal items, as well as for electronic equipment and old clothing. It is important that you separate any items you want to add to our school's recycling bins. Please do not put plastics into our paper bin, or metal into our plastics bin, etc.

Be smart, be a good citizen, be a good community member: Recycle!

What do you think?

1. What is a child-care cooperative?
2. What percent of children live with only one parent?
3. What percent of children under six, whose mothers work, are cared for by non-family member babysitters?
4. What kinds of things can you recycle and get money for?
5. Why is recycling a good idea?

DOWNTOWN JOURNAL

Dear Ms. Know It All

Problem Solving: Lonely Seniors

Dear Ms. Know It All:

A few months ago, my grandfather passed away. My grandmother has been really out of it ever since. She's really down in the dumps. My grandmother is almost eighty years old. She and my grandfather were married forever and she doesn't have any friends her own age to hang out with, so I think she feels like she has nothing to live for. I love my grandmother, and I want to see her perk up and enjoy the rest of her golden years. What can I do to help her?

Sincerely,
Worried About Grandma

Word Help: Underline the idoms in Worried About Grandma's letter. Then write the idioms next to the meanings.

MEANING	IDIOM
1. a very long time	_____
2. the time after retirement	_____
3. died	_____
4. depressed	_____
5. spend time with	_____
6. no reason to continue living	_____
7. not connected with reality	_____
8. revive, become more energetic	_____

CRITICAL THINKING:

Work with a partner or a small group. Talk about Worried About Grandma's problem. Make a list of things he could do to help her. Then complete the letter of advice.

> Dear Worried About Grandma:
> There are certainly some things you can do to bring the spark back to Grandma's eyes. For example, . . .

People and Places

What is happening in the picture?

1 **Read and Listen** Read the story. Then listen to it.

A Night Out

Last week, Andre asked Daisy out. Daisy wanted to go out with him, but she was nervous. So, she asked Elena to go with them. "If the three of us go, it won't be so stressful," she told Elena. "In China, women often bring a friend along on a first date." Elena agreed to come.

They all got together at Elena's apartment. Elena had dropped Sasha off at the babysitter's home earlier. At the apartment, they looked through the entertainment section of the newspaper and tried to decide what to do. They wrote down a few possibilities, but couldn't agree on anything. Finally, Andre suggested that they get on the subway and go to the city. "We'll pick out something fun to do when we get there," he said.

They got off the subway in the middle of Manhattan. There were entertainment possibilities all around them. There was jazz music at a small club, but Daisy doesn't like jazz very much. "I would rather hear classical or rock-and-roll music," she said. There was a comedy club, but Elena thought that her English wasn't good enough to understand American comedy. "They talk so fast," she said, "and they use a lot of idioms." There was a dance club, but the style was salsa and none of them knew how to dance to salsa music. There was a karaoke bar, but Daisy and Elena both hate to sing in public. And there was a movie theater, but each of them wanted to see a different movie.

"There's a nice Italian restaurant," Elena said.

"I'm hungry," Daisy said. "But I'm not crazy about Italian food."

"Well," Andre said, "we need to make a decision."

The three of them stood looking at the bright neon lights blinking at them up the street as far as they could see.

2 **Write** What entertainment choices do Daisy, Andre, and Elena have? List the things they could do on a piece of paper.

CRITICAL THINKING:

Where do you think they should go? Why?

1 Say It Practice the conversation with a partner.

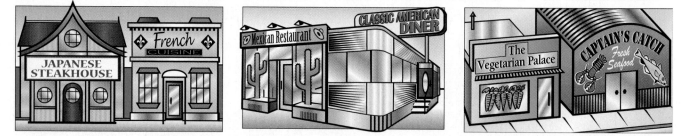

Chinese or Thai?

a movie or a concert?

A: Would you like to get together tomorrow?

B: What do you have in mind?

A: First, we could get some food. Do you prefer <u>Chinese or Thai</u>?

B: I'd rather have <u>Thai</u>.

A: And would you rather go to <u>a movie or to a concert</u>?

B: I think I'd rather go to <u>a movie</u>.

A: OK. Why don't I pick you up and we can get some <u>Thai food and then we'll go to a movie</u>?

B: That sounds good to me.

Practice more conversations. Use the pictures below.

1. **an action movie or a comedy?**

2. **the art museum or the science museum?**

3. **a basketball game or a dance club?**

Word Help: Expressing preferences

We often express preference with *would rather* + the base form of a verb, but you can also use *would prefer*.

> **Would** you **rather go** to the beach or (go) to the park? I**'d rather** go to the beach.
> **Would** you **prefer** going to the beach or (going) to the park? I**'d prefer** going to the park.

2 Group Practice Work with a large group or the whole class. Ask four people if they would like to get together with you tomorrow. Think of some places to go. Use the ideas below or your own ideas.

1. Japanese or Thai?
   a jazz club or a karaoke bar?

2. Russian or Cuban?
   a comedy club or a hockey game?

3. a pizza or a hamburger?
   a soccer game or a play?

4. ice cream or cheesecake?
   a bookstore or a café?

Phrasal verbs

Phrasal verbs are verbs that have two or three parts and have a special meaning.
Ask out is a phrasal verb. It means to ask someone to go out on a date.
 Andre wants to **ask** Daisy **out.**

Check Points:
 ✓ Most phrasal verbs are *separable*—the two parts can be separated by an object.
  Andre **asked** her **out.**
 ✓ Some phrasal verbs are *inseparable*—the parts cannot be separated.
  I'm **getting together with** him tomorrow.

3 **Write** Underline the phrasal verbs in the story on page 82. Which ones do you think are inseparable? Match the phrasal verbs from the story with the meanings below. Write the base form of the phrasal verbs.

SEPARABLE

1. ask on a date   ask out

2. bring with you   _____

3. choose   _____

4. leave some place   _____

5. write on paper   _____

INSEPARABLE

6. meet with someone   _____

7. go on a date   _____

8. enter a bus/train   _____

9. exit a bus/train   _____

10. read quickly   _____

4 **Write** Fill in the blanks with the best phrasal verb from Activity 3. Remember to use the correct verb tense.

1. Why don't we _____ at my place at about six o'clock?

2. Why don't you _____ a nice dress and I'll buy it for you?

3. Can you _____ me _____ at the airport on Saturday?

4. Bill really likes Jen. I think he will _____ her _____ .

5. Do you think that Jen will _____ him?

6. Please _____ the phone number because you might forget it.

7. Let's _____ the subway. I'm tired of walking.

8. If you _____ at the next stop, you'll be right near the theater.

9. Don't forget to _____ your credit card. We might not have enough cash.

10. Why don't you _____ the classified ads for some used furniture?

The passive voice in the past tense

Form the passive voice in the past tense with *was* or *were* and the past participle.

Active Voice
Steven Spielberg **directed** that movie.

Passive Voice
That movie **was directed** by Steven Spielberg.

Check Point:
✓ We often use the passive voice when the subject of an action is not important or not known.

The movie **was shown** five times yesterday. (It's not important who showed the movie.)

5 **Write** Answer the questions about the movie posters with complete sentences in the passive voice.

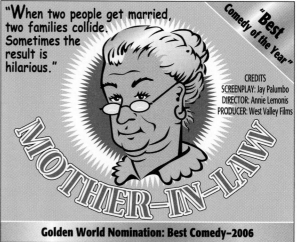

1. Who wrote *The First Kiss*? <u>"The First Kiss" was written by Jack Mears.</u>
2. Who directed *Mother-in-Law*? _____
3. When were the movies made? _____
4. Who produced *Mother-in-Law*? _____
5. What was *Mother-in-Law* nominated for? _____
6. What Oswald awards were won by *The First Kiss*? _____
7. Who was given the Best Director award? _____
8. Which movie was named "Best Comedy of the Year"? _____
9. Who wrote *Mother-in-Law*? _____
10. Who produced *The First Kiss*? _____

6 **Pair Practice** Work with a partner. Ask and answer the questions in Activity 5.

> **Note: Historical present tense**
> When we tell a story, especially from a movie or TV show, we sometimes tell the story in the simple present tense. Instead of telling what happened in the story, we tell what happens every time you see it since the movie or TV show never changes.

7 **Teamwork Task** Work in teams of three or four. Read the review of the movie *The First Kiss*. Then together, finish the review. Pretend that you have seen the movie and describe what happens. Tell who wrote and directed the movie and give your opinion about it. Use the historical present tense.

The First Kiss

The First Kiss is a coming-of-age story about that very special event in life—your first love. The lead role of Jenny Vidal is played beautifully by newcomer Lori Alonso. Jenny is an eighteen-year-old cashier in the neighborhood pet store. One day a young man comes in and buys a bird. He is wearing a T-shirt and has a strange tattoo on his arm. When Jenny leans forward to see the tattoo, the young man kisses her cheek. _____

_____

_____

_____

---

8 **Pair Practice** Work with a partner. Tell your partner about a movie you saw or a story you heard or read recently. Use the present tense to tell what happens. Then give your opinion about the story. Your partner will take notes. Then he or she will tell the class about the story.

9 **Teamwork Task** Work in teams of three. Pretend you are Elena, Daisy, and Andre. Look again at the picture and the story on pages 82 and 83. Work together to make a decision about what to do for the evening. You can use the possibilities given or choose something different to do. When you have made a decision, tell your class about your plans.

Homework

Read the entertainment section of a local newspaper. Find several movie ads. Write down the titles and the names of the writer and director of each one. Write down any information about the movie. If it has won or been nominated for any awards, write that down, too. Then tell the class about two of the movies.

Cultural Differences

1 **Say It** Practice the conversation with a partner.

women get tattoos

A: What are some differences you've noticed between what people do here and what people usually do in your country?

B: I've noticed that in this country some <u>women get tattoos</u>. In my country, <u>women</u> don't usually <u>get tattoos</u>. In fact, before I came here, I had never seen <u>a woman get a tattoo</u>. I was surprised at first, but now I'm getting used to it.

A: In my country, <u>women get tattoos</u> so I didn't have to get used to it.

Practice more conversations. Use the pictures below.

1. men take care of babies

2. elderly people live alone

3. women drive buses

4. men shake hands with women

5. families have several dogs

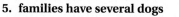

6. people have potluck parties

Note: *Get used to*

We say *get used to* when something that seems strange at first begins to seem normal.

Hearing English every day sounded strange when I first arrived here, but now I'm **getting used to** it.

2 **Write** Do people behave differently in your country from how people behave in the United States? On a piece of paper, write as many differences as you can.

Example: In my country, most people eat dinner late at night. In the United States, most people don't eat late at night. They eat dinner early.

The past perfect tense

Form the past perfect tense with *had* followed by a *past participle*.

I had seen the movie before I read the book.

We usually use the past perfect tense to indicate which of two past events happened first. The action in the past perfect tense happened before the action in the simple past tense.

I moved here three years ago. I studied English five years ago.

    past perfect   simple past

I had studied English before I **moved** here.

---

3 **Pair Practice** Work with a partner. Use the past perfect tense to ask and answer questions about the two events in each item below.

Example: drive a car / you were eighteen years old

    Student 1: **Had** you **driven** a car before you were eighteen years old?

    Student 2: Yes, I **had driven** a car before I was eighteen years old. OR

                 No, I **had not driven** a car before I was eighteen years old.

1. study English / you moved to this city

2. vote in an election / you were twenty-five years old

3. finish high school / you started this English class

4. get married / you moved to your current home

5. ride a bicycle / you were ten years old

6. learn to swim / you started elementary school

7. go to a McDonalds / you moved to this city

8. meet a girl named Elena / you read *Downtown 4*

9. understand past perfect tense / you started this chapter

10. eat a meal / you came to class

11. have a wonderful English teacher / you came to this school

4 **Write** What are some things you had never seen or done before you moved to your current city? Make a list on a piece of paper. Write as many sentences as you can.

Example: I had never taken a taxi before I moved here.

Note: *Present Perfect* vs. *Past Perfect*

We use the *present perfect* tense to ask about things that happened anytime before now. We use the *past perfect* tense to ask about things that happened before *some other* time or other event in the past.

Present Perfect: Have you ever **ridden** a motorcycle? (anytime before now)

Past Perfect: Had you **ridden** a motorcycle before you drove a car?

5 Write Complete the sentences with the past perfect or present perfect forms of the verbs.

1. (shake) _____ you ever _____ hands with a woman?
2. (study) She _____ English for two years before she came here.
3. (be) How long _____ they _____ married before they got divorced?
4. (be) How many times _____ she _____ married?
5. (take) How many English classes _____ you _____ before this one?
6. (find) She _____ already _____ an apartment before she arrived.
7. (see) We _____ already _____ the Statue of Liberty. It's very big.
8. (hear) She _____ a lot about New York before she ever saw it.
9. (drive) He _____ about ten different kinds of cars.
10. (not see) He _____ her picture before he met her, so he was really surprised.

6 Group Practice *Find someone who* . . . Work with a large group or with the whole class. Ask present perfect or past perfect questions for the statements below. Find someone each statement is true about, and write his or her name on the corresponding line.

1. _____ has never been to a basketball game.
2. _____ has seen an American football or basketball game on TV.
3. _____ had driven a car before he or she was sixteen.
4. _____ had not studied English before he or she finished high school.
5. _____ has been to more than two different countries.
6. _____ had known how to swim before he or she could ride a bicycle.

7 Write Write when the holidays are celebrated in the United States. Use the dates in the box. If a similar holiday is celebrated in your country, write the date that it is celebrated.

| first Monday in September | December 25 | December 31 |
| fourth Thursday in November | October 31 | July 4 |

HOLIDAY	DATE IN U.S.	DATE IN YOUR COUNTRY
Thanksgiving Day		
Independence Day		
New Year's Eve		
Christmas Day		
Labor Day		
Halloween		

Write Write about one important holiday that people celebrate in your country. What is the holiday? When is it celebrated? What do people do, eat, drink, or wear on this day?

9 **Pair Practice** Work with a partner from a different country or culture, if possible. Tell your partner about the holiday that you wrote about. Your partner will tell the class about it.

10 **Teamwork Task** Work in teams of five or six.

1. Form a team that has people from two different countries or cultures, if possible. The students from these two countries will be the "experts." (If all of your team is from the same country, then compare your country with the U.S. Choose one U.S. expert.)

2. Choose one student to be the writer for one country and another student to be the writer for the other country. Ask the experts to describe the locations of their countries, the flags, and other general information. Then interview the experts about the people and customs of their countries. Find out the differences between the two countries. The two writers will write the differences.

Example: Do most people eat sushi in your country?

Expert 1: In Japan, most people eat sushi often.

Expert 2: In Bulgaria, most people do not eat a lot of sushi.

Use the ideas below or your own ideas.

- popular foods
- languages
- holidays
- religion
- popular sports
- age people usually marry
- clothes people wear to school, to work, to relax
- popular kinds of music, dances
- greetings (shake hands, kiss, etc.)
- greetings (shake hands, kiss, etc.)
- how people meet their husbands or wives
- the number of children most families want
- how people spend their free time
- who people live with
- number of hours people work, go to church, attend school

Try to find as many differences as you can. Then tell your teacher about some of the differences.

Work Culture

1 **Read and Listen** Read the story. Then listen to the story.

The World of Work

Andre has learned that if you want to get ahead at work, you have to have "people skills," or be able to get along with people well. This is especially important if you work in sales, as Andre does. You have to be friendly with customers and, of course, you have to get along with your boss or, sooner or later, you could get fired.

There are many other things Andre has learned since he got hired at Best Electronics. He has learned that it is important to get up early and get in on time every day. Supervisors expect punctuality at U.S. businesses. They also expect you to be dependable. That means you shouldn't stay home every time you get a cold. If you work in sales, you have to be aggressive. When someone leaves you a message, you have to get back to him or her right away. You can't let a busy signal or answering machine stop you. Keep calling until you get through to your customer.

Managers also expect you to be responsible. If you make a mistake, don't try to get out of it. Just admit your mistake and apologize. Everyone will get over it quickly if you apologize. Managers also expect you to work well with others, to be a good team player. Andre has found that it helps to get together with his coworkers once in a while outside of work. That makes it easier to communicate when they are working together.

Right now, Andre is making enough money to get by. But he is getting better at his job every day. He may not get rich from his job at Best Electronics, but he thinks that he will make enough to live comfortably. Then he might think about getting married!

2 **Write** Answer the questions about the story.

1. If you have "people skills," what can you do well? _____

2. What else do you need if you work in sales? _____

3. What two things do American supervisors expect in business? _____

4. What should a salesman do if someone leaves him a message? _____

5. What should he do if he gets a busy signal? _____

6. What two things do most managers expect? _____

7. What shouldn't you do if you make a mistake? _____

8. What should you do if you make a mistake? _____

9. What is a good team player? _____

10. What might Andre do if he starts making more money? _____

CRITICAL THINKING:

11. What are some things you can do to get along with coworkers? Write as many things as you can.

> **Note: Expressions with *get***
> There are many different expressions that use the verb *get*.
> *get* + adjective = *become* + adjective
> She **got angry** when I arrived late. (She wasn't angry before I arrived late, but she became angry.)

3 Write Underline all the expressions with *get* in the story on page 92. Then match the *get* expressions with the meanings below.

1. lose a job   _get fired_
2. start a new job   _____
3. catch an illness   _____
4. arrive someplace   _____
5. return a communication   _____
6. arise from bed   _____
7. improve   _____
8. have just enough   _____
9. meet with someone   _____
10. escape responsibility for something   _____
11. recover from a bad thing   _____
12. communicate with someone   _____
13. advance or move forward professionally   _____

4 Pair Practice Use the *get* expressions in Activity 3 to ask your partner questions. Use different verb tenses. Use the examples below and think of as many others as you can.

Examples: *(get fired)*   Have you ever *gotten fired* from a job?
(get hired)   How many different jobs have you *gotten hired* for in your life?
(get a cold)   When was the last time you *got a cold*?

Word Help: Communication strategies
Most workers need many different communication strategies to be successful in the workplace. Here are some of the communication strategies people use at work:

interrupt politely	ask for help	show appreciation
disagree politely	offer to help	ask for an opinion
clarify	apologize	check for understanding
ask for clarification	make a request	make a suggestion

5 **Pair Practice** Work with a partner. Identify the communication strategies used in the sentences below.

1. "I'm sorry. I didn't know that . . . "   _apologize_

2. "Excuse me. Do you have a minute?"   _____

3. "Why don't you call his cell phone?"   _____

4. "Thanks for your help. I really needed it."   _____

5. "Which one do you think is better . . ."   _____

6. "Do you need any help with . . ."   _____

7. "Did you say this Saturday?"   _____

8. "Could you give me a hand tomorrow? I'm . . ."   _____

9. "I'm not sure about that. I think it might be better to . . ."   _____

10. "OK?"   _____

6 **Pair Practice** Work together to continue the conversations in Activity 5. Use the communication strategies from page 93.

Example: *Student 1:* I'm sorry. I didn't know that you were the new supervisor.
Student 2: That's OK. It's my fault. I didn't introduce myself.
Student 1: Well, it's nice to meet you. My name is Andre.
Student 2: It's nice to meet you, too.

7 **Listen** Listen to the conversations. Circle the communication strategies you hear in each conversation.

CONVERSATION 1	**CONVERSATION 2**	**CONVERSATION 3**
a. ask for help	a. apologize	a. interrupt politely
b. apologize	b. ask for clarification	b. disagree politely
c. make a request	c. ask for an opinion	c. ask for help
d. make a suggestion	d. offer to help	d. offer to help
e. interrupt politely	e. make a request	e. show appreciation

8 **Say It** Practice the conversations with a partner.

A: Excuse me, Jean. Do you have a minute?

B: Sure, Andre. What can I do for you?

A: My customer is looking for the best printer for a professional photographer. What do you think I should recommend?

B: I'm sorry, I'm not sure about that. Why don't you ask Manuel? That's his specialty.

A: OK. Thanks anyway.

A: Manuel, may I ask you a question?

B: Sure. What is it?

A: My customer is looking for a high-quality printer for a professional photographer. What do you think is the best one?

B: She wants to print photographs?

A: Yes, that's right. I'm thinking of recommending the Landmark 3000.

B: I'm not sure that's the best choice. Why don't you tell her about the Canyon 4000? That's the top-of-the-line printer.

A: The Canyon 4000? Great. Thanks so much for your advice.

B: No problem. I'm happy to help.

Practice more conversations. Pretend your friend is looking for the following:

1. the best Italian restaurant to take his new girlfriend to for dinner.

2. the best English book to give to someone who wants to study English.

9 **Write** Write the sentences from Activity 8 that show a communication strategy. Write the strategy used in each.

SENTENCE	STRATEGY
Excuse me, Jean. Do you have a minute?	interrupt politely

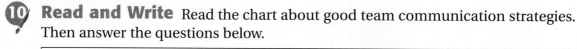

10 **Read and Write** Read the chart about good team communication strategies. Then answer the questions below.

TEAM COMMUNICATION STRATEGIES		
STRATEGY:		**RESULT:**
YOU SHOULD . . .		TEAMMATES WILL FEEL . . .
1. show appreciation for teammates' work	→	more confident
2. ask teammates' opinions about work situations	→	more involved in their job
3. thank teammates who do good work	→	more appreciated
4. ask teammates to make decisions	→	more in control of their job
5. offer teammates rewards for good work	→	more motivated
6. tell teammates how important they are	→	more valued

1. Andre's boss often thanks him for things he does at work. How does she want him to feel? _____

2. Elena's boss wants her to feel valued. What should she do?

   _____

3. Daisy's boss wants her to feel more involved in her job. What could she do?

   _____

4. What could your boss do to make you feel more motivated to work hard?

   _____

5. Cindy always tells her employees how good their work is. How does she want them to feel? _____

11 **Write** Read what the teacher said to her students. How does the teacher want each student to feel? Use the chart in Activity 10 to find your answers.

1. "Your homework was really great. Good job!" _____

2. "I'll give chocolates to anyone who gets 100% on the test." _____

3. "What should we do after the break—grammar or reading?" _____

4. "Did you understand this exercise or should we practice more?" _____

12 **Teamwork Task** Work in teams of three or four. Discuss and decide if your class is more of a "top-down" classroom or more of a "student-centered" classroom. List the reasons why you think so. Give examples to support your conclusion.

TOP-DOWN VS. STUDENT-CENTERED CLASSROOM	
TOP-DOWN	**STUDENT-CENTERED**
• Teacher makes all the decisions.	• Students share in decisions.
• Rules are strict and must be followed.	• Rules are flexible and can be changed.
• Only teachers evaluate.	• Students evaluate each other.
• Students are responsible for themselves only.	• Students are supposed to help each other.
• Students usually work alone.	• Students often work in teams.

1 Read and Write Read the story. Fill in the blanks with the best words you can think of. Remember to use the correct verb tenses.

The Third Wheel

When Andre (1)_____ Daisy out, Elena agreed to go with them on their first date so that Daisy would feel comfortable. Daisy had never (2)_____ out with a Russian man before, so she was nervous about it. "Don't worry," Elena said. "I'm sure you two will (3)_____ _____ fine." But Daisy had asked for her help, so Elena agreed to go with them.

They (4)_____ _____ the subway and took it over the bridge to the city. In the city, they (5)_____ out a nice café and went in. It was very romantic with candles on the tables and soft music playing. Earlier Daisy had (6)_____ down some information about things to do in the city. They sat for a while drinking coffee and (7)_____ over the possibilities. There was a movie playing that (8)_____ _____ by one of Elena's favorite directors. But Andre and Daisy didn't want to see a movie. They wanted to stay in the dark, romantic café. So, they ordered some food and sat listening to the music.

By the time they left the café, Andre and Daisy had gotten (9)_____ to each other's accents and really didn't need Elena at all. On the way back to the subway, they walked together holding hands and Elena could feel herself (10)_____ depressed. She was thinking about her husband, Alex. He (11)_____ sent her an e-mail a couple of days ago, but she hadn't written (12)_____ yet. Now she suddenly couldn't wait to write to him.

Back in Brooklyn, they stopped at the babysitter's and (13)_____ up Sasha. Then Andre and Daisy (14)_____ Elena off at her apartment. As soon as she put Sasha to bed, Elena (15)_____ on her computer and began typing an e-mail. "Hello, Alex," she wrote in her native Russian language, "I miss you very much . . ."

2 Listen Listen to the story and check your answers.

3 Pair Practice Work with a partner. Take turns asking and answering questions about "The Third Wheel." Ask as many questions as you can.

Example:　*Student 1:* Where did Elena, Andre, and Daisy stay most of the evening?
　　　　　　Student 2: They stayed in a dark, romantic café.

CRITICAL THINKING:
Why is the story titled "The Third Wheel"? Why does Elena feel that way?

> **Note: Summarize**
> To *summarize* a story or piece of writing means to tell only the most important parts in your own words. You should not include all the details.

4 Pair Practice Work with a partner.

Student 1: Read "A Night Out" again on page 82. Take a few notes—not complete sentences—on the main ideas. Then close your book and summarize the story for your partner in your own words. Use the historical present tense.

Example: *When Andre asks Daisy out, Daisy invites Elena to go with them.*

Student 2: Read "The Third Wheel" again on page 97. Then close your book and summarize the story for your partner in your own words. Use the historical present tense.

5 Write Correct the mistakes in the sentences. If there are no mistakes, write *correct*.

1. I'll pick up you at your house at 10:00. _____

2. I had never met a famous person. Maybe I will someday. _____

3. That movie has directed by Steven Berg. _____

4. They have written down information before they left Brooklyn. _____

5. Please pick her up at 6:00 and drop her out before 10:00. _____

6. Mother-in-Law was nominated for several awards. _____

7. Every time I watch that movie the same thing happened. _____

8. She didn't like Brooklyn at first, but now she's getting use to it. _____

9. She had drove several cars before she bought her car. _____

10. The First Kiss was been produced by Downtown Studios. _____

6 Write Answer the questions in complete sentences.

1. Who did you get together with recently? _____

2. What is one advantage of an employee-centered workplace?

_____

3. What is something you need to get used to that you aren't used to yet?

_____

4. Where did you pick someone up or drop someone off recently?

_____

5. What is something you were told by someone recently?

_____

6. What are some things you had done before you ate breakfast this morning?

_____

7 **Teamwork Task** Work in teams of three or four. Read the entertainment section of a local newspaper or magazine. Pretend that you are going out together some time soon. Talk about the different places you could go, such as a movie, a museum, a sports event, or a restaurant. Find a place that you all agree on. Then answer the questions about your plans.

1. Where are you going? _____

2. What are you going to do there? _____

3. What time is the event? _____

4. How much will it cost? _____

5. Where is it located? _____

6. How will you get there? _____

7. Why did you choose this place or event? _____

Pronunciation Rising and falling intonation
Listen and repeat the *or* questions using rising and then falling intonation.

1. Would you like coffee (↑) or tea? (↓)

2. Would you rather walk or drive?

3. Should we go on Saturday or Sunday?

4. Should we go alone or with the teacher?

5. Would you rather have a soda or water?

INTERNET IDEA
Go online and use a search engine to find a review of a movie. Who was it written and directed by? Take notes on the review. Write a short summary. Bring it to class and tell the class about the movie.

I can . . .			
• compare entertainment options.	1	2	3
• express preferences.	1	2	3
• read and interpret movie ads.	1	2	3
• write a review.	1	2	3
• describe cultural differences.	1	2	3
• use the past-tense passive voice.	1	2	3
• understand cultural expectations regarding work.	1	2	3
• identify and use various communication strategies.	1	2	3
• summarize a story.	1	2	3
• use the past perfect tense appropriately.	1	2	3

1 = not well   2 = OK   3 = very well

DOWNTOWN JOURNAL

YOUR COMMUNITY NEWSPAPER — VOL. 24 NO. 5 DECEMBER 15

Happy Holidays!

The Downtown Adult School will be closed for the winter holidays from December 19 to January 9. The teachers and staff wish you all a happy holiday break. Don't forget to practice your English over the vacation! There are many ways you can practice outside the classroom:

1. Read. Read. Read.
2. Distance Learning: Use special videos to study at home.
3. See or rent a movie. (See our list of the most popular movies.)
4. Get together with classmates. Speak English together.
5. Watch TV in English.

Most Popular U.S. Movies of All Time

1. *Titanic* (1997)
2. *Star Wars,* Episode 4 (1977)
3. *Shrek 2* (2004)
4. *E.T.* (1982)
5. *Star Wars,* Episode 1 (1999)
6. *Spider Man* (2002)
7. *Star Wars,* Episode 3 (2005)
8. *The Lord of the Rings: The Fellowship of the Ring* (2003)
9. *Spider Man 2* (2004)
10. *The Passion of the Christ* (2004)

Movie Review

By *Daisy Yu*

Titanic is my favorite movie because it is the most romantic movie I have ever seen. It makes me cry every time I see it. *Titanic* was made in 1997 and was directed by James Cameron. It is a story about two young people who meet on the *Titanic* and fall in love. The girl, played by Kate Winslet, is engaged to another man, but she doesn't love him. When she meets the young man, played by Leonardo DiCaprio, she knows that she has found her one true love that will last forever. Even after he dies when the ship sinks, she continues to love him. She knows that he is still with her sixty years later when she is looking back on her life. If you believe in true love, this is a movie you should see!

What do you think?

1. What are some other ways you can practice English?
2. Which of the most popular movies in the list have you seen? How many times?
3. Had you seen any of these movies before you came to the United States? Which ones?
4. What is your favorite movie? Write a review about it.

Dear Ms. Know It All

Problem Solving: Nothing in Common

Dear Ms. Know It All:

    I have been going out with a really great guy for a few weeks. I am really crazy about him, but I'm afraid that our relationship isn't going to work out because we have almost nothing in common. I grew up in Russia, and he is as American as apple pie. We get along great, but we don't see eye to eye about how to spend our free time. I love to go to the ballet, but my boyfriend says he wouldn't be caught dead at the ballet. He likes to go to sports events, but I don't have a clue about sports and I think I would be bored stiff at a sports event. We both like movies, but he calls the movies I like "chick flicks." He likes action movies, but they don't turn me on. Most of the time, I just think they're stupid. Is it possible for us to have a happy relationship with so little in common? Help!

Sincerely,
Not Two Peas In A Pod

Word Help: Underline the idioms in Not Two Peas In A Pod's letter. Then write the idioms next to their meanings.

MEANING	IDIOM
1. like very much	_____
2. be successful	_____
3. very uninterested	_____
4. make me excited	_____
5. romantic type of movies that many women like	_____
6. people who are very similar	_____
7. don't know anything about	_____
8. dating	_____
9. agree	_____
10. be found someplace I'd hate to be	_____

CRITICAL THINKING:

Work with a partner or small group. Talk over Not Two Peas In A Pod's problem. Give your opinion and make suggestions. Then complete the letter of advice.

> Dear Not Two Peas In A Pod:
>   I can certainly see your problem, but there are many people in very good marriages or relationships that have similar problems. I think there are some things you can do, such as . . .

Home and School

What do you like about this house?
What problems do you see?

1 **Read and Listen** Read the story. Then listen to it.

To Buy or Not to Buy

Al and Alice have saved almost $20,000 and they want to buy a house. They want to own a home because they think houses always go up in value if you keep them for a while. Unfortunately, they haven't found any homes in their price range that they really like. The homes they can afford seem to have a lot of problems.

Yesterday they were taken to see a "fixer-upper." (A fixer-upper is a house that has a lot of things that need to be fixed.) It was built in 1935 and Al liked it, but Alice didn't like it very much. Al liked the size of the house and the big window and fireplace in the living room. But Alice didn't like the age or condition of the house. She thought it needed a lot of work. Al liked the swimming pool and barbecue area in the back, but Alice didn't like the broken gate or holes in the concrete. Al liked the fruit trees and the front yard, but Alice didn't like the dog in the yard next door. Al liked the price of the house and the low down payment they would need, but Alice didn't like all the work it would take to make the house look really nice.

It isn't an easy decision because they both like the neighborhood where the house is located. And, according to their real estate agent, the most important thing when buying a home is location. So, they are going back with the agent again tomorrow to look at the house carefully one more time.

2 **Write** Do you think Al and Alice should buy the house? Why or why not? Use the picture and the story to list the reasons for your opinion.

_____

_____

_____

_____

_____

Buy or Rent?

1 **Say It** Practice the conversation with a partner.

HOUSE FOR SALE

3 bedrooms
Nice location
1 1/2 baths
Built in 1960
Asking price:
$425,000

A: I'm calling about the <u>three-bedroom house for sale.</u> <u>The ad says it is in a nice location.</u> Can you tell me if it's still available?

B: Yes, it is.

A: Do you know <u>how many bathrooms it has</u>?

B: Yes. <u>It has one and a half baths.</u>

A: Do you happen to know <u>when it was built</u>?

B: Yes, I do. <u>It was built in 1960.</u>

A: Great. Can you tell me how much the asking price is?

B: Yes. The asking price is <u>four hundred and twenty-five</u> <u>thousand dollars.</u> Would you like to see it?

A: I'm not sure yet. I'll get back to you when I decide. But thanks for your help.

B: No problem.

Practice more conversations. Use the ads below.

Home For Sale
2-bedroom cottage near the beach.
1 bath. Built in 1955.
Asking price: $385,000
or make an offer!

1.

HOME FOR SALE
Nice 3-bdrm in prime
neighborhood. 2 baths;
pool; 2-car garage;
$1,600 per month

2.

CONDO FOR SALE
Beautiful 2-bedroom in quiet area;
3rd floor; close to transportation;
near shops and school;
Asking: $249,000

3.

GRAMMAR CHECK

Embedded (indirect) questions

A short question followed by a noun clause is an *embedded* or *indirect question*. We often use embedded questions because they sound more polite than direct questions. In an embedded question, we reverse the word order of a direct question; that is, we put the subject before the verb instead of after.

Direct question: How much is the rent?

Embedded question: Do you know how much the rent is?

Check Points:

✓ *Yes/No* embedded questions usually start with *if*.

   Can you please tell me **if it is still available?**

✓ Information embedded questions start with a question word:

   Do you know **when** it was built?

2 Pair Practice Work with a partner. Take turns asking embedded questions about the home for sale on pages 102-103.

Example: *Student 1:* Do you know if it has a fireplace?

Student 2: Yes, it does. Can you tell me how many fruit trees are in the front yard?

 3 Write Change the direct questions to indirect questions.

1. How many bathrooms does your home have?

   Can you tell me how many bathrooms your home has?

2. What street is your home on?

   Do you mind telling me

3. Is there a bus stop nearby?

   Do you happen to know

4. What floor is it on?

   Can I ask you

5. Are pets allowed in your building?

   Do you know

6. How much is the rent?

   Can you tell me

7. Does it have a fireplace?

   Can you tell me

8. How much was the security deposit when you moved in?

   Do you happen to know

9. Is it a safe neighborhood?

   Do you have any idea

10. Is it a nice neighborhood to live in?

    Can I ask you

4 Pair Practice Work with a partner. Ask your partner the questions in Activity 3 about his or her home.

Example: *Student 1:* Can you tell me how many bathrooms your home has?
Student 2: Yes, it has two bathrooms.

5 **Listen** Listen to the conversations between a real estate agent and three callers. Take notes in the boxes below about the three properties.

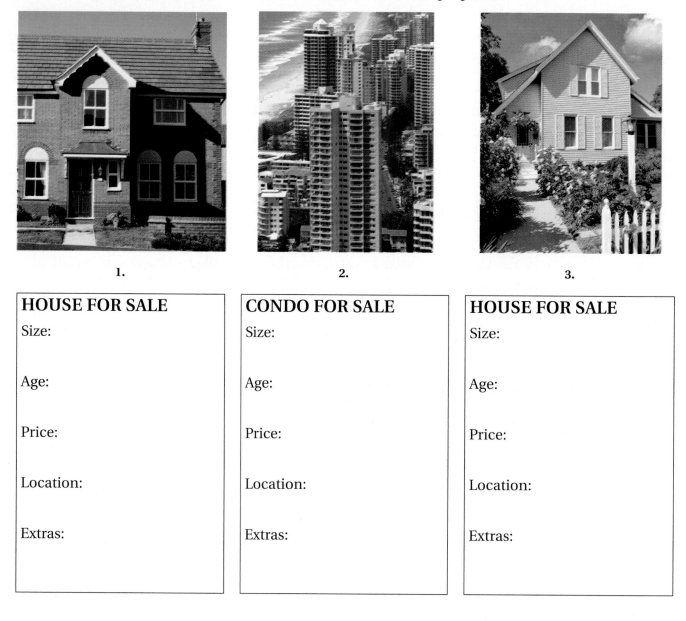

1.

2.

3.

HOUSE FOR SALE	**CONDO FOR SALE**	**HOUSE FOR SALE**
Size:	Size:	Size:
Age:	Age:	Age:
Price:	Price:	Price:
Location:	Location:	Location:
Extras:	Extras:	Extras:

6 **Pair Practice** Work with a partner. Ask and answer embedded questions about the three properties in Activity 5. Take turns playing the real estate agent and the client. Use your notes to answer the questions.

Example: *Can you tell me what the price of the first house is?*

7 **Critical Thinking** Which home in Activity 5 would you buy? Why? Write as many reasons as you can.

_____

_____

_____

_____

8 **Read and Write** Read the story. Then write an underlined word or phrase from the story for each of the definitions below.

Getting a Mortgage

You don't have to have $300,000 to buy a $300,000 home. You just need to be able to get a <u>mortgage</u>. Very few people buy a house without a mortgage. So, what do you need to do in order to get a mortgage?

The first thing you need is to have <u>verifiable income</u> from a job or other source. You also probably need to have some <u>credit history</u>. And, in most cases, you need to have a <u>down payment</u>. <u>Lenders</u> would like you to pay 20% of the house's price as a down payment. But that much isn't really necessary. Many banks or <u>mortgage brokers</u> will approve your loan with only 10% or even 5% down.

The first step for most people is to find out if they can get a mortgage. This is called getting prequalified. When a lender prequalifies you based on your income, <u>debt</u>, and credit history, they will tell you the maximum loan amount you can get. Depending on the bank's mortgage <u>interest rate</u> and the amount of your down payment, this will tell you how expensive a home you will be able to buy.

There are two basic kinds of mortgages—a <u>fixed-rate</u> mortgage and an <u>adjustable-rate</u> mortgage. Adjustable-rate mortgages start out at a lower interest rate than a fixed-rate mortgage, but the rate can become higher over the life of the loan. There are many different agreements that determine how often and how much an adjustable-rate mortgage can change. So, you should get advice from more than one professional before you choose an adjustable-rate mortgage.

1. _____ the amount of money you owe

2. _____ a loan to buy real estate property

3. _____ an interest rate that stays the same

4. _____ an interest rate that changes

5. _____ salary or other earnings that can be proved

6. _____ past use of credit and payments you made

7. _____ someone who loans you money

8. _____ cash you pay that doesn't come from a loan

9. _____ someone who arranges mortgage loans

10. _____ the percent a bank charges to give you a loan

MONTHLY MORTGAGE PAYMENT CHART

MORTGAGE AMOUNT	$150,000	$200,000	$250,000	$300,000	$350,000
5.5% interest rate	$851	$1,135	$1,419	$1,703	$1,987
6.5% interest rate	$948	$1,264	$1,580	$1,896	$2,212
7.5% interest rate	$1,048	$1,398	$1,748	$2,097	$2,447

9 Problem Solving

1. Al and Alice have saved $20,000 for a down payment on a house. If the bank demands a 10% down payment, what is the most expensive home they can buy? _____

2. If Al and Alice take a $200,000 mortgage loan at an interest rate of 6.5%, how much will their monthly mortgage payment be? _____

3. If the interest rate is 7.5%, what will their monthly payment be? _____

4. If Al and Alice can get a loan with only 5% down, how much will they have to put down to buy a $300,000 home? _____

5. If they decide on a $300,000 mortgage with a 6.5% interest rate, how much will their monthly payment be? _____

6. If the interest rate is 7.5% on a $300,000 mortgage, what will their mortgage payment be? _____ How much less will the payment be if they find a loan with a 5.5% interest rate? _____

7. Andre wants to buy a condo for $165,000. He has $15,000 for a down payment. How much will he need to borrow from a lender? _____ If the interest rate is 7.5%, how much will his monthly mortgage payment be? _____

8. Al and Alice are thinking about buying the 1935 fixer-upper on page 103. If they get a mortgage of $284,000 at 6.5% interest, will the mortgage payment be higher or lower than the cost to lease the house? _____

10 Teamwork Task Work in teams of three or four.

1. Together, list the advantages and disadvantages of buying a home. Then list the advantages and disadvantages of renting a home.
2. Look again at the homes for sale or rent in this lesson. Pretend you have to buy or rent one of them. Discuss and decide which house or apartment you want. Then write the reasons why you chose that one.

Homework

Read the real estate section of a newspaper or go on the Internet and use a search engine to find some three-bedroom homes or condos for sale. Where are they located and how much are the asking prices? Write down two or three examples. Bring in your examples to share with the class. What is the relationship between price and location?

1 **Say It** Practice the conversation with a partner.

A: I'm new in the building. Can I ask you some questions?

B: Sure. What do you want to know?

A: <u>When does the rent have to be paid?</u>

B: <u>Rent must be paid on the first of each month. A late fee of 5 percent is charged if it isn't received by the fifth.</u>

A: OK. <u>And what do I do with my garbage? How often is it picked up?</u>

B: <u>All trash must be put in the containers behind the building. It is picked up on Monday and Thursday.</u>

A: OK, thanks. And, finally, <u>what time do you lock the parking lot security gates?</u>

B: <u>The parking lot security gates are locked at midnight every night. Please have your key if you plan to return later than that.</u>

A: OK. Thanks for your help.

B: No problem. That's what I'm here for.

Rules and Regulations

- Rent must be paid by the first of each month. Late fee of 5% is charged if not received by the fifth.

- Trash must be put in containers behind building. Trash is picked up on Monday and Thursday.

- Parking lot security gates are locked at midnight every night. Please have your key if you plan to return late.

Practice more conversations. Use the information below.

RULES AND REGULATIONS

- Security deposit must be paid when lease is signed. Apartment key will not be given without security deposit.
- All cars must be parked in assigned parking spaces.
- Pool and barbecue areas are closed at 10:00 P.M. every night.

1.

Rules and Regulations

- Garage fee must be paid monthly. If not paid, parking privileges will be terminated.
- Dogs should be walked on the street only. Dogs are not permitted behind the building.
- Rear entrance is locked at 11:00 P.M. every night.

2.

GRAMMAR CHECK

Passive voice in the present tense

To form the *passive voice* in the present tense, use the present tense of the verb *to be* with the *past participle* of the main verb.

Active: Someone picks up the garbage on Monday and Thursday.
Passive: The garbage **is picked up** on Monday and Thursday.
Active: Someone locks the security gates at midnight.
Passive: The security gates **are locked** at midnight.

When modals are used in the passive voice, use the modal + *be* + past participle.

Rent **must be paid** on the first of the month.
Cars **should be parked** in assigned parking spaces only.

Write Change the active voice sentences to passive voice.

1. When do they return the security deposit?

   <u>When is the security deposit returned?</u>

2. How often do they clean the pool?

   _____

3. Where do they keep the folding chairs?

   _____

4. When do they turn off the heat?

   _____

5. When do they deliver the newspaper?

   _____

6. Where should I park my truck?

   _____

7. You should drop the rent check in the rent box.

   _____

8. They must repair a clogged toilet within 24 hours.

   _____

9. The landlord must provide heat in the winter.

   _____

10. Someone will fix broken windows as soon as possible.

   _____

Culture Tip

The Fair Housing Act

The Fair Housing Act says that landlords must not discriminate against anyone because of their race, nationality, religion, sex, family status (unmarried couples or couples with children, for example), or disability.

3 Group Practice Work in groups of four or five. Brainstorm a list of things a landlord should and shouldn't do, and a list of things a good tenant should and shouldn't do. Write as many things as you can.

A LANDLORD . . .	A GOOD TENANT . . .
shouldn't refuse to rent to someone	should pay his rent on time
because of his race or nationality	

4 **Say It** Practice the conversation with a partner.

 The Department of Water and Power

∙ ∙ ∙ NOTICE ∙ ∙ ∙

Your service at **2255 Ocean Avenue** may be turned off if this bill is not paid in our office by **5:00 P.M. on Thursday, February 2.**

Do not mail payment

Current Charges:...... $187.45   Past Due Date: Feb. 2

Past Due Amount:.. $134.50   Due Date: Jan. 2

A: Department of Water and Power. Can I help you?

B: Yes, I hope so. When I came home today, there was no water in my apartment.

A: Yes, I see the problem. Your water was turned off this morning.

B: Why was it turned off?

A: We sent you a notice last week. The water is turned off if you don't pay your bill by the past due date. Your past due date was February 2.

B: The reason I didn't pay is because the bill is wrong. It's too high. My bill is usually about sixty or seventy dollars, but we had a water leak. That's why it was so high.

A: If you send a copy of the repair bill from the plumber, your bill can be adjusted. Or you can ask your landlord to pay part of the bill because a water leak is his responsibility.

B: OK. I'll do that. But what can I do now?

A: If you would like to pay the past due amount now, payments are accepted over the phone with a credit card.

B: How much do I have to pay?

A: The past due amount must be paid before the water can be turned on again. Your past due amount is one hundred thirty-four dollars and fifty cents.

B: If I pay it now, how soon will the water be turned on again?

A: It is usually back on within three to four hours. You will also be charged a fee on your next bill. Would you like to pay the past due amount now?

B: I guess I don't have much choice, do I?

Account Number: 3-28-12455

Daisy Yu
2255 Ocean Avenue
Brooklyn, NY 11238

Bill Issued:.........................1/11/06
Due Date:.........................2/02/06
Amount Due:.......................$187.45
Past Balance Due:...............$134.50
Energy Services:...................$62.15
Water Services:...................$115.30
Late Payment Charge:...........$10.00

The Department of Water and Power

Water and Power Bill

PO BOX 456
BROOKLYN
NY 11238

	Meter Information	Electric	Water
THIS YEAR	USE	468 KWH*	40 HFC**
	Days Billed	30	30
	Daily Average	15.6	520 gallons
LAST YEAR	USE	402 KWH	20
	Days Billed	30	30
	Daily Average	13.4	260 gallons

*KWH = kilowatt hours, **1 HFC = 748 gallons

5 **Write** Answer the questions about the water and power bill and notice on page 111.

1. Whose bill is this? _____

2. What is the account number? _____

3. What is the date of the bill? _____

4. When does the bill have to be paid? _____

5. How much are the current charges? _____

6. How much is past due? _____

7. How much is the late-payment charge? _____

8. How much electricity did she use per day this year? _____

9. How many gallons of water did she use per day last year? _____

10. How many gallons of water did she use per day this year? _____

6 **Pair Practice** Work with a partner. Student 1 is Daisy. Student 2 is Daisy's landlord. Daisy thinks that the water leak is her landlord's responsibility and that he should pay for some of her water bill. Create a conversation. Perform your conversation for the class.

7 **Listen** Listen and write the missing information on the rental agreement.

THE TERRIBLE LANDLORD'S RENTAL AGREEMENT

1. All rent _____ in full on the first of the month. If rent is more than three days late, a $500 late fee _____ charged.
2. All dogs and cats _____ on leashes when on the apartment grounds.
3. Landlord _____ supply heat or hot water to tenants.
4. Guests and visitors _____ in apartments after midnight.
5. All TVs and loud music must be _____ by 10:00 P.M.
6. Any leaks or plumbing problems _____ and paid for by the tenant.
7. All furniture _____ and approved by the landlord. Ugly furniture will not _____ in apartments.
8. Children under 18 are not allowed in the pool area, or any other place on apartment grounds, _____.
9. Only church music _____ in apartments on Sundays.
10. Landlord _____ apartment at any time without permission of tenant.

Landlord's Signature: _____   Tenant's Signature: _____

---

8 **Teamwork Task** Work in teams of four or five. Choose one student to play the terrible landlord. The other students read and discuss the rental agreement. Cross out any parts of the rental agreement that you think are terrible and won't accept. Then negotiate a new rental agreement with your landlord. Use your ideas from Activity 3 to help you.

Vocational Education

1 Read Read the story. Then listen to the story.

Vocational Education

In Russia, vocational education is very important. In Russian secondary schools, many students take classes that prepare them to get a special type of job when they graduate. In the U.S., there aren't as many vocational classes available to high school students. But there are a lot of programs and classes available for adults who want to learn skills to get a job. Some vocational classes like nursing and accounting are taught in community colleges. Training for jobs like auto repair and cosmetology is offered at public adult schools. Some job-training programs for fields, such as X-ray technology, are available at hospitals or other community organizations.

Many of Elena's friends have enrolled in vocational training programs in the U.S. Alice studied nursing in Haiti, but she also received an LVN (Licensed Vocational Nurse) degree from a community college that helped her get a job at the hospital. Her husband, Al, received a certificate in culinary arts that helped him get a job as a chef. Vicki is studying cosmetology in a private trade school so she can get a cosmetology license in New York. Andre took several computer classes at Downtown Adult School that helped him get his current job. And Daisy received an Associate of Arts degree from a local community college that was required for her teaching assistant position.

There are other kinds of jobs that you can get with an on-the-job training program, called an apprenticeship. These are usually available in trades, like carpentry or construction. An apprentice usually works for a small amount of pay while learning job skills from an experienced professional. There are also some jobs that let you start as a volunteer to allow you to "get your foot in the door." These are sometimes called internships. Interns usually work without pay in order to gain experience and get a paying job in the same field or business later.

Elena can't afford to work as a volunteer. And she doesn't want to be an apprentice. But she would like to find a vocational training program that would give her the skills or certificate she needs to get a higher paying job. She is thinking about a certificate program in tax preparation or banking. She is also interested in learning about real estate. She can take real estate classes at the local community college, but she will have to pass a state exam in order to become a real estate agent. So, Elena is going to wait until her English is better before she makes a firm decision about her career. She will continue to study English because she knows she will need it for any job she gets.

Write Use information from the story on page 113 to answer the questions.

1. What is vocational education? _____

2. Where are accounting classes usually taught? _____

3. What kind of training is offered at public adult schools? _____

4. What job requires a license from the state? _____

5. What degree can you get from a community college? _____

6. What is an apprenticeship? _____

7. What kind of professions usually have apprenticeships? _____

8. What kind of workers usually work without pay? _____

9. Why do people sometimes work as interns or volunteers? _____

10. What would Elena like to find? _____

CRITICAL THINKING:

11. Do you think it would be a good idea to have more vocational programs offered in high schools in the United States? Why?

3 **Pair Practice** Work with a partner. Ask and answer the questions about the course described below.

```
Course Description                          Medical Records Terminology
                         (5 Credit Units)
This course develops the ability to understand the language of medicine
through word building, analysis of terms, pronunciation, and spelling. You will
learn medical words relating to body systems, including anatomy and physiology,
common diseases, and diagnostic procedures. If you desire to work
in the health industry, this is the class for you.
One-month internships available at conclusion of class.
Prerequisites: Reading level of 10.5. Type 35 wpm.
M—W  5:30 P.M.—9:30 P.M.;  20 wks.  Mr. Rogers—Rm 205.  $25 per credit unit
Medical Records certificate upon successful completion of class.
Space is limited. Register on a first-come, first-serve basis.
```

1. What is the name of the course? _____

2. How often does the course meet? _____

3. How many hours a week is the course? _____

4. How many credit units is the course? _____

5. How much does the course cost? _____

6. What must you do before you start this course? _____

7. What will you get if you pass this course? _____

8. What will you learn in this course? _____

9. Why is it important to enroll in this course as soon as possible? _____

10. How can you get work experience if you take this course?

_____

11. What is the name of the teacher? _____

Say It Practice the conversation with a partner.

A: What would you like to do in the future? What are your long-term goals?

B: I'd like to become <u>an accountant</u>, but I'm not sure if that will be possible.

A: If you want to be <u>an accountant</u>, you will have to <u>get a BA degree from a university</u>.

B: Well, I might do that eventually. But my other idea is to <u>become a real estate agent</u>.

A: If you want to become <u>a real estate agent, you will need to take a state license exam</u>. If you do that, you will be able to work <u>as a real estate agent</u>.

B: Is it hard to do?

A: It's not so hard. I'm sure you'll be able to do it.

Practice more conversations. Use the information below.

1. Ana's long-term goal is to become an elementary school teacher. She will need a BA or BS degree from a college or university in order to become a teacher. Her short-term goal is to be a teacher assistant. She needs an AA degree from a junior college to qualify to be a teacher assistant.

2. Carlos's long-term goal is to be a doctor. He will need to get a degree from a medical school and will have to pass a state license exam for that. His short-term goal is to be an Emergency Medical Technician. For that he needs to get a certificate from a community college or adult school program.

3. Alberto's long-term goal is to be a building contractor. He will need to pass a state contractor's license exam to do that. His short-term goal is to find an entry-level job in construction. For that he needs a certificate in construction fundamentals.

Culture Tip

Vocational Schools

There are many kinds of vocational schools you can attend in the U.S. Some are public and are funded by the government. Others are private and charge tuition. The classes that are offered vary from state to state, and from city to city. In some places, vocational classes are provided by community colleges. In other places, adult schools provide vocational education classes.

5 Listen Read the questions below. Then listen to Elena's telephone conversation. Listen for the information you need to answer the questions. Take notes if necessary. Then write the answers to the questions.

1. What is the first thing Elena will have to do if she wants to attend the college?

   _____

2. What will she need to bring to the registration office?

   _____

3. When is the registration office open?

   _____

4. What will she have to do before she can register for English class?

   _____

5. When will she have to pay the fees for her classes?

   _____

> **Note: Future ability and future necessity**
> Use *will + be able to* to talk about future abilities.
>   I **will be able to** speak English better when I finish this class.
> Use *will have to* or *will need to* for things that will be necessary in the future.
>   She **will have to** pass a state exam to be a real estate agent.

6 Teamwork Task Work in teams of four or five. Together create an educational plan for each of your team members. Start with a long-term goal. Then list the courses he or she will have to take and the types of schools he or she will have to attend to reach this goal. Follow the example.

Name: Elena
Long-term goal: Accountant
Future plan: First she will have to complete her English classes at Downtown Adult School. Then she will need to get an AA degree from a community college. After that she can transfer to a university. She will have to get a BA degree in accounting. Then she will be able to work as an accountant.

Homework

Visit a school in your city and get a schedule of classes, or go online and find the schedule. Choose three classes that sound interesting. Write down the number of units, the cost of the class, and any prerequisites you need to register for this class.

1 **Read and Listen** Read the story. Then listen to the story.

Buying a Home

Al and Alice went to a real estate agent (1) <u>a couple of months ago</u> (2) <u>to get some help and advice about buying a home</u>. The first question the real estate agent asked was, "How much do you have for a down payment?" They told her that they had about $20,000. She seemed happy about that. "The next step," she said, "is to go to a bank or a mortgage broker to get prequalified. It's important to get prequalified (3) <u>so you will know how expensive a house you will be able to buy</u>."

After they were prequalified, (4) <u>they were taken around the city by the agent to look at homes in their price range</u>. They looked at (5) <u>about twenty</u> different places. Then finally they found a house that they both liked. It was not too small, not too old, and in a good neighborhood. They talked it over with their agent. Then they made an offer for the house that was $10,000 below the asking price. Their first offer wasn't accepted. They were both really depressed that night. But then, (6) <u>the next day</u>, they received a counter offer from the seller. This counter offer was (7) <u>$5,000 below the original asking price</u>.

Al and Alice had another meeting with their agent to discuss the counter offer. Then Al called (8) <u>his father</u> for some last-minute advice. His father told him that they should buy it if they really liked it. So, the next day they decided to accept the counter offer. They gave the seller a deposit of 2% of the asking price. Then they had the house inspected (9) <u>to make sure there weren't any problems that the seller hadn't told them about</u>.

The inspector didn't find any big problems, so six weeks later they moved in. Pretty soon they will be able (10) <u>to invite all their friends to a party at their very own home</u>. The thought of that makes both of them very happy.

2 **Write** Complete an indirect question for the underlined parts of the story.

1. Do you happen to know when <u>Al and Alice went to a real estate agent?</u>

2. Can you tell me why _____?

3. Do you know why _____?

4. Do you have any idea what happened _____?

5. Do you know how many _____?

6. Do you happen to know when _____?

7. Can you tell me how much _____?

8. Do you know who _____?

9. Can you tell me why _____?

10. Do you know what _____?

3 **Pair Practice** Work with a partner. Ask and answer the questions in Activity 2.

Example: *Student 1:* Do you happen to know when Al and Alice went to a real estate agent?
Student 2: Yes. They went a couple of months ago.

4 **Pair Practice** Work with a different partner. Take turns asking each other indirect questions. Ask as many as you can.

Example: *Student 1:* Can you tell me when this class ends?
Student 2: Yes, it ends at 11:30. Do you know if the teacher is married?

5 **Teamwork Task** The Grammar Bowl

1. This is a grammar competition for two teams (a Blue Team and a Red Team) of six to eight students each. Each team should separate into pairs. Pairs are allowed to help each other, but not other members of the team. When your teacher says "Go," you will have ten minutes to fill in the blanks in the sentences below with **passive voice verbs**. When the teacher says "Stop," put down your pens and begin the next part of the competition.

2. Your teacher will give each student a number from 1 to 16 to match the sentences below. Students then go to the board and write their sentences—the Red Team on one side and the Blue Team on the other. When all the sentences are written, the teacher will check them and give one point for each correct sentence. The team with the most points wins. If it is a tie, the team that wrote their sentences the fastest wins. So, it is important to be both FAST and ACCURATE. Good luck!

1. (pick up) The garbage _____ _____ _____ twice a week.
2. (park) All cars should _____ _____ in assigned parking spaces.
3. (pay) Rent must _____ _____ on the first of the month.
4. (deliver) The mail _____ usually _____ about 11:00 A.M.
5. (turn off) All loud music must _____ _____ _____ by 10:00 P.M.
6. (lock) The security gates _____ _____ at midnight.
7. (take) Showers must _____ _____ before entering the pool.
8. (give) Up to three keys _____ _____ to each condo owner.
9. (drive) Cars may not _____ _____ faster than 10 mph on condo grounds.
10. (eat) Food should not _____ _____ inside the pool area.
11. (keep) Dogs must _____ _____ on leashes in all public areas.
12. (hold) Meetings _____ _____ on the first Monday of every month.
13. (buy) Most homes _____ _____ by married couples.
14. (make) The pizza _____ _____ by the pizza cook.
15. (bring) Weapons should not _____ _____ to the school.
16. (drink) Alcohol may not _____ _____ on school property.

Pronunciation Word stress: *can/can't*

It is not only the contracted sound of "t" that distinguishes the pronunciation of the two modals *can* and *can't*. English speakers rely on stress. *Can* is **not** stressed in normal conversation. *Can't* **is** stressed. Listen and repeat the sentences with *can* and *can't*.

1. I can **have** a pet here. Pets are allowed.
   I **can't** pay that much rent. It's too expensive.

2. You can **park** over there, at the meter.
   You **can't** park there. You'll get a ticket.

3. I can **call** you tomorrow.
   I **can't** call you tomorrow. I'm working.

I can . . .			
• understand housing ads.	1	2	3
• use embedded or indirect questions.	1	2	3
• understand steps to buy a home.	1	2	3
• evaluate homes for sale.	1	2	3
• interpret information about mortgages.	1	2	3
• interpret housing rules and regulations.	1	2	3
• discuss landlord and tenant rights and responsibilities.	1	2	3
• identify types of vocational education.	1	2	3
• understand a course description.	1	2	3
• identify and discuss long-term and short-term goals.	1	2	3
• use the passive present-tense voice.	1	2	3
• express future necessity and ability.	1	2	3

1 = not well   2 = OK   3 = very well

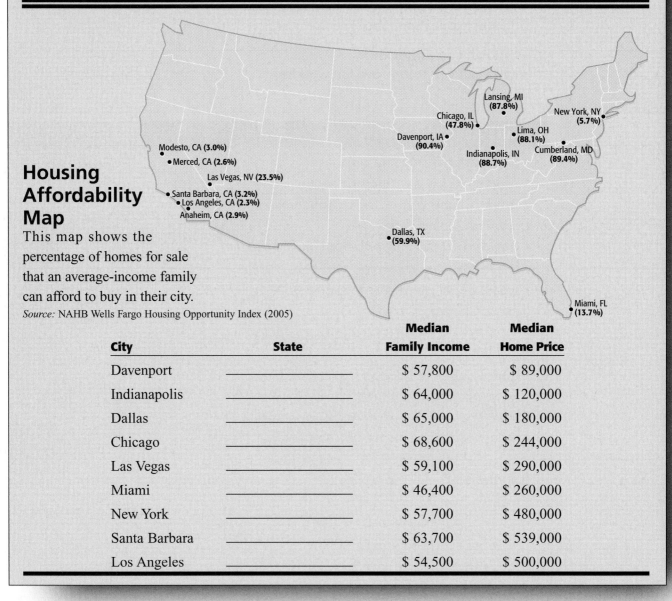

Housing Affordability Map

This map shows the percentage of homes for sale that an average-income family can afford to buy in their city.

Source: NAHB Wells Fargo Housing Opportunity Index (2005)

City	State	Median Family Income	Median Home Price
Davenport	_____	$ 57,800	$ 89,000
Indianapolis	_____	$ 64,000	$ 120,000
Dallas	_____	$ 65,000	$ 180,000
Chicago	_____	$ 68,600	$ 244,000
Las Vegas	_____	$ 59,100	$ 290,000
Miami	_____	$ 46,400	$ 260,000
New York	_____	$ 57,700	$ 480,000
Santa Barbara	_____	$ 63,700	$ 539,000
Los Angeles	_____	$ 54,500	$ 500,000

What do you think?

1. Find the cities listed in the table on the map. Write the name of the state on the line in the table.
2. On a piece of paper, list these cities in order from the most affordable to the least affordable. What can you say about the most affordable cities? What part of the country are they located in? What can you say about the least affordable cities?

DOWNTOWN JOURNAL

Dear Ms. Know It All

Problem Solving: Debt

Dear Ms. Know It All:

My husband and I have been putting away money for a couple of years to buy a house. Unfortunately, saving money is no piece of cake for us. We have already cut down on a lot of things, and have cut out some things completely, but we still have only $11,000. That's not just a drop in the bucket, but it also isn't enough for a down payment on the kind of home we want to buy.

My mother-in-law has offered to lend us another $10,000. But my mother-in-law is a very pushy, difficult woman. I think that money from in-laws always comes with strings attached, so I don't want to take her money. My husband and I usually see eye to eye on everything, but in this case we are miles apart. He thinks we should take the money and be grateful. He thinks I'm being stubborn and ridiculous. But I think he's seeing things through rose-colored glasses. What do you think?

Sincerely,
Stubborn and Ridiculous

Word Help Underline the idoms in Stubborn and Ridiculous's letter. Then write the idoms next to their meanings.

MEANING	IDIOM
1. agree	_____
2. far away from each other	_____
3. saving	_____
4. do or use less of something	_____
5. stop doing or using something	_____
6. aggressive	_____
7. expectations	_____
8. seeing only positive things	_____
9. not easy	_____
10. a very small amount of something	_____

CRITICAL THINKING:

Work with a partner or small group. Talk about Stubborn and Ridiculous's problem. Give your opinion and make suggestions. Then complete the letter of advice.

> Dear Stubborn and Ridiculous:
>
> Nobody likes to take money from other people . . .

Health and Safety

GOALS

✓ Distinguish between healthy and unhealthy behavior

✓ Describe symptoms of an illness

✓ Understand and describe preventative health practices

✓ Identify principles of good nutrition

✓ Interpret a health insurance policy

✓ Interpret a medicine label

✓ Follow directions from a health professional

✓ Create a list of health-care providers

✓ Understand procedures for avoiding accidents

✓ Describe unsafe conditions

What do you see in the picture? What can you say about healthy behavior from the doctor's waiting room?

1 **Read and Listen** Read the story. Then listen to it.

The Flu

Sasha has the flu. It started with a headache and a sore throat. At first, Elena thought that he just had a cold. Kids get colds all the time. But he was coughing, too, and he couldn't get out of bed. Elena gave him some over-the-counter cough medicine, but it didn't work. Finally, she called the doctor. When she called the doctor's office, the nurse told her to take Sasha's temperature. His temperature was 103 degrees. He also had chills and body aches. The nurse asked her to bring him in to see the doctor.

At the doctor's office, Elena filled out a Medical History form for Sasha. Then the doctor took him to the examination room and checked him over. "He has the flu," the doctor said. He told Elena to give Sasha plenty of liquids and to make sure he got a lot of rest. He told her to keep him home from school for at least a week. Sasha didn't seem too unhappy about that. But Elena felt terrible.

"I should have gotten him a flu shot," she told Daisy on the phone later. "They were giving free flu shots at the clinic last month."

"Maybe we all should have gotten flu shots!" Daisy said.

Elena thought for a minute about trying to get a flu shot for herself. But she was already getting a headache and a sore throat, so it was probably too late. She told herself she'd be sure to get a flu shot next year!

 Write Answer the questions about the story.

1. What are Sasha's symptoms?

   _____

2. What did the doctor tell Elena to do?

   _____

3. What should Elena have done last month?

   _____

1 Say It Practice the conversation with a partner.

A: I'm worried about <u>getting the flu</u>. What do you think I should do?

B: Did you talk to a <u>doctor</u> about it?

A: Yes, I did.

B: What did the <u>doctor</u> tell you?

A: She told me <u>to wash my hands a lot</u>.

B: That's a good idea.

A: She also told me <u>to stay away from sick people</u>.

B: That's a good idea, too.

A: And she told me <u>to get a flu shot</u>.

B: That's a really good idea. If you <u>wash your hands a lot, stay away from sick people, and get a flu shot, you probably won't get the flu</u>.

A: Yes. That's probably true.

getting the flu

wash my hands a lot / stay away from sick people / get a flu shot

Practice more conversations. Use the pictures below.

losing my teeth

1. brush twice a day / floss every day / stay away from sweets and soft drinks

gaining weight

2. stop eating desserts / eat more fruits and vegetables / exercise every day

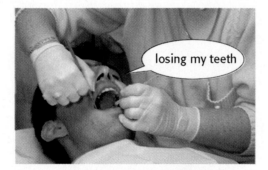

getting skin cancer

3. wear a hat / try to stay out of the sun / put on sunblock every day

feeling stressed out

4. exercise regularly / stay away from caffeine / find a healthy way to relax

Reported speech

When we report what someone said or told us, we change the *direct quote* to *reported speech*. With commands or advice (things someone told or advised us to do), use an infinitive for the reported verb. For a request, use *ask* + an infinitive.

Direct quote	Reported speech
"Lose some weight."	He told me to lose some weight.
"You really should quit smoking."	He advised me to quit smoking.
"Please sign the insurance form."	He asked me to sign the insurance form.

Check Point:

✓ When reporting negative commands, advice, or requests, use *not* before the reported verb.

He told me **not to eat** donuts.

 Write Change the direct quotes to reported speech.

1. Dr. Diaz: "Bring him in right away!"

   Doctor Diaz told me . . . _____

2. Dr. Garcia: "Brush your teeth at least twice a day."

   _____

3. Dr. Garcia: "You should also get a cleaning every six months."

   _____

4. Dr. Garcia: "Please bring your insurance card next time you come in."

   _____

5. My personal trainer: "Exercise at least three times a week."

   _____

6. Dr. Diaz: "Find a way to relax. That's important."

   _____

7. Mr. Jones: "Please don't smoke in here. It's annoying."

   _____

8. Dr. Diaz: "Don't worry so much about everything, OK?"

   _____

 Write Complete the sentences with advice people have given you about your health.

1. My mother told me to _____ .

2. My doctor advised me to _____ .

3. My dentist told me to _____ .

4. My friend told me to _____ .

5. My grandmother told me to _____ .

6. My _____ advised me to _____ .

4 **Pair Practice** Work with a partner. Ask your partner about the information in Activity 3.

Example: *Student 1:* What did your mother tell you to do about your health?

Student 2: My mother told me not to eat a lot of junk food.

5 **Listen** Listen to the conversation between Lucy and her doctor. Take notes on the healthy things he tells her to do and the unhealthy things he tells her not to do.

Healthy Habits   **Unhealthy Habits**

_____   _____

_____   _____

_____   _____

_____   _____

_____   _____

6 **Write** Write sentences about the doctor's advice to Lucy.

1. _He advised Lucy to get at least seven hours of sleep a night._____

2. _____

3. _____

4. _____

5. _____

6. _____

7. _____

8. _____

9. _____

10. _____

7 **Group Practice** Work in groups of four to five. Each group member must choose to be one of the students listed below. (It doesn't have to be true.) Ask your group members to give you advice about how to fix your problem. Take notes on what they tell you.

Student 1 wants to lose weight.
Student 2 wants to quit smoking.
Student 3 wants to have a healthier diet.
Student 4 feels stressed and wants to be able to relax more.
Student 5 is tired all the time and doesn't have any energy.

Notes

_____

_____

_____

_____

Tell your teacher or class about the advice you received from your classmates.

Say It Practice the conversation with a partner.

THE FIVE MAJOR FOOD GROUPS

1. Grains:
(bread, rice, cereal, pasta)

2. Milk:
(yogurt, cheese)

3. Meat & Beans:
(poultry, fish, eggs, nuts)

4. Fruits

5. Vegetables

A: I want to have a healthier diet, and I'd like to lose some weight.

B: That's a good idea. If you eat a healthier diet, you will probably lose weight.

A: What do you advise me to do to have a healthy diet?

B: First of all, I'd advise you to eat a balanced diet. That means eating food from all of the five major food groups. Do you know what those are?

A: Yes, I think so.

B: And then I'd advise you to cut back on saturated fats, sugar, and salt.

A: OK. I can do that.

B: If you do that, I'm sure you'll have more energy and feel a lot better.

Note: A healthy diet
- emphasizes fruits, vegetables, whole grains, and fat-free or low-fat milk and milk products.
- includes lean meats, poultry, fish, beans, eggs, and nuts.
- is low in saturated fats, trans fats, cholesterol, salt, and sugar.

Most of your fats should be polyunsaturated or monounsaturated fats. These can be found in nuts, fish, cooking oil, and salad dressing.

---

9 **Pair Practice** Work with a partner.

1. Recommend two foods from each food group that you would advise your partner to eat. Be specific.

Example: I would advise you to eat a lot of fish, especially salmon.

Grains: _____

Milk: _____

Meat and Beans: _____

Fruits: _____

Vegetables: _____

2. Recommend some foods your classmate shouldn't eat if he or she wants to cut back on fat, sugar, or salt.

Example: I would advise you not to eat too many donuts if you want to cut back on fat.

Conditionals to show a possible or expected result

Use a conditional (*If* clause) to show what will or could be true under certain conditions. Use a present tense verb for the *If* clause (the condition). Use a future tense verb or a modal for the result.

If you eat less food, you **will lose** weight.

If you eat too much salt, you **could get** high blood pressure.

10 **Write** Match the conditions with a possible result. Then write a complete sentence for each.

Example: *If you smoke a lot, you could get heart disease or cancer.*

CONDITION
1. If you smoke a lot, . . .
2. If you eat a lot of sweets and fats, . . .
3. If you don't brush or clean your teeth, . . .
4. If you stay in the sun too much, . . .
5. If you drink a lot of alcohol, . . .

POSSIBLE RESULT
a. get liver disease
b. get cavities and gum disease
c. get skin cancer
d. get heart disease or cancer
e. get diabetes or heart disease

11 **Teamwork Task** Work in teams of four or five. Discuss the things you should or shouldn't do to stay healthy. Choose ideas from this chapter or use your own ideas. Then work together to rank the five most important things a person should or shouldn't do to stay healthy. Number one is the most important.

TO STAY HEALTHY . . .

1. _____

2. _____

3. _____

4. _____

5. _____

Game Time

Game Time: What is it?

Work in two teams of five or six. A student volunteer (or the teacher) will write the name of a food on a piece of paper. The two teams will try to guess what it is by asking yes/no questions.

Example: Student 1: Is it a vegetable?

Volunteer: Yes, it is.

Student 2: Is it green?

Volunteer: No, it isn't.

When one team gets a "No" answer, the other team guesses. The team that guesses the food first gets a point. The first team to get five points wins.

1 **Say It** Practice the conversation with a partner.

coughing a lot/
muscle aches/
a 103-degree
temperature

son / the flu

A: I'm worried about my <u>son</u>. I'm thinking about bringing <u>him</u> to the doctor.

B: What's wrong with <u>him</u>? What are <u>his</u> symptoms?

A: Well, <u>he's been coughing a lot</u>. And <u>he</u> has <u>muscle aches</u>.

B: Anything else?

A: Yes, <u>he</u> also has <u>a 103-degree temperature</u>.

B: If <u>he</u> has <u>a 103-degree temperature</u>, plus the other symptoms, that could be <u>the flu</u>. Why don't you take <u>him</u> to the doctor today?

A: OK. I think I will. Thanks.

Practice more conversations. Use the pictures below.

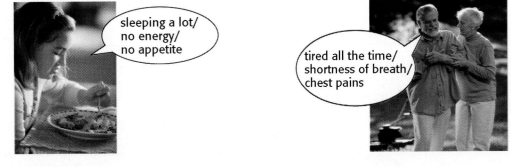

sleeping a lot/
no energy/
no appetite

tired all the time/
shortness of breath/
chest pains

1. **daughter / depression**

2. **father / heart disease**

Culture Tip

Health Insurance

In the United States, 84 percent of people have some form of health insurance that pays for all or part of their medical bills. Do most people in your country have health insurance or do they pay cash for medical services?

Source: U.S Census Bureau, Current Population Survey

GRAMMAR CHECK

Conditional for present possibility

Conditionals are also used to show possibility in the present.

If his fever is very high, he **could have** pneumonia. (It's possible.)

2 Write Match the information in the boxes to write present conditional sentences.

IF SOMEONE . . .	HE OR SHE COULD HAVE . . .
has chronic pain in joints like knees or hips	pneumonia
has severe stomach pain that gets worse and worse	arthritis
gets a sudden high fever after having the flu	bipolar disorder
eats very little but always thinks she's fat	appendicitis
hears voices that aren't there	schizophrenia
has extreme mood swings —very happy or very sad—for no real reason	anorexia nervosa

1. *If someone has chronic pain in the joints like knees or hips, he or she could have arthritis.*

2. _____

3. _____

4. _____

5. _____

6. _____

3 Listen Listen to the pharmacist and complete the information on the medicine label.

NATICK PHARMACY

Rx #410967   Dr. Bijan
AMOCILLIN   0 REFILLS
3/29/06   Use by: 3/29/07

One capsule every four hours.

4 Pair Practice
Look at the pictures and tell your partner about Elena's recent visit to her doctor's office. Tell what everyone said and did.

1. She made a copy of Elena's health insurance card.

2. _____

3. _____

4. _____

5. _____

6. _____

5 Write
Write a past tense sentence under each picture above. Write all the things the health professionals did at Elena's doctor's visit.

6 Listen
Listen and check your answers to Activities 4 and 5.

7 Write
Write a paragraph about Elena's medical checkup. Write what each person asked or told Elena to do, and what each person did.

Elena's Checkup

In the waiting room, the receptionist asked Elena for her health insurance card. She made a copy of the card. Then the nurse took Elena into the doctor's office. Then . . .

8 **Write** Use the chart to answer questions about Daisy's health insurance costs.

BLUE DIAMOND INSURANCE	Employee: **Daisy Yu** Employee Number: **660-3115**	Effective: **8/1/06** Plan: **Blue Diamond HMO Plus**	
	Blue Diamond HMO *Health Maintenance*	**Any Blue Diamond Network Provider**	**Any Non-Network Licensed Provider**
Annual Deductible	None	$250	$500
Maximum Lifetime Benefit	Unlimited	$1,000,000	$1,000,000
Physician Office Visits	$10 co-pay	70% after deductible	70% of approved and customary charges
Well-Baby Care	100%	Not covered	Not covered
Emergency Room Treatment	$50 co-pay (waived if admitted)	70% after deductible	70% after deductible
Surgery and Other Inpatient Care	100%	70% after deductible	70% after deductible to $1,200 per day
Chiropractic Care	70%	70%	70% of approved charges
Inpatient Mental Health Care	80% - maximum of 30 days/year	80% - maximum of 30 days/year	Not covered
Outpatient Mental Health Care	$10 co-pay	$10 co-pay	Not covered
Substance Abuse Treatment	80% - annual maximum of 30 days	80% - annual maximum of 30 days	Not covered

1. Daisy's doctor charges $100 for an office visit. How much will she have to pay with her HMO option? _____

2. How much will Daisy have to pay if she goes to a non-network doctor?

   _____

3. With her HMO, how much will Daisy have to pay for an emergency room visit if she isn't admitted? _____ If she is admitted? _____

4. How much will Daisy have to pay for surgery with her HMO provider? _____ With a non-network licensed provider? _____

5. How many days is Daisy covered for inpatient mental health care with her HMO? _____

9 **Pair Practice** Work with a partner. Ask and answer more questions about Daisy's insurance coverage. Ask as many questions as you can.

10 **Teamwork Task** Work in teams of five or six. Together, list health providers in your community. Include hospitals, doctors, dentists, clinics, and any other providers you know about. Use a phone book, the Internet, or any other source to help you. Share your list with the class.

Work and Play Safely

1 **Read and Listen** Read the story. Then listen to the story.

Emergencies

In the last few months, several of Elena's friends have experienced emergencies on their jobs. Some of them were prepared and knew what to do, but some did not. Elena decided that everyone should know more about safety, so she asked Al and Alice, along with several other friends, to come to her house for dinner. Al, who is a chef, and Alice, who is a nurse, agreed to give everyone some information about safety and about what to do in an emergency.

First, Al talked about an emergency that happened at his job. There was a fire in the kitchen. Al was in the office talking to the restaurant manager when the fire started. A kitchen helper left a pot holder on the stove and it caught on fire. The fire spread to some grease, and the helper tried to put it out by throwing water on it. "You never throw water on a grease fire, " Al said. "He should have used baking soda to put out a grease fire." And, of course, he shouldn't have left the pot holder so close to the burner."

Another emergency happened on the street in front of Andre while he was walking to work. There was a car accident and a man was seriously hurt. Andre tried to help. He pulled the man out of his car. "My leg!" the man screamed. Andre tried to move his leg to see how serious the injury was, but the man screamed even louder. Andre didn't know where the nearest emergency room was, so he left the man on the street and ran into his manager's office and called 911.

"Andre," Alice said, "you shouldn't have moved his leg. Actually, you probably shouldn't have even pulled him out of the car unless there was some danger of another car hitting him. And you should always know where the nearest emergency room is. But it was good that you called 911."

The third emergency happened at Daisy's school. An eight-year-old boy was walking too fast in the cafeteria with food in his mouth. He tripped and fell, and then started to choke on a piece of meat. By the time Daisy got to him, he couldn't talk or breathe. Daisy didn't know who to call or what to do. Finally, another teacher heard Daisy calling for help. She ran over and put her arms around the boy from behind. She held her hands together and pushed up and in on the top part of the boy's stomach. The piece of meat popped out of his mouth.

"First of all," Alice said, "the boy shouldn't have been running with food in his mouth. But, Daisy, you should have known how to do the Heimlich maneuver, which is what the counselor did to save the boy. Would you like to learn how to do it?" Alice went around the room and taught everyone how to do the Heimlich maneuver.

GRAMMAR CHECK

Past modals: *should have, could have*

To use a modal in the past tense, use the modal + *have* + a *past participle*.

She **should have called** 911 right away. (She didn't call right away. That was a mistake.)

He **could have come** earlier. (He didn't come earlier, but it was possible.)

Check Points:

✓ Use *should have* for an opinion about a past event or to comment on a mistake.

✓ Use *could have* to talk about a past possibility.

 Write Read the story on page 133 again. List the things that people did wrong. Use *should have* or *shouldn't have* to describe their mistakes.

Al's kitchen helper shouldn't have left a pot holder on the stove.

_____

_____

_____

_____

_____

_____

3 Write Answer the questions about the handbook page.

Handbook of Company Safety Policy   p. 12

SMOKING POLICY

Because smoking is harmful to everyone's health—to smokers as well as to nonsmokers who could be affected by second-hand smoke—smoking is prohibited on all company property. Employees, during designated time periods—lunch or during break—may choose to smoke outside of company grounds.

SAFETY EQUIPMENT

Hard hats must be worn in all work areas. Cover all hair when operating machines. Employees are responsible for wearing appropriate safety equipment when working with company machinery. Please obey all posted safety signs, including speed limits. When safety equipment is required, be sure to use it.

---

1. Where are workers not allowed to smoke? _____

2. When may employees smoke? _____

3. Who is the company policy trying to protect? _____

4. Where must employees wear hard hats? _____

5. What must be covered when operating machines? _____

6. What are employees required to obey? _____

7. When must employees use safety equipment? _____

SAFETY TIPS

1. Never use ladders with broken steps.
2. Don't stand on the top rung of a ladder.
3. Don't let plugs or electrical cords get wet.
4. Don't plug in electrical equipment when you are wet.
5. Never put anything with electrical parts (plugs, wires, appliances) in water.
6. Unplug all electrical appliances before opening or trying to repair them.
7. Never barbecue with charcoal indoors.
8. Open a window when using gas-powered equipment.
9. Never smoke or light matches around gas-powered machines.
10. Open a window and call the gas company if you smell a gas leak.
11. Keep paper, cloth, and all flammable products away from heat or fire.
12. Keep chemical products away from small children.
13. Keep pins, nails, and other sharp things away from children.
14. Never leave small children alone.

 Write Write the problem you see in each picture. Then write what could have happened. Use the information from the Handbook and the Safety Tips as needed.

1. fall and get hurt

A: What did someone do wrong?

B: Someone left the baby alone on a table. They shouldn't have left him alone.

A: Why not?

B: He could have _____

_____

A: I guess that's true. Fortunately, he didn't.

2. drink it and get poisoned

A: What did someone do wrong?

B: _____

_____

A: Why not?

B: _____

_____

A: Yes, I guess that's true.

3. start a fire

A: What did someone do wrong?

B: _____

_____

A: Why not?

B: _____

_____

5 **Teamwork Task** Work in teams of three or four. You are the safety inspection team from the New York State Inspector's Office. You want to close down The Brooklyn Tire Company because of safety violations. List the safety violations you see in the picture. Explain why these violations are mistakes. Use the Handbook page and the Safety Tips on pages 134-135 as guidelines.

Example: When we arrived, several men were smoking cigarettes. They shouldn't have been smoking in the warehouse.

Review

① Read and Listen Read the story. Then listen to the story.

Help!

One of the members of Elena's child-care co-op had an emergency at her home last Saturday. Irina was babysitting for three children along with her own two kids. Maybe that was too many children for one parent to handle. She left a four-year-old boy named Rudy alone in her bathroom for a few minutes. She was supervising the other children playing a board game and trying to cook dinner at the same time. Then suddenly she heard Rudy screaming.

Irina dropped everything and ran into the bathroom. Little Rudy was sitting on the floor next to the toilet rubbing his eyes and crying. There was a spray-top bottle of household cleaner on the floor next to him. Irina could see blue liquid from the bottle on the floor and on Rudy's face and hair. When she saw the blue liquid on Rudy's face, Irina panicked and screamed. Her own two children heard her and started to cry, too.

Irina picked Rudy up, but he just kept crying. She didn't know what to do. She had left the cleaner in the cabinet under the sink, but there wasn't a lock on the cabinet. She didn't think anyone would open it and try to play with anything inside. Her children had never done that. And she never thought a child would squirt himself in the eyes with a cleaning bottle! Irina didn't know if she should take him to an emergency room, try to call a doctor, or do something to try to help him. She didn't have a car and she hadn't written down an emergency-room or hospital phone number. She did have Alice's number, and Alice was a nurse, so she ran to the phone and called Alice.

Rudy was still crying as Irina told Alice what had happened. "Look at the bottle," Alice said. "And read the label. What does it say?"

"It says, 'Keep away from children' and 'Harmful if swallowed'."

"Read more. What does it say about eyes?"

Irina found it. "In case of eye contact, immediately flush with water and continue flushing for fifteen minutes. Get medical attention right away!"

"OK," Alice said. "Start flushing his eyes with water. Use slightly warm water. I'll be there in a few minutes."

② Write Answer the questions about the story with complete sentences.

1. What was Irina's first mistake? _____

2. What are some other things she shouldn't have done? _____

3. What are some things she should have done, but didn't do? _____

4. What is the first thing Alice told Irina to do? _____

5. What else did Alice tell Irina to do? _____

6. What did the label on the cleaner say to do? _____

CRITICAL THINKING:

7. What do you think was Irina's biggest mistake?

3 Write Complete the sentences with information from the chapter.

1. If you don't have a fever and body aches, you probably don't have
   _____.

2. If you don't eat any fruit or vegetables, you probably don't have a
   _____.

3. If you don't get dental checkups and regular cleanings, you could develop
   _____ and _____.

4. If someone has extreme mood swings, he could have
   _____.

5. If you have very high blood pressure, you are in danger of having a
   _____.

4 Listen Listen to the conversations. Write what the doctor tells, advises, or asks each patient to do.

1. _____

2. _____

3. _____

4. _____

5. _____

5 Teamwork Task The Grammar Bowl II

1. Work in two teams of six students each—a Red Team and a Blue Team. You will have ten minutes to write sentences below that describe what each person did wrong. Each description should include *should have* and a past participle. You must stop writing after ten minutes.

2. When you finish writing, the teacher will give each student a number to match one of the twelve sentences. Students take turns going to the board in numerical order to write their sentences. The Red Team writes on one side and the Blue Team writes on the other. For each sentence that is 100% correct, your team gets a point. The team with the most points wins!

Example: He didn't take a shower.   *He should have taken a shower.*

1. Irina didn't write down the phone number.

   _____

2. Daisy didn't do the Heimlich maneuver.

   _____

3. Vicki didn't keep her appointment.

   _____

4. He didn't have a first-aid kit.

   _____

5. She didn't pay her bill on time.

   _____

6. He didn't bring his medicine.

_____

7. She didn't choose a good dentist.

_____

8. She didn't give him the correct information.

_____

9. He didn't know where the hospital was.

_____

10. He didn't read about his insurance coverage.

_____

11. She didn't tell the doctor her problem.

_____

12. She didn't think before she spoke.

_____

Pronunciation *Shoulda, coulda, woulda*

The contracted forms of past modals are often pronounced with strong reductions:

should've = shoulda   *could've = coulda*   *would've = woulda*

Listen and repeat the sentences with the reduced pronunciation.

1. You **shoulda** quit smoking years ago.
2. She **shoulda** called first.

3. He **woulda** gone with you.
4. They **coulda** gotten lost.

I can . . .			
• distinguish between healthy and unhealthy behavior.	1	2	3
• describe symptoms of an illness.	1	2	3
• understand and describe preventative health practices.	1	2	3
• identify principles of good nutrition.	1	2	3
• interpret a health insurance policy.	1	2	3
• interpret a medicine label.	1	2	3
• follow directions from a health professional.	1	2	3
• create a list of health-care providers.	1	2	3
• understand procedures for avoiding accidents.	1	2	3
• describe unsafe conditions.	1	2	3

1 = not well   2 = OK   3 = very well

DOWNTOWN JOURNAL

YOUR COMMUNITY NEWSPAPER   VOL. 24 NO. 7 FEBRUARY 15

It's Flu Season

Follow these steps to avoid the flu and not pass it on to other people.

1. Wash your hands often with soap and warm water, or use antibacterial hand sanitizer.
2. Cover your mouth when you cough or sneeze.
3. Avoid contact with sick people.
4. Eat a healthy, balanced diet.
5. Don't come to school if you think you have the flu.

Is It a Cold or the Flu?

Adults average two to four colds a year. Women have more colds than men, possibly because of their closer contact with children. Colds are most prevalent among children. They have about six to ten colds a year. It seems to be related to their relative lack of resistance to infection and to contact with other children in day-care centers and schools. The flu is a much more serious illness, involving much stronger symptoms, and it can even be life threatening. Fortunately, most people get the flu less than once a year.

Important Phone Numbers:

Emergencies: <u>Call 911</u>

Personal Physician: _____

Hospital Emergency Room: _____

Domestic Abuse Hotline: _____

Child Abuse Hotline: _____

Psychiatric Emergency Services: _____

AIDS/HIV Hotline: _____

Alcohol and Drug Abuse Information: _____

Fill this chart in and keep it for your refrigerator.

SYMPTOMS	A COLD	THE FLU
fever	rare	high (102°-104°), lasts 3-4 days
headache	rare	prominent
general aches and pains	slight	usual, often severe
fatigue, weakness	mild	can last up to 3 weeks
extreme exhaustion	never	early and prominent
stuffy nose, sore throat	common	sometimes
complications	earache, sinus congestion	bronchitis, pneumonia, can be life threatening
prevention	none	annual vaccination
treatment	only temporary relief of symptoms	antiviral medicines—see your doctor

What do you think?

1. What is more common—a cold or the flu?
2. What is more serious—a cold or the flu?
3. What are some serious complications you can get from the flu?
4. What can you do to prevent the flu?

Dear Ms. Know It All

Problem Solving: Running Grandma

Dear Ms. Know It All:

My husband's mother has taken up a new hobby this year and we are on the fence about whether it is a good thing or a bad thing. She has become a runner. The problem is that she is seventy years old. My husband thinks that seventy is way over-the-hill for someone to begin a sports career. He doesn't have a problem with a seventy-year-old working out. But the idea of his mother jogging through the park in a pair of shorts makes him think that she is losing her marbles.

Actually, I think my husband is embarrassed about it. He's kind of a couch potato himself, and I think he's afraid that she'll be in better shape than he is before too long. I think the old lady is kind of a hero. Besides, she's a big girl, capable of making up her own mind about things. What do you think? Is running at seventy a good thing, or is she out of her mind?

Sincerely,
Worried About Grandma

Word Help: Underline the idioms on Worried About Grandma's letter. Then write the idioms next to their meanings.

MEANING	IDIOM
1. undecided	_____
2. exercising	_____
3. make her own decisions	_____
4. crazy	_____
5. becoming crazy	_____
6. begin something new	_____
7. advanced in age	_____
8. a person who doesn't exercise	_____

CRITICAL THINKING:

Work with a partner or a small group. Discuss Worried About Grandma's problem. Give your opinion and talk about some suggestions. Then complete the letter of advice.

Dear Worried About Grandma :
    Staying fit is important at any age. However, . . .

Work: Getting a Job

GOALS

✓ Prepare for a job interview

✓ Use different ways to talk about the future

✓ Interpret and compare two letters of recommendation

✓ Use character adjectives to describe personal strengths

✓ Write a cover letter

✓ Write a letter of recommendation

✓ Fill out a job application form

✓ Describe nonverbal communication

✓ Discuss work history and job duties

✓ Role-play a job interview

✓ Use participial adjectives

✓ Understand various employee benefits

✓ Review verb tenses

Elena is planning for a job interview. What questions do you think the interviewer might ask her?

1 🎧 **Read and Listen** Read the story. Then listen to it.

A Great Job?

"Elena," Daisy said excitedly, "I think I've found a great job for you."

Elena listened closely and agreed that it did sound like a great job for her. It was a job as an administrative assistant in a small law office. The boss, Mr. Christov, was the father of one of Daisy's students. He wanted to hire someone who spoke Russian, was organized, and knew about accounting and record keeping. The pay was $20 an hour.

Elena was very interested. The next day she called Mr. Christov. They spoke in Russian and in English for twenty minutes. He asked her to send him a resume and a cover letter that included her job skills and her personal strengths. He also told her to go online to fill out an application on his law office Web site. Then he made an appointment for her to come in for an interview.

Elena was nervous. She sat down and made a list of things she needed to do to get ready. She had to look at, and probably rewrite, her resume. She had to write a cover letter to send with her resume. She wanted to ask her aunt for a letter of recommendation that she could bring with her to the interview. And then she wanted to think about questions Mr. Christov could ask her at the interview and how she would answer them. Finally, she had to decide what to wear to the interview because she wanted to look good. She wanted to look organized and professional—like someone Mr. Christov would want to represent his business.

This job interview could be a real opportunity for her in the "land of opportunity," and she wanted to be prepared for it.

2 **Write** How is Elena going to prepare for her job interview? List the things she will probably do to get ready.

1. _____

2. _____

3. _____

4. _____

5. _____

1 **Say It** Practice the conversation with a partner.

A: Well, I spoke to Mr. Christov. He is interviewing me next Wednesday.

B: That's wonderful, Elena.

A: I'm really excited about it. But I'm also terrified. What if I mess it up?

B: You won't mess it up. Just make sure you are prepared. Make sure you know how to get to his office and get there on time. And think about what you are going to say.

A: The first thing I'm going to do is rewrite my resume. Mr. Christov told me what kind of skills he's looking for, so I want to make sure my resume shows the right skills.

B: Good idea.

A: Then I have to make a list of my personal strengths. He wants me to send a cover letter that describes my skills and personal strengths.

B: Maybe I can help you with that.

A: Then I'm going to buy something really nice to wear to the interview. Maybe I'll get a dark blue business suit.

B: I can definitely help you find that.

A: I might even get my hair cut.

B: You don't need to do that. Your hair looks great.

A: I have to ask my aunt for a letter of recommendation because she is my current employer.

B: I'm sure she'll give you a great one.

A: And then I'm going to think about questions they might ask me at the interview, and I'm going to write down the best answers I can think of. Maybe I'll even do a practice interview. Would you be willing to help me practice?

B: Of course. But all you really need to do is be yourself. I'm sure Mr. Christov and his partners will like you.

A: I hope so, Daisy. I'll be really disappointed if I don't get the job.

B: Don't worry. I really think you will get the job. Just try not to be too nervous. The most important thing at a job interview is to be confident.

A: Then I'll try my best to sound and act confident, even if I don't feel it!

Culture Tip

How many interviews?

Most people don't get hired from their first job interview. The average unemployed applicant has 21 interviews before getting a job.

Talking about the future

There are several ways to talk about future time in English:

1. Use *be + going to* + a verb to express a future plan.
   I am **going to rewrite** my resume tomorrow.
2. Use *present continuous* to show a future arrangement with someone.
   He **is interviewing** me on Wednesday.
3. Use *will* for a promise, an offer to help, a prediction, or a decision made right now.
   I **will love** you forever. (a promise)
   I think you **will get** the job. (a prediction)
4. Both *going to* and *will* can be used for future statements of fact and for predictions.
   But, when there is a strong reason for the prediction, use *going to.*
   I heard the weather report, so I'm pretty sure it **is going to rain.**
5. Use *might* or *may* for future possibility.
   I **might** even get my hair cut.

2 Write Read the conversation on page 144 again. Make a list of Elena's future plans. Then make a list of predictions or possibilities about Elena's future.

FUTURE PLANS	PREDICTIONS AND POSSIBILITIES
Elena is going to rewrite her resume.	Elena might get a dark blue business suit.

3 Pair Practice Work with a partner.

A. Ask your partner about his or her future plans. Use follow-up questions to get as much information as possible.

Example: *Student 1:* What are you going to do in the future?
Student 2: I'm going to write a resume and start looking for a job.
Student 1: What kind of job are you going to look for?

B. Ask your partner to tell you about any future arrangements or plans he or she has with a person or with a company.

Example: They are interviewing me on Wednesday. *OR*
I'm going to the dentist tomorrow.

C. Ask your partner to make some predictions about Elena.

Example: I think Elena probably won't get the job. What do you think?

4 Group Practice Work in groups of three or four. Together, make ten predictions about the future. Your predictions can be about people or ideas.

Example: We think the next president of the U.S. will be a Democrat.
We think that José will have a lot of kids in the future.

Mr. Michael Christov
Christov Law Office, Inc.
2305 Sheepshead Bay Rd.
Brooklyn, N.Y. 11230

March 12, 2007

Dear Mr. Christov:

   I am writing to you in support of the application of Elena Petrova for a position as administrative assistant in your law office. Elena has worked in my office in a similar position for over a year. Her computer skills are excellent and include detailed knowledge of both Excel and Money Management accounting programs. In the last few months, she has completely reorganized our business records system.

   Elena is reliable, always punctual, flexible—willing to take on any job we need her to do—and very sociable, with the ability to make everyone around her feel relaxed and comfortable. She was born and raised in Russia, so her Russian language skills are excellent. Her English has been improving rapidly, too.

   I am happy to give Elena my highest recommendation. If she is hired, I'm sure she will be a great asset to your office.

Sincerely,
Sonia Schaffer

Mr. Michael Christov
Christov Law Office, Inc.
2305 Sheepshead Bay Rd.
Brooklyn, N.Y. 11230

March 13, 2007

Dear Mr. Christov:

   I am writing to you in support of Dora Brodsky's application for a position as administrative assistant in your law office. I have worked closely with Dora as her immediate supervisor for the last four months. In those four months, Dora has impressed all of us with her creative and outgoing personality. She always seems to have new ideas and new ways of trying to solve old problems. Dora has excellent oral communication skills in English. She also speaks Russian, but I have no idea how fluent her Russian is. Dora has excellent knowledge of the Internet as we have seen from the many hours she spends surfing for bargains.

   I am happy to recommend Dora for this position. In the right situation, I believe that Dora could have a positive impact on any business's bottom line.

Sincerely,
Robert Johnson

1. What is an example of Elena's excellent computer skills?

   _____

2. What is her biggest accomplishment at her current job?

   _____

3. What is an example of her flexibility?

   _____

4. What other personal strengths does she have?

   _____

5. Why does Sonia think that Elena is sociable?

   _____

6. What is Robert's relationship to Dora?

   _____

7. What is an example of Dora's creativity?

   _____

8. How is Dora's English?

   _____

9. What is an example of her knowledge of the Internet?

   _____

CRITICAL THINKING:

10. Which do you think is a stronger recommendation? Why? Give as many reasons as possible.

Word Help: Match the character adjectives with a behavior.

1. _____ flexible
2. _____ efficient
3. _____ patient
4. _____ organized
5. _____ outgoing

6. _____ independent
7. _____ ambitious
8. _____ punctual
9. _____ reliable/dependable
10. _____ fast learner

a. understands things quickly
b. stays calm, doesn't get upset easily
c. does things quickly and accurately
d. likes to work alone
e. knows where everything is; keeps records and schedules
f. always arrives on time
g. strong desire to succeed
h. friendly, likes to meet and talk with people
i. willing to do many different kinds of jobs
j. always does what he or she is supposed to do

6 **Write** Which of the character adjectives above describe you? List the adjectives that describe you and write a sentence for each one explaining why.

Example: **Ambitious.** I am *ambitious because I want to be president of a big company, and I'm willing to work hard to do it.*

7 **Write** Help Elena write a cover letter for her resume by filling in the missing words in the letter below.

THE BROOKLYN NEWS- March 9

HELP WANTED

Administrative Assistant wanted for busy law office. Friendly, flexible person with good computer skills to organize and maintain business records. Heavy client contact with mostly Russian clients. Good people skills. Strong Russian oral and writing skills pref. Send resume with cover letter to: Michael Christov, Christov Law Office, Inc., 2305 Sheepshead Bay Rd., Brooklyn, N.Y. 11230

Mr. Michael Christov
Christov Law Office, Inc.
2305 Sheepshead Bay Rd.
Brooklyn, N.Y. 11230

March 14, 2007

Dear Mr. Christov:

I am enclosing my (1)_____ for the (2)_____ _____ position that was advertised in The Brooklyn News on March 9. I am an administrative assistant in my current job, so I believe that my background, (3)_____, and personality match what you are looking for this position.

I have a degree in accounting from a major Russian university, so my (4)_____ and (5)_____ skills in Russian are very strong. I am friendly and I enjoy meeting and talking to people, so I believe that I have good (6)_____ _____ . I also have the kind of experience you are looking for because at my last job I used my computer skills to (7)_____ and (8)_____ the company's business records.

Thank you for considering me for this position. I look forward to meeting with you soon.

Sincerely,
Elena Petrova

8 **Listen** Listen and check your answers to Activity 7.

9 **Teamwork Task** Work in teams of three or four. Choose a volunteer from your team. Pretend the volunteer is applying for a job as a teacher's assistant. Work together to write a letter of recommendation for him or her. Describe the volunteer's skills and personality and tell how long you've known him or her. Give any other information you know. Try to convince the teacher to hire the volunteer for the job.

1 **Say It** Practice the conversation with a partner.

business travel

Elena: schedule appointments, make travel arrangements, keep track of business expenses

A: Please have a seat.

B: Thank you.

A: Tell me a little about your present job. I see that you are currently working as an administrative assistant.

B: Yes, that's right.

A: What are your main duties at your present job?

B: I am in charge of <u>business travel</u>. That's the main thing I do.

A: What does that mean exactly? Can you explain that a little?

B: Yes. I <u>schedule appointments, make travel arrangements</u> for the sales people, and <u>keep track of business expenses</u>.

A: This job requires a lot of contact with clients. Are you good with people?

B: Yes, I think I have very good people skills. I'm friendly and outgoing. I like meeting and talking with new people.

A: Good. That's definitely a plus.

Practice more conversations. Use the pictures below.

internet research

1. **Dora: make purchases online, keep purchase records, keep track of budgets**

client relations

2. **Greg: communicate with clients, send out advertising brochures, make follow-up phone calls**

2 **Group Practice** Work in groups of three or four. Look at the three job candidates: Elena, Dora, and Greg. Describe how they look. What are they wearing? How are they sitting? Which one looks the most professional? Together, make a list of things people should and shouldn't wear and do at a job interview. Write as many things as you can.

3 **Say It** Practice the conversation with a partner.

reliable, flexible, good people skills

Elena: "If I say I'm going to do something, I always do it."

2006   2007

Moved to N.Y.: 7/06   Admin. Asst. 8/06–present

A: How long have you been living in New York? When did you move here?

B: I came here in <u>July, 2006</u>. So, I've been living here <u>almost a year</u>.

A: How long have you been at your present job?

B: I've been there since <u>August, 2006</u>.

A: Have you had any other jobs in the U.S.?

B: <u>No, I haven't</u>.

A: Tell me a little more about yourself. What are your best personal qualities?

B: I think that I'm <u>reliable and flexible</u>, and I have <u>good people skills</u>.

A: Can you give me an example?

B: I think that I'm <u>reliable because if I say I'm going to do something, I always do it</u>.

A: Excellent. Now, tell me more about your computer skills.

B: Well, I know how to use several accounting programs. I've been doing computerized record keeping for several years, so I have a lot of experience with that. And, of course, I am very familiar with the Internet.

Practice more conversations. Use the information below.

creative, outgoing, good communication skills

2006   2007

Moved to N.Y.: 7/05   Office Asst. 11/05–10/06   Admin. Asst. 1/07–present

1. Dora: "I always have new ideas about how to do things."

organized, efficient, strong sales skills

2005   2006

Moved to N.Y.: 9/04   Sales Rep. 10/04–9/06   Admin. Asst. 10/06–present

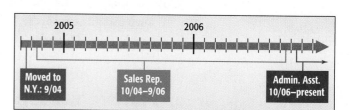

2. Greg: "I keep a schedule on my desk and always follow the schedule."

4 **Say It** Pactice the conversation with a partner.

Work History

POSITION: *Accountant*

FROM: 6/03 TO: 5/06

DUTIES: *kept payroll and other business records; did taxes*

REASON FOR LEAVING: *moved to U.S.*

Elena

A: Tell me a little more about your work history. What did you do in your previous job?

B: In my previous job, I was <u>an accountant</u>.

A: How long did you work at that job?

B: I worked there for <u>two and a half years, from June 2003 to December 2005.</u>

A: What were your primary duties on that job?

B: <u>I kept payroll and other business records, and I did the taxes for the company.</u>

A: Why did you leave that job?

B: I moved to the United States.

Practice more conversations. Use the information below.

Work History

POSITION: Office Assistant

FROM: 11/05 TO: 10/06

DUTIES: *typed letters, answered phones and did light filing*

REASON FOR LEAVING: *bored— needed a change*

1. Dora

Work History

POSITION: *Sales Representative*

FROM: 10/04 TO: 9/06

DUTIES: *sold health club memberships*

REASON FOR LEAVING: *tired of commission work— wanted a steady paycheck*

2. Greg

5 **Group Practice** Work in groups of four. Write these names on four small pieces of paper: Elena, Dora, Greg, and Mr. Christov. Fold the names, mix them up, and give one to each member of your group. Then pretend you are the person whose name you received and role-play the interview from Activities 1, 3, and 4.

6 **Critical Thinking** Which of the three candidates (Elena, Dora, or Greg) do you think Mr. Christov will hire for the job? Make a list of reasons for your choice. Write as many reasons as you can.

_____

_____

_____

_____

_____

7 **Write** Change the negative answers to positive by adding an explanation.

1. Do you have local references? *No, I don't, but* _____

2. Do you have any experience with sales? *No, but* _____

3. Did you bring a resume? *No, but* _____

4. Have you ever used an Excel program? *No, but* _____

8 **Write** Answer the following questions on a piece of paper.

1. List the simple present and present continuous verbs in Activity 1. How many can you find?

2. List the present perfect and present perfect continuous verbs in Activity 3. How many can you find?

3. List the past tense verbs in Activity 4. How many can you find?

9 **Pair Practice** Work with a partner. Pretend you are at a job interview. Introduce yourself and shake hands. Then ask your partner questions from the list below. Answer with your own information or give pretend answers. Answer with complete sentences in the correct verb tense.

1. What position are you applying for?
2. What is your current position?
3. What are your main duties at your current job?
4. How long have you been working at your present job?
5. Why do you want to leave that job?
6. How many different jobs have you had in the United States?
7. What did you do on your previous job?
8. How long did you work there?
9. Tell me about yourself. How would you describe your personal strengths?
10. What skills do you have that might be useful for this job?
11. What are your goals for the future?
12. Do you have any questions for me?

⑩ Teamwork Task Work in teams of four. Choose one member of your team (Student 1) to be the job applicant. Then together, fill out the job application for the applicant. **Student 1**—fill out Part I: Employment Desired. **Student 2**—fill out Part II: Personal Information. **Student 3**—fill out Part III: Education and Skills. **Student 4**—fill out Part IV: Work History. Students 2, 3, and 4 should ask Student 1 questions to find the information necessary to complete the form.

http://www.online.jobapplications.com/

I. EMPLOYMENT DESIRED

POSITION

DATE YOU CAN START   AVAILABILITY: FULL-TIME ☐   PART-TIME ☐   WEEKENDS ☐   EVENINGS ☐

II. PERSONAL INFORMATION

NAME: LAST   FIRST   MI

SOCIAL SECURITY NUMBER

STREET ADDRESS

CITY   STATE   ZIP CODE

TELEPHONE [   ] – [   ]   E-MAIL ADDRESS

ARE YOU OVER 18 YEARS OLD?   YES ☐   NO ☐   HAVE YOU EVER BEEN CONVICTED OF A FELONY?   YES ☐   NO ☐

III. EDUCATION AND SKILLS

LAST SCHOOL ATTENDED   LOCATION

DATES   DEGREE OR CERTIFICATE

SKILLS: List any skills relevant to the position

IV. WORK HISTORY   List your current or most recent job. Please complete even if you are attaching a resume.

EMPLOYER   LOCATION

TELEPHONE [   ] – [   ]   SUPERVISOR

DATES WORKED   POSITION

DUTIES PERFORMED

REASON FOR LEAVING

Homework

Go to a nearby department store or go on the Internet to find a job application. Complete it with true information about yourself. Bring it to class and show it to your teacher and classmates.

Benefits

1 **Read and Listen** Read the story. Then listen to the story.

Benefits

Elena got the job!

Elena was very excited because getting a new job is always exciting. She was pleased with the amount of money she was going to make and thrilled about the benefits of the job. She was also interested in getting to know the people at her new job because they all seemed to be smart and interesting. So, there was a lot to be happy about after Mr. Christov told her the good news.

The benefits Mr. Christov offered were excellent for a small business. First of all, he told her they would provide medical and dental insurance for her and Sasha. She would get eight paid holidays—days when the office would be closed—and two weeks paid vacation after one year. She would get one paid sick day, or personal necessity day, for every two months that she worked. Also, she could have a flexible schedule on days when they didn't have any clients coming in for a meeting.

Mr. Christov told her that they expected her to look professional every day because she would often be meeting with clients in addition to answering phones and keeping business records. Most of their clients were Russian and part of Elena's job would be to speak with them in their own language and to make them feel relaxed and comfortable. "One of the reasons we chose you for this job is because we thought you would make the best impression on our Russian clients," Mr. Christov said.

Elena found it amusing that it wasn't her accounting or computer skills that had helped her get the job. It was her ability to speak Russian and to make people feel comfortable that had gotten her first real job in the United States.

2 **Write** Answer the questions about the story.

1. Why was Elena excited? _____

2. What was she thrilled about? _____

3. What was she interested in doing? _____

4. What was Elena pleased with? _____

5. How many paid holidays will Elena get per year? _____

6. When will she get two weeks paid vacation? _____

7. How do they expect her to look every day? _____

8. What did Elena find amusing? _____

CRITICAL THINKING:

9. What do you think is the best thing about Elena's job? Why?

_____

GRAMMAR CHECK

Participial adjectives

Both the present participle *(exciting)* and the past participle *(excited)* of a verb can be used as adjectives to describe feelings. The *present participle* (the *-ing* form) is used to describe a cause or a reason. The *past participle* describes a result or receiver of a feeling.

The class was **interesting,** so the students were **interested.**

Check Points:

✓ A person can be both a cause and a result of a feeling.
The teacher was **boring,** so the students were **bored.**

✓ A nonliving thing can be a cause, but cannot be a result. (Because nonliving things don't feel anything.)
My job is **tiring.** <u>NOT</u> My job is **tired.**

Some common paired participles include the following:

amazing	amazed	exhausting	exhausted
amusing	amused	frightening	frightened
annoying	annoyed	frustrating	frustrated
boring	bored	interesting	interested
confusing	confused	satisfying	satisfied
disappointing	disappointed	surprising	surprised
embarrassing	embarrassed	terrifying	terrified
exciting	excited	tiring	tired

 Write Circle the correct participial adjectives.

1. Dora was (disappointing / disappointed) that she didn't get the job.

2. Greg's job is really (boring / bored). He is (boring / bored) most of the day.

3. The news report last night was really (frightening / frightened).

4. We were (terrifying / terrified) when we heard the news.

5. Working ten hours is (tiring / tired). I usually go to bed feeling (tiring / tired).

6. Elena was very (confusing / confused) by her boss's difficult question.

7. I was really (embarrassing / embarrassed) by her childish behavior.

8. The long wait to see the counselor was (annoying / annoyed).

4 Write On a piece of paper, write five sentences using a past participle as an adjective and five sentences using a present participle as an adjective. Use at least five different participles.

Examples: Looking for a job can be very **frustrating.**
I was **embarrassed** when I discovered I was wearing one blue sock and one red sock.

5 **Listen** Listen to the conversation. Write a participial adjective that describes how each person felt.

1. She was _____   4. She was _____

2. He was _____   5. He was _____

3. They were _____

6 **Pair Practice** Work with a partner. Ask your partner questions with a participial adjective.

1. When were you confused?

2. When were you disappointed?

3. When were you exhausted?

4. When were you embarrassed?

5. What is a movie you thought was really exciting?

6. What is an interesting place you have been?

Ask more questions with participial adjectives. Ask as many as you can.

7 **Teamwork Task** Work in teams of three or four. Read the list of benefits below that some employers give their employees. Together, rank them from 1 to 10 in order of how important each one is for you. Then rank them in order of how important each one would be if you were Elena—a single parent with a small child. Compare your team's ranking with your classmates' rankings.

ME	ELENA	
____	____	opportunity to work overtime
____	____	dental insurance
____	____	medical insurance with low deductible
____	____	eight to ten paid holidays a year
____	____	two or three weeks paid vacation a year
____	____	flexible work schedule
____	____	six to ten paid sick days a year
____	____	employer provided child care
____	____	tuition assistance for more education
____	____	retirement or pension plan provided by employer

Game Time

Two truths and a lie

Your teacher will give you a participial adjective (for example, *embarrassed*). On a piece of paper, write three sentences about a time when you were embarrassed. Two sentences should be true and one not true. (Write *T* or *F* next to each sentence.) The teacher will read your sentences to the class. If nobody guesses which sentence is a lie, you win.

1 Read and Listen Read the story. Then listen to the story.

I Got a Job!

Finding a job can be a long and difficult process. Elena realizes that she was lucky. She found a job through word of mouth—by networking. And she got the first job she interviewed for. Most people don't get the first job they apply for. But, on the other hand, she had been looking for a long time before she found something she wanted to apply for.

Mr. Christov wants her to start on Monday, so now she is getting ready for her first day. First, she is going to buy some new clothes because she wants to look professional. Next, she is going to study a list of legal vocabulary words that Mr. Christov gave her because part of her job will be to interview Russian-speaking clients and translate for them, if necessary. She hopes it won't be necessary in the first few days at least. She has been studying English since she arrived in the U.S., but there are still a lot of English words and idioms she doesn't know. It takes a long time to speak another language really well.

The night after her job interview, Elena called Alex in Russia. "I got a job!" she said. "The pay is $20 an hour," she said. "And I will have medical insurance for Sasha and me." Alex sounded happy. The salary was a lot more money than she had ever made in Russia. She told Alex a little about her job duties and a little about Mr. Christov. "He speaks Russian," she said, "but not very well. That's what he needs me for." She told him how nice Mr. Christov was and how much she was going to learn on this job. Alex was quiet for a moment.

"Elena," he asked, "is Mr. Christov married?"

"Yes, Alex," she said, "he's married. And so am I." She hesitated for a moment. "I haven't forgotten that," she said. "Have you?"

"No, Elena," Alex said. "I haven't forgotten either."

2 Write Read the story again. Find an example of each of the following verb forms. Write them on a piece of paper.

1. a simple present tense verb
2. a simple past tense verb
3. a future plan
4. a future statement
5. a simple present negative
6. a future negative
7. a present perfect verb
8. a present perfect continuous verb
9. a past perfect tense verb
10. a past perfect continuous
11. a gerund
12. an infinitive

3 Critical Thinking What do you think will happen in Elena's future? Make predictions about Elena and her family and friends. Use *going to* and *will*. Write as many predictions as you can on a piece of paper

Write Complete the sentences with the best character adjective.

1. She always arrives on time. She's very _____.

2. We need somebody who likes to work alone; someone who is very _____.

3. This place gets very busy. We need someone who won't get upset—a very _____ person.

4. I need a secretary to keep all my records and make weekly schedules for the staff—someone who is very _____.

5. Every day brings a different challenge. We need someone who can do a lot of different things—someone who is very _____.

5 Write Complete the sentences with the best participial adjective.

1. The movie was really _____. I almost fell asleep.

2. I was really _____ by what he said. I couldn't believe it.

3. I was very _____ by the question. I didn't know what he meant.

4. My English class is very _____. I learn a lot every day.

5. I wouldn't say I was angry. That's too strong. I was more _____ by his behavior.

6 Teamwork Task Grammar Bowl III

Work in two teams of six or eight students each—a Blue Team and a Red Team. You will have ten minutes to complete the sentences below with the correct forms of the verbs in parentheses. After ten minutes, the teacher will give each student a number. Write the number and the complete sentence on the board—the Blue Team on one side and the Red Team on the other. If the verb is correct, including spelling, the team gets a point. The team with the most points wins!

1. (begin) Two months ago she _____ looking for a new job.

2. (ask) _____ they _____ a lot of different questions at your last interview?

3. (apply) She _____ _____ for many jobs since she moved here.

4. (have) Every time he _____ a job interview he gets nervous.

5. (celebrate) I have only one plan. When I get my first paycheck, I'm _____.

6. (not get) My prediction is that she _____ _____ the job. They'll make the decision tomorrow.

7. (quit) _____ you ever _____ a job? I haven't.

8. (not come) The interview was scheduled for 9:00, but she _____ _____ until 9:15. That's bad.

9. (sit) I _____ _____ _____ here for twenty minutes. I hope he comes soon.

10. (take) _____ you ever _____ a job that you didn't really want?

11. (know) _____ you _____ how many positions they have open?

12. (enjoy) She usually _____ talking to new people. She's very sociable.

13. (not meet) I _____ never _____ anyone yet who works at a bank.

14. (leave) She decided _____ after just a few months.

15. (not speak) They _____ _____ to each other in years before he came to visit.

16. (have) How many job interviews _____ you _____ in your life?

Pronunciation Sentence stress

Negative words are usually stressed in a sentence, but sometimes we don't want to stress the negative. Listen and repeat the negative sentences, and the "*No, but . . .*" sentences.

1. I <u>don't</u> have a resume.
   I don't have a <u>resume</u>, but I brought an <u>application</u>.

2. I <u>don't</u> have a car.
   I don't have a <u>car</u>, but I have a <u>motorcycle</u>.

3. I <u>haven't</u> worked in sales.
   I haven't worked in <u>sales</u>, but I'm <u>sure</u> I'd be <u>good</u> at it.

I can . . .			
• prepare for a job interview.	1	2	3
• use different ways to talk about the future.	1	2	3
• interpret and compare two letters of recommendation.	1	2	3
• use character adjectives to describe personal strengths.	1	2	3
• write a cover letter.	1	2	3
• write a letter of recommendation.	1	2	3
• fill out a job application form.	1	2	3
• describe nonverbal communication.	1	2	3
• discuss work history and job duties.	1	2	3
• role-play a job interview.	1	2	3
• use participial adjectives.	1	2	3
• understand various employee benefits.	1	2	3
• review verb tenses.	1	2	3

1 = not well   2 = OK   3 = very well

DOWNTOWN JOURNAL

YOUR COMMUNITY NEWSPAPER   VOL. 24 NO. 8 MARCH 15

How Is Your Body Language?
Ten Tips for Positive Nonverbal Communication

1. Arrive on time.
2. Dress for success—look professional.
3. Make eye contact.
4. Introduce yourself.
5. Shake hands—firmly.
6. Sit up straight.
7. Don't slouch or cross your legs.
8. Don't fold your arms or put your hands in your pockets.
9. Avoid nervous habits.
10. Smile.

Story of the Week: Oscar's Job Interview

Oscar was at a job interview recently. It was a job that required speaking with clients. Oscar had studied a lot of English grammar but hadn't spent much time on listening and speaking skills. The interviewer liked Oscar, but he didn't think his English was good enough for the job. Oscar, always positive, insisted that it was. "If you don't believe me," he said, "give me a test."

"OK," the interviewer said. "Here is your test. Tell me a sentence with the words *green*, *pink*, and *yellow*. "

"Just one sentence?"

"That's right," the man said. Oscar thought about it for a moment. Then he thought about it a little more. "OK," he said. "I've got it."

The interviewer waited.

"I come home from work," Oscar said, "and walk into my apartment and suddenly I hear the telephone say 'green, green, green,' so I pink it up and say 'yellow, yellow'."

What do you think?
Do you think Oscar got the job? Why or why not? What is the moral of this story?

1. Know your colors before you speak.
2. It's better to clarify than to say something wrong.
3. Job interviewers ask crazy questions.
4. Pronunciation is more important than you think.
5. _____
   (your own idea)

INTERNET IDEA
Go on the Internet and use a search engine to search for job interview tips and body language. Write down what you learn about body language at a job interview.

DOWNTOWN JOURNAL

Dear Ms. Know It All

Problem Solving: Grooming

Dear Ms. Know It All:

My hard-headed husband—let's call him Fred—has been looking for a job for several weeks and so far he hasn't had any luck. He is a pro at what he does. He is a top-of-the-line salesperson, and he is as sharp as a tack in an interview, so I think the problem might be the way he looks. I think the problem might be his beard. He has a full, dark beard.

My husband is only twenty-eight years old and is real eye candy without the beard. But the beard hides his handsome face and makes him look like a lot older. He thinks it makes him look more like an alpha male. He sees the beard as a plus. I definitely see it as a minus.

I don't want to see my wonderful husband out pounding the pavement any longer, so I think the beard's got to go. What do you think?

Sincerely,
Worried About the Beard

Word Help: Underline the idioms in Worried About the Beard's letter. Then write the idioms next to their meaning.

MEANING	IDIOM
1. someone nice to look at	_____
2. looking for a job	_____
3. something positive	_____
4. something negative	_____
5. success at something	_____
6. one of the best	_____
7. very proficient	_____
8. a leader of a group	_____
9. very smart	_____
10. stubborn	_____

CRITICAL THINKING:

Work with a partner or a small group. Discuss Worried About the Beard's problem. Give your opinion and make some suggestions about what she *should* or *shouldn't* do. Then write an answer to her letter.

Dear Worried About the Beard:
_____

Work: On the Job

GOALS

- ✓ Take and deliver telephone messages
- ✓ Report what someone said or wrote
- ✓ Understand organizational charts
- ✓ Call for transportation
- ✓ Use short questions for clarification
- ✓ Use the Internet to make airline reservations
- ✓ Contrast and compare travel options
- ✓ Interpret a work schedule
- ✓ Interpret an office memorandum
- ✓ Interpret a technical manual
- ✓ Program a cell-phone calendar
- ✓ Interpret a job performance evaluation form

What office equipment do you see in Elena's office?

1  **Read and Listen** Read the story. Then listen to it.

Work

Elena likes her new office a lot. It is a nice, big office with a lot of new modern equipment. She sometimes shares it with Amy, who is a legal secretary and the person Elena relies on to teach her all the new things she has to learn. Amy has her own office, too. She told Elena that she would only come in when Elena needed help with something or someone.

On her desk, Elena has a large, modern, flat-screen computer monitor. When he hired her, Mr. Christov told Elena that he would get her a new computer with a large, flat-screen monitor because she would be spending a lot of her time typing or doing Internet research. Mr. Christov kept his word.

There are a lot of things Elena has to learn. There is a new filing system, as well as a fax machine, a copy machine, a fancy printer, and even a paper shredder that she has to learn how to use. There are new accounting programs she has to operate. And she has to learn how to research many new Internet Web sites. But, with Amy to help her, she is pretty sure she will be able to learn all that sooner or later. The thing she worries most about is her English. Part of her job is to answer the phone and take messages. Another part is to help translate things for Russian clients if necessary. So, she is still working hard to improve her English as much as she can. Elena doesn't know what she will be doing a year from now, but for now she is very happy with her new job.

 Write What are Elena's job duties? List as many as you can.

_____

_____

_____

_____

_____

Oral Communication

Lesson 1

1 **Say It** Practice the conversation with a partner.

Date: 4/2   Time: 11:15 A.M.
To: Mr. Christov
From: Mr. Ford—Lincoln Industries
MESSAGE
Can I come in tomorrow afternoon at 2:00?
☑ WILL CALL BACK   ☐ PLEASE CALL
Taken by: Elena

A: Are there any messages for me, Elena?

B: Yes, there is one. A <u>man</u> from <u>Lincoln Industries</u> called at <u>11:15</u>.

A: Did <u>he</u> say what <u>his</u> name was?

B: Yes. <u>He</u> said <u>he</u> was <u>Mr. Ford</u>.

A: What did <u>he</u> want?

B: <u>He</u> wanted to know <u>if he could come in tomorrow afternoon at 2:00</u>.

A: That's fine. Does <u>he</u> want me to call <u>him</u> back?

B: No. <u>He said he would call again</u>.

Practice more conversations. Use the information below.

Date: 4/3   Time: 10:30 A.M.
To: Mr. Christov
From: Mr. Carter—Johnson Insurance
MESSAGE
Will you be available for a consultation on Friday?
☐ WILL CALL BACK   ☑ PLEASE CALL
Taken by: Elena

1.

Date: 4/4   Time: 3:20 P.M.
To: Ms. West
From: Ms. Hakopyan—Black Sea Imports
MESSAGE
Can you see me ASAP?
☑ WILL CALL BACK   ☐ PLEASE CALL
Taken by: Elena

2.

Date: 4/5   Time: 4:05 P.M.
To: Amy
From: Mr. Kennedy—Brooklyn College
MESSAGE
Will you be at the meeting on Friday?
☐ WILL CALL BACK   ☑ PLEASE CALL
Taken by: Elena

3.

GRAMMAR CHECK

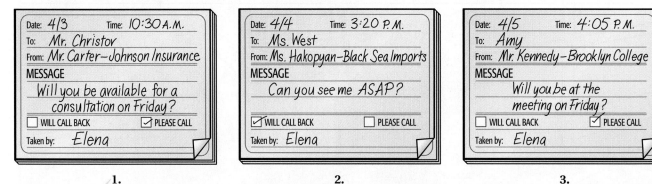

Reported speech with *can* and *will*

When we report what someone said or asked in the past, we usually change *can* to *could* and *will* to *would*.

When the direct question is a *yes/no* question, we usually use *if* as the question word in reported speech.

   Can she call me tomorrow? (direct question)

   He asked **if** she **could** call him tomorrow. (reported speech)

Check Point:

   ✓ Don't forget to change the pronouns as necessary.

2 **Pair Practice** Work with a partner. Ask your partner to tell you several interesting things he or she can do. Take notes. Then report to the class what your partner told you.

Example: She told me that she could type fifty words per minute.

Reported speech

When the main verb is in the past tense, we usually change present tense verbs in a direct quote to the past tense in reported speech.

"I'm going to get a job."   He said that he **was going** to get a job.

"I **don't have** time today."   He said that he **didn't have** time today.

When reporting questions, drop *do* or *does* and replace it with *if* or *whether*.

"**Do** you have an appointment?"   He asked me **if/whether** I had an appointment.

Check Points: There are exceptions to the change-of-tense rule.

✓ If we are repeating something someone just said for someone who didn't hear it, we don't usually change tenses.

"I **can't** find my glasses."

"What did he say?"

"He said he **can't** find his glasses."

✓ If we are talking about a general truth, we don't usually change tenses.

"The earth **revolves** around the sun."

"He said the earth **revolves** around the sun."

3 Say It Practice the conversation with a partner.

```
Elena,

Please call Sid Kane. Tell
him I am going out of town.
I won't be back until Friday.

Thanks,
Mr. C.
```

A: Could I speak with <u>Mr. Kane</u>, please?

B: This is <u>Mr. Kane</u>. What can I do for you?

A: This is Elena Petrova from Mr. Christov's office. Mr. Christov asked me to call you.

B: About what?

A: <u>He asked me to tell you that he was going out of town. He said that he wouldn't be back until Friday</u>.

B: OK. Thank you for calling.

Practice more conversations. Use the information below.

1.
```
Elena,
Please call Mr. Carter. Tell him
I'm in a meeting all day.
I'll call him at about 6:30.
Thanks,
Mr. C.
```

2.
```
Elena,
Please call Ms. Nixon. Tell her I need
another day to finish the papers.
I'll get back to her tomorrow.
Thanks,
Mr. C.
```

3.
```
Elena,
Please call Mr. Jackson. Tell him that
Arnold is dropping the case because
he doesn't think that we can win.
Thanks,
Mr. C.
```

Culture Tip

Business e-mails

E-mail at work can be less formal than a business letter. But be careful. Think before you write! E-mails may cause misunderstandings if the tone is TOO informal.

 4 **Write** Change the direct quotes to reported speech.

1. Mr. Arnold: "I will be back."

   <u>He said that he would be back.</u>

2. Mr. King: "I have a dream."

   _____

3. Ms. West: "I need to talk to John."

   _____

4. John: "Love makes the world go 'round."

   _____

5. Mrs. Carter: "I'm going to be late."

   _____

6. Daisy: "I prefer chocolate to vanilla."

   _____

Now change the reported speech to direct quotes.

7. Greg said that he was a lawyer. Greg said, "_____"

8. Vicki told me that she had a headache. Vicki said, "_____"

9. Vito said he would make me an offer. Vito said, "_____"

10. My boss said that he wanted to talk to me. My boss said, "_____"

5 **Listen** Listen to the conversations and take down the messages.

Date:	Time:
To:	
From:	
MESSAGE	
☐ WILL CALL BACK	☐ PLEASE CALL
Taken by:	

1.

Date:	Time:
To:	
From:	
MESSAGE	
☐ WILL CALL BACK	☐ PLEASE CALL
Taken by:	

2.

Date:	Time:
To:	
From:	
MESSAGE	
☐ WILL CALL BACK	☐ PLEASE CALL
Taken by:	

3.

6 **Pair Practice** Work with a partner. Report the three messages to your partner.

> **Note:** *Should* in reported speech
> *Should* and *should have* do not change from direct to reported speech.
> "You **should** call 911." They told me I **should** call 911.
> "He **should have** called home." I said he **should have** called home.

BLACK SEA INDUSTRIES—CALL ROUTING CHART			
PROBLEM	**DEPARTMENT**	**EXTENSION**	**NAME**
Problems with bills or payments	Billing	221	Mr. Ming
Customer complaints, returns	Customer Service	222	Mr. O'Neil
Job applications, resumes	Personnel	223	Mr. Bryant
Telephone orders, prices, product questions	Sales	224	Ms. Bill or Mr. Reddy
Questions about delivery, items that have been shipped out	Shipping	225	Ms. Brown
Questions about equipment	Technical Services	226	Ms. Fixit

7 **Say It** Practice the conversation with a partner. Use the chart above.

I have a problem with my bill.

A: I'm calling because <u>I have a problem with my bill</u>. Who should I talk to about that?

B: You need to speak with <u>the billing department. I'll connect you to extension 221. You should speak to Mr. Ming</u>.

A: Thank you very much.

Practice five more conversations. Use the information in the chart above.

1. "I have a question about prices. Who should I talk to?"

2. "I need some technical help with my new equipment. What extension should I call?"

3. "I want to complain about the person who installed my equipment. What number can I call to make a complaint?"

4. "I need to know when my new printer will be delivered. Who can I talk to about that?"

5. "I'm looking for a job. Do you have any job openings?"

Write Look at the phone calls in Activity 7. Report what each caller said.

Example: *She said she was calling because she had a problem with her bill. She asked who she should talk to about the problem.*

1. _____

_____

2. _____

_____

3. _____

_____

4. _____

_____

5. _____

_____

9 **Group Practice** Work in groups of five or six. Sit in a circle. Whisper a sentence to the person next to you. Use a present or future tense verb, or a sentence with *can*. When each person has whispered a sentence to another student, go around the circle and report what was whispered to you.

Example: *Student 1:* (whispering) I'm going to quit my job soon.
Student 2: (reporting) She told me that she was going to quit her job soon.

10 **Teamwork Task** Work in two teams of six people each.

1. On a piece of paper, write your name and a sentence underneath it. The sentence should be in the present or future tense and should be at least six words long. Give the piece of paper to your teacher and **don't forget** your sentence.

2. Next, each team will line up in front of the chalkboard—the "A" Team on one side and the "B" Team on the other side. Each person in line should whisper the sentence he or she wrote to the person in front of him. The first person in line should whisper his sentence to the last person in line.

3. When the teacher says, "Go," one person from each team goes to the board and writes a reported speech sentence about what their classmate whispered. After all of the sentences have been written, the teacher will look at the sentences on the pieces of paper and check to see if they were reported correctly. The team with the most correct sentences wins. If both teams have an equal number of mistakes, the team that writes the sentences the fastest wins! Good luck!

1 **Say It** Practice the conversation with a partner.

> Elena,
>
> I need a cab to the airport (JFK) for Tuesday morning at 8:15. It's Air America. Have them pick me up in front of the office. Find out how much it is.
>
> Thanks,
> Mr. C.

A: Good morning. This is Elena from Christov Associates.

B: I'm sorry. From where?

A: Christov Associates, on Kings Highway.

B: OK. What do you need?

A: We need a cab to the airport.

B: Which airport?

A: JFK Airport, at 8:15 A.M. on Tuesday.

B: I'm sorry. What day?

A: Tuesday morning, April 17th. We'd like to be picked up here, in front of the office.

B: Picked up where?

A: Here at the office—222 Kings Highway.

B: OK. 222 Kings Highway, Tuesday morning at 8:15 A.M. It'll be $30.

A: That's fine. See you then.

GRAMMAR CHECK

Short questions for clarification

We often use short questions for clarification when one part of a sentence is not heard or understood. A short question might be just a question word and one or two more words, rather than a complete sentence.
   "She lives in Apartment 3303." "I'm sorry. Which apartment?"
   "I'm meeting Mr. Dillon for dinner." "'Meeting who?"

Check Point:
   ✓ Question words can come first or last in a short question, depending on what information is being questioned.

2 **Write** Write a short clarification question for the underlined words.

1. I saw <u>Elmer Fudd</u> at the party. _You saw who?_

2. I need a cab on Monday morning to <u>Newark</u> Airport. _____

3. <u>Boris</u> called yesterday after you left. _____

4. She told me that she called <u>thirty-five</u> people yesterday. _____

5. We're going to have to leave before <u>five o'clock</u>. _____

6. <u>Thirteen</u> applicants came in for the interview. _____

7. They'll pick us up around the corner in front of <u>the bank</u>. _____

8. She said she would come in <u>by train</u>. _____

3 **Listen** Listen to the conversation between Elena and Mr. Christov. Help Elena fill in the information on the travel Web site.

```
http://www.DownTown-TravelAir.com/stepone
```

| STEP 1 | QUICK SEARCH - *FLIGHTS* | Home Contact SiteMap |

Please answer the 5 questions and press the ENTER button. You will be taken to the next page.

1. I need a hotel room with this flight ☐

2. From [＿＿＿＿＿＿＿] ▼ To [＿＿＿＿＿＿＿] ▼

3. Departure [＿＿＿＿＿＿＿] ▼ Return [＿＿＿＿＿＿＿] ▼

4. I can travel ☐ Exact dates only

☐ Within 1 to 3 days of date for lower price

☐ Within 30 days for lowest price

5. Adults ☐   Seniors ☐   Minors ☐   **ENTER**

```
http://www.DownTown-TravelAir.com/steptwo
```

| STEP 2 | *CHOOSE YOUR DATE* | Home Contact SiteMap |

Please CLICK on the price that matches your preferred departure and return dates.

LEAVING	RETURNING				
	Fri. 4/20	Sat. 4/21	Sun. 4/22	Mon. 4/23	Tues. 4/24
Mon. 4/16	$273	$350	$362	$313	$373
Tues. 4/17	$279	$350	$352	$319	$373
Weds. 4/18	$279	$380	$390	$313	$375
Thurs. 4/19	–	$380	$413	$313	$353
Fri. 4/20	–	$407	$384	$313	$353

4 **Problem Solving** Use the travel site above to answer the questions.

1. What box should Mr. Christov check in Step 1 if he wants to change his travel dates? ＿＿＿＿＿＿＿＿＿＿＿＿＿＿＿＿＿＿＿＿＿＿＿＿＿＿＿

2. What box should he check if his schedule is flexible and he wants the lowest possible fare? ＿＿＿＿＿＿＿＿＿＿＿＿＿＿＿＿＿＿＿＿＿＿＿

3. What should he do if he wants to bring his wife and two children? ＿＿＿＿＿＿

＿＿＿＿＿＿＿＿＿＿＿＿＿＿＿＿＿＿＿＿＿＿＿＿＿＿＿＿＿＿＿＿＿＿＿

4. How much will he pay for one person if he leaves on 12/17 and returns on 12/21? ＿＿＿＿＿＿＿＿＿＿＿＿＿＿＿＿＿＿＿＿＿＿＿＿＿＿＿＿＿＿

5. What is the cheapest fare he can get in the table above? ＿＿＿＿＿＿＿＿＿

6. How much could he save if he left on Thursday and came home on Monday instead of Sunday? ＿＿＿＿＿＿＿＿＿＿＿＿＿＿＿＿＿＿＿＿＿＿＿

7. On what return day are the fares generally the most expensive? ＿＿＿＿＿＿＿

8. Which is the most expensive leave-and-return combination? ＿＿＿＿＿＿＿＿

9. Mr. Christov has decided to leave on Tuesday and will return on Sunday. How much is he going to spend on airfare? ＿＿＿＿＿＿＿＿＿＿＿＿＿＿＿

5 **Say It** Practice the conversation with a partner.

```
http://www.FoundURL-Flight.com/Jetpink/info-4/17
```

YOUR FLIGHT

DATE:	April 17
AIRLINE:	Jet Pink
DEPARTURE TIME:	6:55 A.M.
ARRIVAL TIME:	9:42 A.M.
TOTAL TRAVEL TIME:	5 HR. 47 MIN.—Nonstop
ROUND-TRIP FARE:	$390.00

Home   Contact   SiteMap

A: I'm on a travel Web site. There is a flight on Jet Pink that leaves at . . .

B: I'm sorry. What airline?

A: Jet Pink. It leaves New York at 6:55 A.M. and arrives in L.A. . . . .

B: I'm sorry. Leaves when?

A: At 6:55 . . . five minutes to seven in the morning. And arrives in L.A. at 9:42 A.M. The total travel time is five hours and forty-seven minutes. It's a nonstop flight. The fare is $390.

B: 6:55 A.M. is really early. Is there a flight that leaves a little later?

A: That's the latest flight available on Jet Pink on April 17th. Do you want me to try another airline?

B: Yes, please. Let me know what you find out.

> **Note: Simple present tense for future**
> For future scheduled events, we often use the simple present tense.
> The movie **starts** at 8:00. The plane to New York **leaves** at 6:00.

6 **Pair Practice** Work with a partner. Tell your partner about the four different travel possibilities for April 17th. The four circled items represent problems your partner has with those flights. Your partner will complain about those problems. Then he or she will make a decision about which one he or she wants to book.

```
http://www.DownTown-TravelAir.com/stepthree
```

STEP 3   *CHOOSE YOUR FLIGHT*   Home   Contact   SiteMap

Please CLICK on your preferred flight choice.

AIRLINE	DEPARTURE NY–JFK	ARRIVAL LA–LAX	TOTAL TRAVEL TIME	ROUND-TRIP FARE
Air America Flight 192	6:25 A.M.	8:55 A.M.	5 hr. 30 min. Nonstop	$279
Western Air Flight 17	8:10 P.M.	12:30 A.M. (next day)	7 hr. 20 min. Change planes in Chicago	$315
Slow Air Flight 111	4:20 P.M.	10:40 P.M.	9 hr. 20 min. Change planes in Dallas	$330
Golden Air Flight 14	6:30 P.M.	8:48 P.M.	5 hr. 18 min. Nonstop	$485

7 Say It Practice the conversation with a partner.

Agenda	
Beverly Hill Hotel, 4/17–4/20	
	WEDNESDAY, 4/18
8:00	*Breakfast–Alberto & Cindy*
9:00	*Meeting–Bob Schwartz,* *Tennis International*
11:00	—
12:30	*Lunch–Jessica Vidal*
2:00	*Meeting–Mr. Geffen,* *Music Video Inc.*
4:00	—
6:00	*Movie Screening–The Last Kiss*
8:00	*Dinner–Jen and Marc*
10:00	—

A: Do you have my schedule for the California trip?

B: Yes, everything is arranged. You'll be staying at the Beverly Hills Hotel from April 17th to the 20th.

A: What's on the agenda for Wednesday?

B: On Wednesday, you are having breakfast with Alberto and Cindy Gonzalez. Then you will be meeting with Bob Schwartz at 9:00.

A: How long will I be meeting with Bob?

B: The meeting is scheduled for two hours.

A: And after that?

B: After that you have some free time until 12:30. At 12:30 you are having lunch with Jessica Vidal.

A: OK. For 11:00 write in "relax by the pool." That sounds like a good thing to do after a two-hour meeting with Bob.

Ask and answer more questions about Mr. Christov's Wednesday agenda.

GRAMMAR CHECK

> **Present and future continuous**
>
> We often use the *present continuous tense* for future arrangements—things that have been planned with someone in advance.
>   We **are meeting** for lunch at noon.
> The *future continuous tense* is used to talk about a continuing future action or to tell the duration of a future event—how long you will be doing something.
>   I **will be staying** in L.A. for three days.

8 Write Answer the questions with complete sentences on a piece of paper.

1. Who are you having dinner with tonight?
2. How long will you be studying at this school?
3. What will you be doing between 8:00 and 9:00 tonight?
4. When are you taking your final exam?

9 Teamwork Task Work with a team of three or four. Choose a volunteer from your team. The volunteer is going on a trip to Hawaii that is partly business and partly vacation. Create a two-day schedule for him or her. Include two business meetings a day. Fill in the rest of the day with your own ideas.

Following Directions

1 **Read and Listen** Read the story. Then listen to the story.

Following Directions

One of the hardest things about starting a new job is learning the rules and expectations of the job. There are a lot of things Elena has to learn about her new job. There are a lot of new directions she has to follow. Fortunately, she has a boss who is very patient.

The first thing she had to learn was how to answer the phone properly. She is supposed to say, "Christov Associates, how may I help you?" That isn't a sentence she hears in her everyday life. It is more formal English that is appropriate for a law office.

Elena also has to learn about the rules of the office. One way to learn is to read memos and the employee handbook. But, fortunately, she has her coworker Amy, who is willing to help her. On the second day of her job, Elena brought a cup of coffee from lunch back to the office. "If I were you," Amy said, "I wouldn't drink coffee in the office." "If I were you, I wouldn't . . ." is Amy's favorite expression. That is how she warns Elena whenever she does something wrong.

"If you spill coffee on any of Mr. Christov's legal papers,'" she said, "he'll hand you your walking papers." She explained that that meant she would be fired. Idioms are another thing that Amy is helping Elena with.

Elena has to learn how to operate several new machines. She has to learn how to access several important Web sites. She has to learn a lot of legal vocabulary and terminology. She has to learn several organizational charts. But she realizes that if she were Daisy, she would have to learn rules about the school district. If she were Vicki, she would have to learn rules about customer service. If she were Alice, she would have to learn a lot of medical vocabulary and terminology. So, everybody has to learn the rules of his or her job. Elena's plan is to learn it all as quickly as she can.

2 **Write** Complete the sentences with words from the story. Try not to look back at the story. Then scan to check your answers.

1. One of the hardest things about starting a new job is learning the _____ and _____ of the job.

2. There are a lot of new _____ she has to follow.

3. Fortunately, she has a boss who is very _____.

4. It is more _____ English that is appropriate for a law office.

5. One way to learn is to read _____ and the employee _____.

6. Fortunately she has her coworker Amy, who is _____ to help her.

7. "If I _____ you," Amy said, "I _____ drink coffee in the office."

8. "If you spill coffee on any of Mr. Christov's legal papers," she had said, "he'll hand you your _____."

9. She has to learn how to _____ several important Web sites.

10. She has to learn several _____ charts.

Present unreal conditional

We use the *present unreal conditional* to talk about a condition that isn't true, or real, at the present time.

For present unreal conditionals, use a past tense verb in the *if* clause and *would* or *could* in the main, or result, clause.

In unreal conditions, use *were* (not *was*) for *I, he, she,* and *it*.

Condition	**Result**
If I had a million dollars, (I don't have it)	**I would** give half to my teacher.
If I were rich, (I'm not rich)	**I could** buy my mother a house.

Check Point:

✓ When we see a past tense verb in an *if* clause, we know that the situation is unreal or not true.

 Write Complete the sentences with your own ideas. Use *would* or *could* in the result clause.

1. If I spoke English perfectly, _____.

2. If I had a very big house, _____.

3. If I were the president of the United States, _____.

4. If I were the president of my native country, _____.

5. If I lived close to the beach, _____.

6. If I were on vacation right now, _____.

7. If I could live any place in the world, _____.

8. If I were Elena, _____.

4 **Pair Practice** Work with a partner. Ask and answer questions from Activity 3.

Example: *Student 1:*   What would you do if you spoke English perfectly?
                 Student 2:   If I spoke English perfectly, I wouldn't be in this class!

5 **Read** Read the interoffice memo.

Black Sea Industries—*Interoffice Memoranda*

All employees must read and be aware of the following information.

Time-Off Request Form

All employees should plan to attend a training session regarding our new **Time-Off Request Form**. This new form must be filled out by all employees who want to be paid for vacation time or for absences due to illness or personal necessity, including bereavement. Vacation leave must be requested at least two weeks in advance. Written sick-pay requests should be turned in by employees on the day they return to work. Bereavement leave applies only to the loss of an immediate family member and is limited to five working days without loss of pay.

Pair Practice Work with a partner. Use the interoffice memo on page 174 to answer the questions below.

1. If you worked for Black Sea Industries, what would you have to do?
2. Who should attend this training session?
3. What is the purpose of this training session?
4. If you wanted to be paid for time off, what would you have to do?
5. If you wanted a paid vacation, how far in advance would you have to request it?
6. If you were out sick, when would you turn in your sick-pay request?
7. If your close friend died, would you be paid for bereavement leave?
8. Could you take two weeks off with pay if an immediate family member died?

7 Read Read the instructions for using the cell-phone calendar.

> You may schedule up to eight events for any day by indicating each event's start and end time.
> Events scheduled for future days will appear on your TODAYS EVENTS schedule when the day arrives.

WEEK
Monday
Tuesday
Wednesday
Thursday
Friday
Saturday
Sunday

DISPLAY

RIGHT NAVIGATION KEY

RIGHT SOFT KEY

MENU

LEFT NAVIGATION KEY

ENTER KEY

LEFT SOFT KEY

TO ADD A NEW EVENT

1. In standby mode, press MENU,
   then press the right navigation key to SETTINGS & TOOLS.
   When you see the TOOLS menu, press CALENDAR.
   The calendar will appear in the display.

2. To view available options,
   press the right soft key—OPTIONS.
   A pop-up menu will appear showing the following options:

Weekly:	View the curent week
Go to Date:	Go to any date you specify
Go to Today:	View today's events
Erase Old:	Delete past events
Erase All:	Delete all events in your calendar

3. Press the left soft key to ADD a new event.

8 Write Use the technical manual above to answer the questions.

1. If you wanted to add a new event to your calendar, what would you do first?

_____

2. What would you do next? _____

3. If you wanted to see all the options, what key would you press?

_____

4. If you wanted to delete all the events in your calendar, what would you press?

_____

5. What key would you press to add a new event?

_____

9 **Teamwork Task 1** Work in teams of four or five. Look at the job performance evaluation form below. Choose a volunteer to play Vicki. The other students are the store supervisors. Vicki wants a raise. Decide together if you would give her a raise. Make a list of things she could do to improve her ratings. Use conditional sentences. Tell Vicki what she could do to get a raise.

Example: Your punctuality rating needs improvement. If you came in on time every day, you could get a raise.

JOB PERFORMANCE EVALUATION FORM

NAME: *Vicki Martinez*

TITLE: *Customer Service Representative*

SUPERVISOR: *Mr. Burns*

DATE: *April 15, 2007*

OVERALL RATING: *3*

CATEGORY	RATING	COMMENTS
Punctuality	2	comes in late about once a week
Dependability	3	good attendance, but has missed three meetings
Customer Service	3	gets along well with coworkers, but sometimes gets upset with customers
Organizational Skills	4	good paperwork, but sometimes forgets to sign forms
Work Habits	4	hard worker, but sometimes takes long breaks

Rating Scale: 5 = Excellent, 4 = Good, 3 = Acceptable, 2 = Needs Improvement, 1 = Poor

10 **Teamwork Task 2** Work together to evaluate your teammates in the five categories on the job performance evaluation form. Ask questions as necessary. (How many times have you been absent?) Which of your teammates has the best rating for each of the categories? Give your teammates advice about how they could improve their ratings.

1 **Read and Listen** Read the story. Then listen to the story.

Changes

Having a new full-time job has made Elena's life better in some ways, but more challenging in other ways. A full-time job takes time. It requires not just eight hours a day on the job, but also time to learn the new things that she needs to know to do her job well. Mr. Christov told her at her job interview that he wanted a dedicated, hard worker for the position. Of course, nobody asked her if she had any children because that is an illegal question to ask at a job interview. But Elena has a child. If she didn't have Sasha, it would be a lot easier to work long hours. But her child needs time, too.

After she got her new job, Elena had to explain to Sasha that she wouldn't be able to pick him up from school anymore. She told him that his grandma would be picking him up and he would be staying at Grandma's house for a while after school every day. He looked very sad, and asked if Grandma would help him with his homework after school like Elena always did. "Honey," she told him, "you know your grandma doesn't speak English very well."

Elena's friends were sympathetic about her problem. Daisy told her that it was going to be difficult to get used to the new schedule, but she eventually would. Alice told her that she would just have to make the best of it.

After her first week of full-time work, Elena was feeling depressed. She decided to call Alex in Russia. When he answered the phone, he sounded excited. "Did you get my message?" he asked. She told him that she hadn't gotten any message. She started to talk about the problems with her new schedule, but he stopped her. "Elena," he said, "it was approved."

For a moment, she didn't know what he was talking about.

"Elena," he said, "my application was approved! I'm coming to New York."

"You're coming to New York?"

"Yes," he said. "Soon. As soon as possible."

"Is it true?" she said. "I can't believe it!"

She had never felt so happy in her whole life.

2 **Write** Who said each of these things? Who did they say them to?

WHO?	TO WHOM?	
1. _____	_____	"I want a dedicated, hardworking person."
2. _____	_____	"I won't be able to pick you up from school."
3. _____	_____	"Will she help me with my homework after school?"
4. _____	_____	"It's going to be difficult, but you'll get used to it."
5. _____	_____	"You will just have to make the best of it."
6. _____	_____	"No, I didn't get any message."

Write Correct the mistakes in the sentences on a piece of paper. If there are no mistakes, write *correct*.

1. If I am a rich man, I would buy all my classmates new cars.

2. If he can, he would. But he can't.

3. I don't like coffee. But if I like it, I would go out for coffee with you.

4. He told me that the earth revolves around the sun. But who doesn't know that?

5. If she were my wife, I would be a very happy man.

6. If you have questions about delivery, you should probably call the personnel department.

7. She told me I should get a job.

8. "You should call the shipping department." "Department which?"

9. "I saw him in the cafeteria." "Saw him who?"

10. The train leaves at 7:00 sharp. Don't be late.

11. Tomorrow at 6:00 I be eat dinner with my family.

12. We're meeting for lunch at 1:00.

4 **Write** Answer the questions about the memo.

> **Black Sea Industries—*Interoffice Memoranda***
> ## Travel Training Now Required
> If you travel as part of your job, or plan to work off site at any time this year, please plan to attend a special training session to discuss our new travel policy. The training session will be held in Conference Room D on the second floor and will last about an hour. Contact your floor supervisor to make arrangements to attend.

1. If you planned to work off site this year, what would you have to do?

_____

2. If you went to this training session, what would you learn about?

_____

3. If you went to this training session, how long would it probably last?

_____

4. How would you make arrangements to attend a travel training session?

_____

5 **Teamwork Task** Work in teams of three or four. Write a story about Elena's future. What do you think she will be doing next year? Two years from now? Five years from now? How about Alex and Sasha? What will they be doing? Will they be happy? What will change in their lives? Talk with your teammates. Then, together, write a story of at least ten sentences about Elena's future life.

Pronunciation Sentence rhythm and stress

A. In most English sentences, only the important words are stressed. If we stress every word equally, the speaker sounds angry. Listen to the sentences with equal stress.

1. I won't be attending the meeting.

2. I am ready to leave now.

3. Can I please have a check?

B. Now listen and repeat the same sentences with normal stress.

1. I **won't** be **attend**ing the **meet**ing.

2. I'm **ready** to **leave** now.

3. Can I **please** have a **check?**

INTERNET IDEA
Go to an online travel Web site. Find the least expensive fare you can find for a round-trip ticket from New York to Los Angeles for two weeks from today. Write down the airline and the fare. Compare your results with your classmates.

I can . . .			
• take and deliver telephone messages.	1	2	3
• report what someone said or wrote.	1	2	3
• understand organizational charts.	1	2	3
• call for transportation.	1	2	3
• use short questions for clarification.	1	2	3
• use the Internet to make airline reservations.	1	2	3
• contrast and compare travel options.	1	2	3
• interpret a work schedule.	1	2	3
• interpret an office memorandum.	1	2	3
• interpret a technical manual.	1	2	3
• program a cell-phone calendar.	1	2	3
• interpret a job performance evaluation form.	1	2	3

1 = not well   2 = OK   3 = very well

DOWNTOWN JOURNAL

YOUR COMMUNITY NEWSPAPER   VOL. 24 NO. 8 APRIL 15

Survey

1. If you could have any job, what job would you choose?
   I would be a . . .
   _____

2. If you could live any place in the world, where would you live?
   _____

3. If you could have dinner with any person who ever lived, who would you choose?
   _____

4. If you could change one thing about your appearance, what would you change?
   _____

5. If you had one wish with a magic lamp, what would you wish for?
   _____

Interview the students in your class. Create a bar graph and a pie chart of your class's opinions from the student survey. Follow the examples.

1. If I could have any job, I would be a . . .

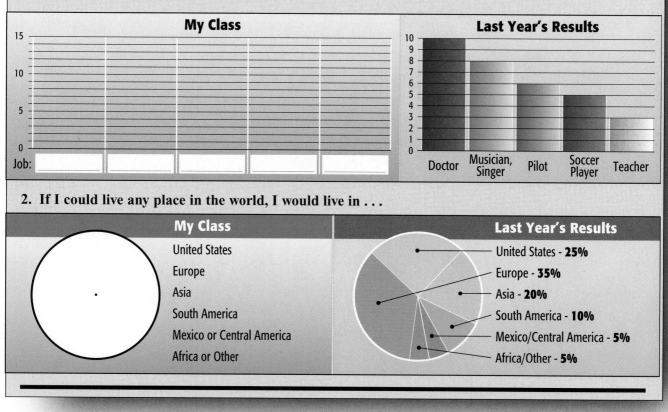

2. If I could live any place in the world, I would live in . . .

My Class	Last Year's Results
United States	United States - **25%**
Europe	Europe - **35%**
Asia	Asia - **20%**
South America	South America - **10%**
Mexico or Central America	Mexico/Central America - **5%**
Africa or Other	Africa/Other - **5%**

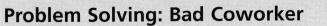

Dear Ms. Know It All

Problem Solving: Bad Coworker

Dear Ms. Know It All:

I have a coworker, let's call her Judy, who drives me up the wall. Since I spend half my life at work, I would like to try to do something about the problem. If you were a fly on the wall in my office for five minutes, you would see that Judy thinks she's the cat's meow. Everything is always about her.

The problem is that I work in a small office, just a handful of people, so it's important that we all get along and help each other. Of course, I'm willing to pitch in and help Judy whenever she needs something. I sometimes work overtime to help Judy when she can't finish something that has a tight deadline. But when the shoe is on the other foot, she won't lift a finger to help me.

I have complained to our boss about Judy more than once. He seems to get it when I explain the problem. But then Judy goes in and bats her eyelashes at him and he turns to jelly. Is there anything I can do to make Judy see that the world doesn't revolve around her? Or should I start looking for a new job?

Sincerely,
Up the Wall

Word Help: Underline the idioms in Up the Wall's letter. Then write the idioms next to their meanings.

MEANING	IDIOM
1. an unseen observer	_____
2. make some effort	_____
3. a very special person	_____
4. become weak	_____
5. understand	_____
6. flirt	_____
7. the situation is reversed	_____
8. a lot of time	_____
9. work together	_____
10. makes me crazy	_____

CRITICAL THINKING:

Work with a partner or a small group. Discuss Up the Wall's problem. Give your opinion about things she might do to improve her situation. Then write an answer to her letter.

Dear Up the Wall:

_____

Government and the Law

What illegal activities can you see in this neighborhood?

① Read and Listen Read the story. Then listen to it.

The Law

Now that Elena works in a law office, she has been thinking a lot about the law. She is now aware of how many people break the law every day. Today she took a walk on Ocean Avenue and counted all the illegal activities she saw along the way. She saw a motorcycle rider, not wearing a helmet, speed through a red light. She saw numerous people cross streets in the middle of a block or at a red light. Although it is against the law to write on someone's property, she saw graffiti on several walls that she passed. Hitchhiking is illegal in New York, but she saw a teenage girl doing just that.

The law says that all dogs must be licensed and on leashes, but she saw several people walking dogs without leashes. Although it's against the law to sleep on the street, she saw two homeless men sleeping in alleys. The law prohibits littering, but she saw plenty of trash on the street. The law says you are not allowed to sell or give cigarettes to minors, but she saw several teenagers smoking anyway. She even saw two guys who were probably selling and buying stolen watches.

She also saw people breaking traffic laws: people not wearing seat belts, making illegal turns, double parking, and speeding. And what about the violations she couldn't see? How many people were driving without insurance or without a license? How many people didn't file their tax returns? How many young men hadn't registered with the selective service? There are so many laws to keep track of, Elena thought, and so many people who are breaking them. Maybe that's why there are so many lawyers!

 Write List the laws mentioned in the story on a piece of paper. Use an appropriate modal for each law.

Example: *Motorcycle riders must wear helmets.*

① Say It Practice the conversation with a partner.

throwing trash on the street / get a ticket

A: I saw someone <u>throwing trash on the street</u> today. That's against the law, isn't it?

B: Yes, it is. You can <u>get a ticket for throwing trash on the street</u>.

A: I thought so.

B: The law says that you're not allowed to <u>throw trash on the street</u>. I personally think it's a good law, don't you?

A: Yes, I think so, too. **OR** Actually, I don't think so. I would vote to get rid of that law.

Use the pictures below to practice more conversations.

1. writing graffiti on someone's property / get arrested

2. walking her dog without a leash / get a ticket

3. sleeping on the street / get arrested

4. crossing in the middle of the street / get a ticket

5. stealing / go to prison

6. selling drugs / go to prison

Note: Some violations of law are *infractions.* You can get a ticket for them. Other violations are *misdemeanors.* You can get arrested for them. Some more serious violations are *felonies.* You can go to prison for them.

Tag questions

A *tag question* is a short question "tagged" on to the end of a statement. Tag questions are often used to confirm something that we think is true but are not sure about.

You are from Mexico, **aren't you?** (I think you are from Mexico.)

The verb or modal in the tag should be the same tense as the verb in the main statement. For a positive statement (with an expected "yes" answer), we use a negative tag question. For a negative statement (with an expected "no" answer), we use a positive tag question.

Simple Present:	You like pizza, **don't you?** (Yes, I do.)
Present Continuous:	She is studying English, **isn't she?** (Yes, she is.)
Simple Past:	You got a speeding ticket, **didn't you?** (Yes, I did.)
Present Perfect:	You haven't met Mr. Christov, **have you?** (No, I haven't.)
Modals:	You can't speak Russian, **can you?** (No, I can't.)

Check Point:

✓ Tag questions are sometimes used just to make conversation when both speakers already know the answer.

It's a beautiful day, **isn't it?**

2 **Write** Complete the sentences with the correct tag questions.

1. You speak Spanish, *don't you?* _____

2. You don't have a driver's license, _____?

3. You were in class yesterday, _____?

4. You are married, _____?

5. You like this English class, _____?

6. You aren't looking for a job, _____?

7. You haven't lived here very long, _____?

8. You are going to buy a car this year, _____?

9. You won't be in class tomorrow, _____?

10. You know a lot about U.S. laws, _____?

3 **Pair Practice** Work with a partner. Ask and answer the questions in Activity 2. If you think the answer is going to be "yes," ask the question with a positive statement and a negative tag question. ("You speak Spanish, don't you?") If you think the answer is going to be "no," ask the question with a negative statement and a positive tag question. ("You don't speak Spanish, do you?") See if you can guess how your partner will answer all the questions.

Say It Practice the conversation with a partner.

don't have automobile insurance

A: You <u>don't have automobile insurance, do you</u>?

B: No, I <u>don't</u>, as a matter of fact.

A: Well, you should. The law says that all <u>drivers must have automobile insurance</u>.

B: I don't like that law very much.

A: You may not like it, but you'd better obey it. It's the law!

B: OK, fine. I'll <u>get automobile insurance</u>. If the law says I'm supposed to, I will. I don't want to break the law.

Practice more conversations. Use the information below.

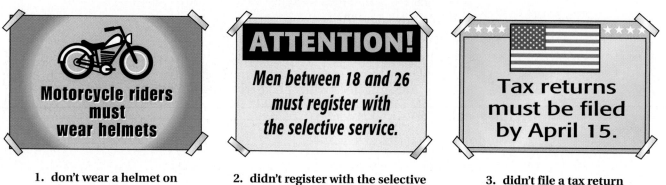

1. don't wear a helmet on your motorcycle

2. didn't register with the selective service

3. didn't file a tax return

GRAMMAR CHECK

Review: Using modals and related expressions

To express . . .	use . . .
warning	had better
strong or formal necessity	must
personal or informal necessity	have to, have got to
prohibition	must not
obligation	(be) supposed to
advice or suggestion	should, ought to, shouldn't
permission	(be) allowed to, can, may
lack of necessity	don't have to

Write Explain the law for each street sign. Use the modals and related expressions in the Grammar Check on page 186.

1. You had better stop at the stop sign or you will get a ticket.

2. _____

3. _____

4. _____

5. _____

6. _____

7. _____

8. _____

 Write Find the safety sign above for each sentence below. Fill in the blanks with the best modal or related expression.

1. You _____ come to a full stop here.

2. You _____ turn right, but you _____ _____ _____ turn left or you might get killed.

3. You _____ _____ make a U-turn here.

4. If you have a handicapped sticker on your dashboard, you _____ park here.

5. You _____ speed up when you see this, even though many people do it. You actually _____ slow down and get ready to stop.

6. You are _____ to park here all day on Sunday. You don't _____ _____ put money in the meter on Sunday.

7. You _____ _____ pass on this part of the road.

8. You probably won't get a ticket, but you aren't _____ _____ park here if you are driving a big SUV.

7 Group Practice *Find someone who . . .* Work with a large group or the whole class. Ask tag questions to find people who answer "yes" to the statements below. When someone answers "yes," write his or her name on the line.

Example: You always wear a seat belt in the car, don't you?

1. _____ always wears a seat belt in the car.

2. _____ has a driver's license.

3. _____ sometimes crosses a street at a red light.

4. _____ thinks there are too many laws in the United States.

5. _____ thinks smoking should be allowed in bars and restaurants.

Now find people who answer "no" to the following questions.

6. _____ has never gotten a ticket.

7. _____ has never been in a courtroom.

8. _____ has never filed a federal tax return.

8 Teamwork Task Work in teams of three or four. Discuss the legal notices. Then work together to answer the questions.

No. 312156232
Downtown Police Department

**TRAFFIC VIOLATION CITATION
-Notice to Appear**

FIRST NAME	Maria	LAST NAME	Quinteros	INITIAL
ADDRESS	5161 Queens Road
CITY Brooklyn	STATE NY	ZIP 11215
LIC. NUMBER GF2290	YEAR 99	MAKE Fort	MODEL Tourer
COLOR Blue	DATE 12/12/06	TIME 6:15 P.M.

THE DESCRIBED DID THEN AND THERE COMMIT THE FOLLOWING OFFENSE(S)

☐ Exceed speed limit ☐ +5mph ☐ +10mph ☐ +15mph ☐ other
☐ Illegal turn   ☐ Failure to signal turn
☐ Illegal lane change   ☐ Reckless driving
☑ Failure to stop at stop sign   ☐ Failure to yield to traffic
☐ Failure to stop at red signal light ☐ Aggressive driving
☐ Nonfunctioning lights   ☐ Excessive noise

I AGREE TO APPEAR IN COURT ON OR BEFORE 1/31/07.

OPERATOR'S SIGNATURE *Maria Quinteros*

BAIL/FINE OF $50 MAY BE SENT IN LIEU OF APPEARANCE
Failure to appear in court will be considered a guilty plea and bail will be forfeited

---

SUMMONS

CIVIL COURT
OF THE CITY OF NEW YORK

FILED AT CIVIL COURT
OF THE CITY OF NEW YORK
BY G. Smith
CASE NUMBER 00231

Black Sea Industries

PLAINTIFF

vs.

Mike Jagged

DEFENDANT

COMPLAINT: Action for money damages, for $16,600 due and owing plaintiff.

ATTORNEY for PLAINTIFF:

Mike Christov
222 Kings Highway
Brooklyn, NY 11230

Mike Christov

Plaintiff's of Attorney for Plaintiff

BY SIGNING THIS CLAIM, The Plaintiff verifies that 1) the plaintiff is the true owner of the claim, 2) the defendant resides in Kings County, and 3) the information above is true and correct to the plaintiff's best knowledge.

---

1. Who received a traffic citation?

2. What is she accused of doing?

3. What was the date of the alleged violation?

4. What does she have to do on or before 1/31/07?

5. Who is being sued in the summons?

6. What is the legal term for the person or business who is suing?

7. How much is the plaintiff asking for?

8. Who is the lawyer for the plaintiff?

1 **Say It** Practice the conversation with a partner.

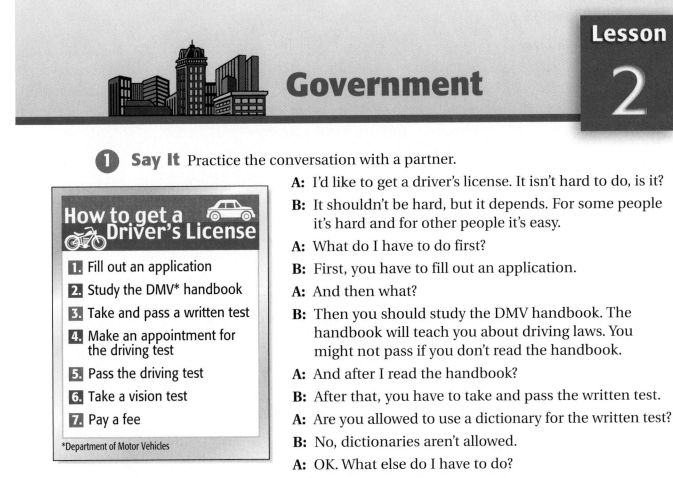

How to get a Driver's License

1. Fill out an application
2. Study the DMV* handbook
3. Take and pass a written test
4. Make an appointment for the driving test
5. Pass the driving test
6. Take a vision test
7. Pay a fee

*Department of Motor Vehicles

A: I'd like to get a driver's license. It isn't hard to do, is it?

B: It shouldn't be hard, but it depends. For some people it's hard and for other people it's easy.

A: What do I have to do first?

B: First, you have to fill out an application.

A: And then what?

B: Then you should study the DMV handbook. The handbook will teach you about driving laws. You might not pass if you don't read the handbook.

A: And after I read the handbook?

B: After that, you have to take and pass the written test.

A: Are you allowed to use a dictionary for the written test?

B: No, dictionaries aren't allowed.

A: OK. What else do I have to do?

B: If you pass the written test, you can make an appointment for the driving test. You don't have to do it right away. You shouldn't take the test until you practice driving for a while.

A: What do I have to do on the driving test?

B: You are supposed to do whatever the tester tells you to do. And you'd better not break any laws or get into an accident, or you won't get a license.

A: So, if I pass the driving test, will I get my license?

B: Not yet. You also have to take a vision test and pay a fee.

A: OK. I think I'll get started tomorrow.

2 **Write** Complete the sentences with a tag question.

1. If I fail my driving test, I can take it again, _____?
2. I don't have to rent a car for the test, _____?
3. I should probably study the DMV handbook, _____?
4. I have to pass the written test first, _____?
5. I'm not allowed to use my dictionary, _____?
6. I can wear my glasses for the vision test, _____?
7. They will send my license in the mail, _____?
8. I don't have to make an appointment right away, _____?
9. It's not a good idea to speed on the driving test, _____?

Motor vehicle laws

Most motor vehicle laws are made by individual states, so speed limits and other motor vehicle laws may vary from state to state. The state that allows people to get a license at the youngest age is South Dakota—14 years old. However, in New Jersey you have to be 18 to get a driver's license. How about in your state?

3 **Pair Practice** Work with a partner. Explain how to file a federal tax return. Use the information and the correct modals in the box below. Your partner will ask short questions as you explain the process.

Example: *Student 1:* First, you have to get the right tax forms.
Student 2: OK, then what?

FILE A TAX RETURN

1. Get the right tax forms. (**have to**) Use form 1040 EZ if you don't have many deductions. (**can**) Use Form 1040 if you have a lot of deductions. (**should**)
2. Get a copy of your W2 form, and any other documents related to your income. (**have to**)
3. Find a tax preparation program or a tax preparer to help you. (**should**) Get free help from the IRS* if your income is low. (**can**)
4. Use the information from your W2 form to fill out the tax return form. (**should**)
5. Read the instructions on the tax return carefully. (**should**) Make sure you copy the numbers from your W2 form correctly. (**have to**)
6. Don't forget to check the boxes for your filing status and for your exemptions. (**shouldn't**)
7. Sign the form. (**must**) The IRS won't accept a tax return if it isn't signed.
8. Attach a copy of your W2 form to the tax return. (**supposed to**)
9. Mail your tax return on or before April 15 or you might have to pay a penalty. (**had better**)

*Internal Revenue Service

 Write Complete the sentences with a tag question.

1. Tax preparers are easy to find, _____ ?
2. I can get help from the IRS, _____ ?
3. It doesn't take long to fill out the 1040 EZ, _____ ?
4. My W2 form will come in the mail, _____ ?
5. I have to sign the form myself, _____ ?
6. It isn't necessary to attach my pay stubs, _____ ?
7. It should be mailed by April 15th, _____ ?
8. I don't need to hire an accountant to help me, _____ ?
9. I need to check the form before sending it, _____ ?

Some tag questions don't expect an answer. (Nice day, isn't it?) But confirmation tag questions that expect an answer end with rising intonation. Ask a partner the questions in Activity 4. Practice using rising intonation with the tag questions.

5 🎧 **Listen** Listen and fill in the missing words in the story.

Taxes

Vicki didn't file her tax return on time this year. She knew she (1)_____ file her return by April 15th, but she was going on vacation and just didn't want to think about taxes. "It's OK," Elena told her, "you (2)_____ file a Form 4868 instead. Form 4868," Elena explained, "is a request for an automatic four-month extension. When you file Form 4868, you (3)_____ file your return until (4)_____." "The bad news," Elena said, "is that you still (5)_____ all your taxes by the normal tax deadline. And if you owe money and you don't pay by the deadline, you will have to pay penalties and interest, too."

Vicki didn't like that idea at all. But, Elena cheered her up again. "Actually, you (6)_____ a problem. You don't have a very high income so you (7)_____ owe very much. In fact, you (8)_____ owe any taxes at all. If your employer withheld the right amount from your paychecks, you (9)_____ owe anything. You will probably get a refund. And if the government owes you money, you (10)_____ to wait as long as you want to file your tax return."

Now it is August and Vicki has decided that she (11)_____ wait any longer. She got her W2 form and a 1040 EZ form and copied the information from her W2 to the (12)_____. She put in her exemptions and standard deduction. When she subtracted that from her gross income, she saw that she didn't owe any money! Then she signed the form. She wasn't filing a joint return so she (13)_____ have anyone else sign it. Then she went to the post office and sent it by certified mail. There are two addresses where all returns (14)_____ to be sent. She sent hers to the one for people who are getting a refund. Now she just (15)_____ what she is going to do with the money!

Word Help: Match the words from the story with their correct meanings.

1. _____ file
2. _____ extension
3. _____ deadline
4. _____ penalty
5. _____ amount withheld
6. _____ refund
7. _____ exemptions
8. _____ standard deduction
9. _____ a joint return
10. _____ the bottom line

a. amount of money returned to you
b. a fine you have to pay
c. a longer amount of time
d. a return filed by husband and wife together
e. how much you owe or will get back
f. date when something must be done
g. number of dependents (children, for example) you have
h. complete and send in
i. money taken out of your paycheck
j. accepted amount you can subtract from your income

Write Use Vicki's W2 form and the tax table to answer the questions.

a Control number		This information is being furnished to the Internal Revenue Service	
b Employer identification number (EIN) 96-236832		**1** Wages, tips, other compensation $29,440.00	**2** Federal income tax withheld $2,944.00
c Employer's name, address, and ZIP code Downtown Department Store 330 Flatbush Ave. Brooklyn, NY 11228		**3** Social security wages	**4** Social security tax withheld
		5 Medicare wages and tips	**6** Medicare tax withheld
d Employee's social security number 225-XX-7575		**7** Social security tips	**8** Allocated tips
e Employee's name, address, and ZIP code Vicki Martinez 219 E. 26th Street Brooklyn, NY 11230		**9** Advance EIC payment	**10** Dependent care benefits
15 Employer's state ID number NY, 904-3353	**16** State wages, tips, etc. $29,440.00	**17** State income tax $455.00	

Form **W-2** Wage and Tax Statement
Copy B—To Be Filed With Employee's FEDERAL Tax Return

Department of the Treasury — Internal Revenue Service

How Much You Owe

If your taxable income is		and you are			
at least	but less than	Single	Married filing jointly	Married filing separately	Head of a household
		Then you owe			
$21,000	$21,050	$2,789	$2,424	$2,789	$2,631
$21,050	$21,100	$2,796	$2,431	$2,796	$2,639
$21,100	$21,150	$2,804	$2,439	$2,804	$2,646
$21,150	$21,200	$2,811	$2,446	$2,811	$2,654
$21,200	$21,250	$2,819	$2,454	$2,819	$2,661
$21,250	$21,300	$2,826	$2,461	$2,826	$2,669
$21,300	$21,350	$2,834	$2,469	$2,834	$2,676
$21,350	$21,400	$2,841	$2,476	$2,841	$2,684
$21,400	$21,450	$2,849	$2,484	$2,849	$2,691
$21,450	$21,500	$2,856	$2,491	$2,856	$2,699

Department of the Treasury — Internal Revenue Service

1. What should Vicki do with this W2 form? _____

2. How much money did Vicki earn for the year? _____

3. How much federal tax was withheld from her paychecks? _____

4. If Vicki's taxable income is $21,025 and she files as a single person, how much tax is she supposed to pay? _____

5. If Vicki's taxable income is $21,025, and she files as a single person, will she owe money or will she get a refund? _____

6. If someone files as a head of household with $21,425 taxable income, how much federal tax will she have to pay for the year? _____

7 **Teamwork Task** Work in teams of three or four. Together, complete a 1040EZ tax return for Vicki. Use the information from her W2 form and the tax table above to see whether she will get a refund or pay more money. Download a 1040 EZ tax form from the Internet at *www.1040.com*.

1 **Read and Listen** Read the story. Then listen to the story.

Congratulations

On a rainy Monday, Elena went to an office in downtown Brooklyn for her citizenship interview. She was nervous even though she had studied everything she needed to know. "All you have to do is be polite," Mr. Christov told her, "and answer any questions they ask you. You are the smartest young lady they will see all month."

The first thing Elena had to do was sit down and be patient because the interviewer was running behind schedule. When she finally went into the office, she smiled and shook the interviewer's hand. He invited her to sit down. Then he asked her a few questions from her application form. After that, he asked her about her job. And then he asked her a few questions about U.S. history and government. He asked her what the colors of the American flag were. Elena smiled because the flag was right behind him in his office. He asked her if she knew who wrote the Declaration of Independence. "That beautiful document was written by Thomas Jefferson," she said, "wasn't it?"

"Yes," he said, "that's right."

He asked her about the three branches of government, and she described them for him. Then he asked her who the Chief Justice of the Supreme Court was. That was a hard one and her mind went blank for a minute. "The Chief Justice," she finally said, "is John Roberts, isn't it?"

The interview looked surprised and then he smiled for the first time. "Yes," he said, "it certainly is."

When she left the building, Alex and Sasha were outside waiting for her. "What happened?" Alex asked. "Was it hard?"

"No," she said, "it wasn't hard at all."

"Congratulations, Mom," Sasha said. "I'm proud of you."

Elena put her arms around her husband and her son and hugged them both tight.

Write Answer the questions about the story with a statement and a tag question for confirmation.

1. Where did Elena go for her citizenship interview? <u>She went to Booklyn, didn't she?</u>

2. How did Elena feel when she arrived for her interview? _____

3. What had Elena studied before her interview? _____

4. What did Elena do when she finally went into the office? _____

5. What was the first thing the interviewer asked her? _____

6. What did Elena do when he asked her about the colors of the flag?

_____

 Write Correct the mistakes in the sentences below. If there are no mistakes, write *correct.*

1. Today is Monday, doesn't it? _____

2. The law says that dogs can be licensed or you can get a ticket.

_____

3. You must not to throw trash in the street. That's littering.

_____

4. She'll pass her test, will she? _____

5. Elena is ready to become the citizen. _____

6. It's going to be an easy test, isn't it? _____

7. I have to file a tax return, haven't I? _____

8. You don't pay taxes, are you? _____

9. The Declaration of Independence guarantees freedom of speech.

_____

10. The first ten amendments to the Constitution are called the Bill of Freedoms.

_____

 Teamwork Task The Good Citizen Bowl

1. Work in three teams of five. You will have ten minutes to answer the questions below and practice the answers. Then close your books and stand up in a line.

2. Each team member will get one question to answer. You must answer with a correct answer and a tag question for confirmation. Your team gets a point for each correct answer.

Example: *Teacher:* What are the colors of the flag?
    Student: The colors of the flag are red, white, and blue, aren't they?

1. What do the stars on the flag represent? _____

2. How many original colonies were there? _____

3. Who was the first president of the United States? _____

4. When is Independence Day? _____

5. How many branches of government are there? _____

6. How many states are there today? _____

7. What are the first ten amendments to the Constitution called?

_____

8. When was the Declaration of Independence written? _____

9. What is the supreme law of the land? _____

10. Who is the head of the executive branch of government? _____

11. Who wrote the Declaration of Independence? _____

12. Who was the president during the Civil War? _____

13. Who is the commander-in-chief of the army? _____

14. How long is the term of a president? _____

15. How many senators are there in the U.S. Senate? _____

Pronunciation Tag questions

When we think we know something but aren't sure, a tag question can be used for confirmation. In this case, a tag question has rising intonation like a *yes/no* question. Listen and practice saying the tag questions with rising intonation.

1. You passed the test, didn't you?
2. You have a license, don't you?
3. You aren't a citizen, are you?
4. She isn't your sister, is she?

Sometimes tag questions are used just to make conversation and we don't really want an answer. In this case, we use falling intonation.

1. Nice day, isn't it?
2. Terrible storm last night, wasn't it?

I can . . .			
• identify illegal behavior.	1	2	3
• discuss common laws.	1	2	3
• use tag questions for confirmation.	1	2	3
• interpret safety signs.	1	2	3
• read and interpret a citation and a summons.	1	2	3
• understand procedures for getting a driver's license.	1	2	3
• understand information about tax returns.	1	2	3
• read and interpret a W2 form.	1	2	3
• read a tax table and fill out a simple tax return.	1	2	3
• understand the process of becoming a U.S. citizen.	1	2	3
• read and interpret information about U.S. history and government.	1	2	3

1 = not well   2 = OK   3 = very well

DOWNTOWN JOURNAL

YOUR COMMUNITY NEWSPAPER   VOL. 24 NO. 10 APRIL 15

April 15 Is Tax Day

If your filing status is . . .	and on 12/31 you were . . .	You must file a return if your gross income was more than . . .
Single	under 65	$8,200
	65 or older	$9,450
Married filing jointly	under 65 (both spouses)	$16,400
	65 or older (one spouse)	$17,400
	65 or older (both spouses)	$18,400
Married filing separately	any age	$3,200
Head of household	under 65	$10,500
	65 or older	$11,750

In general, you *have to* file if your income is high.

You *should* file if your income is low because you will probably get money back.

TIP: Even if you do not *have to* file a return, you *should* if any federal income tax was withheld from your paycheck. You will likely get a refund. You should also file if you are eligible for the earned income credit or the additional child tax credit.

Earned Income Credit: You may be eligible for the earned income credit if . . .

1. a child lived with you AND you earned less than $34,458, (or $35,458 if filing a joint return).

2. no child lived with you, but you earned less than $11,750, (or less than $13,750 if filing a joint return).

*Numbers are for 2005 tax year

Where can you find federal or state tax forms?

1. You can download forms from the Internet at www.1040.com
2. You can call this toll free number: 1-800-829-3676.
3. You can find forms at your local library.

Note: For people with a low income, free tax help is available at any IRS office.

DOWNTOWN JOURNAL

Dear Ms. Know It All

Problem Solving: Completing a tax return

Dear Ms. Know It All:

Help! This year I have to complete a tax return for the first time. I want to get started early because I think I will receive a refund but I don't know where to begin! Can you explain the process for me? What documents do I need and where can I get them? How do I know which form to fill out?

Where can I get the forms? Is there any place I can go for help because I think I will receive a refund?

Sincerely,
Taxed About Taxes

CRITICAL THINKING:

Work with a partner or a small group. Talk about Taxed About Taxes' problem. List the documents he needs and the steps he should follow to complete a tax return. Then write an answer to his letter.

Documents

_____

_____

Steps

_____

_____

_____

_____

Dear Taxed About Taxes,

_____

Chapter 1:
Nice to Meet You

Page 2 (Chapter Opening, Activity 1)

Read and Listen *Read the story. Then listen to it.*

Hello, New York

Elena and her son, Sasha, recently moved from Russia to New York. They have been living in New York for about a month, but Elena still feels like a visitor. New York is the third city Elena has lived in. She thinks it is the most difficult to get to know, but also the most interesting. Every day she walks around the streets with her eyes wide like a tourist. Sometimes she visits tourist attractions like the Statue of Liberty and the Empire State Building.

Elena grew up in a small city in Russia. After she got married, she moved to Moscow for three years. Then she came to the United States with her parents and Sasha. They are all living in a section, or borough, of New York called Brooklyn.

In Brooklyn, Elena likes to see all the different ethnic shops when she walks around her neighborhood. Right now she is carrying a bag of groceries from a Russian market and a pretty shirt from a Chinese clothing store. She enjoys meeting people from all over the world. She has already met some interesting neighbors in her own building. One is a Chinese woman whose name is Daisy.

Tomorrow Elena is going to register her son for school. The elementary school has classes for adults too, so she is also going to register herself for an English class. She hopes that when her English is better, she will be able to find a good job in her new city.

Page 10 (Lesson 2, Activity 3)

Listen *Listen and check your answers to Activity 2.*

All ESL students <u>must</u> take an assessment test before registering. However, students <u>don't have to</u> register for the level indicated on their assessment result form. Students <u>may</u> register for one level higher or one level lower than the test result indicates. For example, if test results show a Beginning High level, students are <u>allowed</u> to register for a Beginning Low or an Intermediate Low class. All students <u>have to</u> complete a registration form before the first day of class.

Students <u>may</u> register for as many as three classes, but <u>may not</u> register for two classes given during the same time period. Students <u>are supposed</u> to attend all class sessions. Students <u>must</u> bring a note of explanation after each absence.

Please note: Students who want to register for only distance learning <u>don't have to</u> take the assessment test. It isn't required.

Students <u>are not allowed to</u> smoke on campus. Smoking is prohibited.

Page 10 (Lesson 2, Activity 5)

Listen *Listen to the conversation between Elena and the office clerk. Fill out the registration form for Elena with the information you hear.*

Clerk: Please spell your last name.
Elena: Petrova. P-e-t-r-o-v-a.

Clerk: And your first name?
Elena: My first name is Elena.
Clerk: And your address?
Elena: 1950 Ocean Avenue.
Clerk: And do you have a telephone number where we can reach you?
Elena: Yes. It's 718-555-5868.
Clerk: Do you have an e-mail address?
Elena: Yes. It's EllaPet @ coldmail.com.
Clerk: Where were you born?
Elena: What do you mean exactly? The city where I was born?
Clerk: No, just your native country is good enough.
Elena: Russia.
Clerk: And what is your date of birth?
Elena: With the year, too?
Clerk: It's optional, but most people don't mind.
Elena: My birthday is May 5th, 5/5. But I'd rather not give the year, if it's not necessary.
Clerk: That's fine. Are you currently working, unemployed, or not looking for work?
Elena: I have a part-time job, but I'm looking for a better job. Should I say working or looking for work? Because I am actually doing both of these things.
Clerk: They just want to know if you are working, so that would be "yes."
Elena: OK.
Clerk: And your native language is Russian?
Elena: Yes.
Clerk: What is the highest grade you completed in school?
Elena: I went to university in my country. I studied accounting and graduated.
Clerk: So, you graduated from college. Great. That would be sixteen years of school here. Is it the same in Russia?
Elena: Yes, I think so.
Clerk: Just one last question.
Elena: OK.
Clerk: What is your primary reason for studying English?
Elena: Primary?
Clerk: The most important reason.
Elena: I guess the most important reason is that it will help me get a good job here.

Page 12 (Lesson 3, Activity 1)

Read and Listen *Read the story. Then listen to the story.*

A New Job

Elena graduated from college with a degree in accounting. She worked as an accountant for three years in Russia before she came to the United States. But she hasn't worked as an accountant in the United States. Accounting in the U.S. is very different from accounting in Russia, so now she has to retrain herself. She has to start by learning English.

Elena studied English in high school, but she didn't take it very seriously and, unfortunately, she didn't learn very much. She also took English classes for a year when she lived in Moscow, but she still doesn't speak English well enough to get the kind of job she wants. So, she is going to register for some more English classes in New York.

Other than English, Elena isn't sure yet what classes she is going to take. She could take an accounting class, but she thinks she isn't ready for that yet. She could take a banking class, or a tax preparation class, because those classes train you to get a job right away. But she hasn't made a decision yet.

Page 13 (Lesson 3, Activity 4)

Listen *Listen and take notes. Then create a time line for Freddy with the information you hear.*

First of all, I was born in Cuba. I came to the U.S. with my family in 1992 when I was 13 years old. It wasn't my decision, of course. My whole family came here, so I didn't have any choice. I went to high school here in Brooklyn and I graduated in 1997. June. I also got my first real job in July right after I graduated. I was a cashier and assistant manager of a convenience store. I met Maria in my last year of high school and we got married in January of '99. The next month I changed jobs and became a cashier at the A&B market. Unfortunately, in June of 2002, Maria and I split up. We were separated for a little while and then got divorced in the summer of 2003. I wasn't doing so well for about a year, but in the beginning of '04 I got a new job—they made me assistant manager at A&B. That's the job I still have now. What else do you want to know?

Page 17 (Chapter 1 Review, Activity 1)

Read and Listen *Read the story. Then listen to the story.*

A Difficult Decision

Elena has been a single parent since she moved to the United States. Sasha's father, Alex, is still in Russia. He is waiting for permission to join his wife and child in the U.S. Nobody knows how long that will take. It could be a short time or it could take many years. In the meantime, Elena is determined to be strong and to do the best she can for her son and herself. But she has already learned that being a single parent is not easy.

Before she got married, Elena made a decision to apply, along with her parents and brother, for a visa to immigrate to the United States. Her aunt and uncle were willing to sponsor her, but it still took several years for her application to be approved. When it was approved, she had to make a very difficult decision.

She decided to come to the U.S. with the rest of her family, but without her husband.

In New York, Elena has her parents and her aunt and uncle to help her. Her Aunt Sonia and Uncle Morris have lived in the U.S. for ten years. They have a small but successful business. Her aunt is her sponsor, so she is supposed to help Elena get started in her new country. Aunt Sonia found her an apartment before she arrived. She also gave Elena a part-time job in her business. But Elena understands that the job is temporary and that she has to find a "real" job and a new career as soon as she can.

It was a very difficult decision for Elena to move to a new country with her little boy and without her husband. She hopes she made the right decision.

Page 19 (Chapter 1 Review)

Pronunciation *Lost /h/ sound*

A. *The /h/ sound of he is usually lost when we ask yes/no questions. Listen and repeat the linked sounds.*

1. Is he . . . (izzy)	Izzy from Mexico?	Yes, he is.
2. Does he . . . duzzy)	Duzzy have a car?	No, he doesn't.
3. Has he . . . (hazzy)	Hazzy had lunch yet?	Yes, he has.
4. Was he . . . (wuzzy)	Wuzzy in class yesterday?	No, he wasn't.
5. Did he . . . (diddy)	Diddy pass the test?	Yes, he did.

B. *Work with a partner. Point at male students in your class and ask your partner the yes/no questions above. Use the fast, linked pronunciation.*

Chapter 2:
Love and Marriage

Page 22 (Chapter Opening, Activity 1)

Read and Listen *Read the story. Then listen to it.*

Changes

Elena sometimes thinks about how different her life has become since she and Sasha moved to the United States. In some ways, their lives are better. New York is an interesting place to live. There are more job opportunities for Elena and more educational opportunities for both her and Sasha. But, in some ways, their lives are more difficult now.

In Russia, Elena used to live with her husband. She had someone who could help her with all the household chores. Her husband used to cook some of their meals, and he used to help take care of Sasha. She used to have time to relax and read a magazine after dinner. Now the only thing she reads is children's books with Sasha to help him learn English. In Russia, Elena didn't have to take care of everything by herself.

When she thinks about her life in Russia, Elena feels homesick. She misses her husband, of course. But it isn't just him. She misses everything about her old life. In Russia, Elena had a good job in an accounting office. In Russia, she didn't need a resume to find a job. She got her jobs by networking with her friends and former classmates. Now Elena needs a resume and more education in order to get a good job. Tomorrow she is going to get started writing her resume. Then maybe she'll get a good job and stop feeling homesick!

Page 27 (Lesson 1, Activity 9)

Listen *Listen and write the positive or negative gerund phrases you hear. Then check whether you agree or disagree with each statement.*

1. <u>Not teaching</u> children right and wrong is a problem in many American families.
2. <u>Allowing children to watch</u> too much TV causes anxiety for children and makes their behavior worse.
3. <u>Not helping</u> children with their homework makes them better students.
4. <u>Allowing</u> teenagers to date in high school makes them better students.
5. <u>Giving</u> children too much freedom makes them confused and anxious.

Listen *Listen and write the adjectives in the correct box. Then add a few more of your own.*

Let me tell you about my brother. He's very tall and thin. And he's bald. He likes that look. He shaves his head. And I would say that he's quiet. He doesn't say much, but what he says is usually right. He's a very smart guy.

My sister? Well, she's pushy. She always has to get her way. But she's also generous. She always gives great gifts for special occasions. She's kind of short and a little bit plump. She could lose about twenty pounds, I'd say. But men usually find her attractive, so I guess she's attractive.

Jack? He's big and muscular. Very strong. And he has a strong personality, too. He's aggressive. And very ambitious. But in his case I guess it's a good thing because he's very successful at what he does.

Kevin? He's cute. No, I'd say handsome more than cute. Cute sounds too boyish and he looks more like a man. He's romantic. Women are always attracted to him. But he doesn't take advantage. He's actually a very sweet guy. He's warm and open-minded. Nothing seems to bother him.

Donna? She's pretty. No, I'd say beautiful. No, actually she's gorgeous. She's a knockout. She has long, straight hair. And she's nice, too. She's easygoing and dependable. And she's actually very funny when she wants to be. She can always make me laugh.

Listen *Listen to the three dating service profiles. Complete the profiles by filling in the missing gerunds.*

1: I think of myself as a lover, not a fighter. I try to get along with everybody. I am the kind of guy who will bring you flowers every time we go out. I believe in (1)<u>opening</u> doors for women and in (2)<u>making</u> a woman feel like a queen. I dream about (3)<u>saying</u> "I love you" every morning. If you want to wake up with a kiss every day and always be surrounded by flowers, I might be the guy for you. I look forward to (4)<u>hearing</u> from you soon. Thank you for (5)<u>reading</u> my profile.

2: I am not good at (1)<u>talking</u> about myself. I am the kind of man who lets his actions speak for him. I am quiet and serious. I am a man who works hard and plays hard. I believe in (2)<u>doing</u> my best at everything I do. I believe in (3)<u>telling</u> the truth all the time and I insist on (4)<u>hearing</u> the truth from you. If you want a man who will never lie to you and will always be there when you need someone to take care of you, I am the man for you. I look forward to (5)<u>hearing</u> from you soon.

3: I am very successful and generous. I believe in (1)<u>setting</u> high goals and in (2)<u>working</u> hard to achieve them. I have always succeeded in (3)<u>doing</u> everything I wanted to do except in (4)<u>finding</u> my perfect mate. Could it be you? I have a good job, a high income, and a nice home. (5)<u>Traveling</u> is my love and I want to see as many different countries as possible. (6)<u>Eating</u> in good restaurants is one of my hobbies. I am looking forward to someday (7)<u>finding</u> a soul mate to travel around the world with me.

Read and Listen *Read the story. Then listen to the story.*

Writing a Resume

Elena has been thinking about writing a resume for several days, but she hasn't been able to do it yet. The main problem is that she needs to write an objective. The objective should be the job she is looking for right now. But she doesn't know what job she wants right now. She just wants a full-time job with a good paycheck that will teach her something new and help her to pay her bills. Unfortunately, she can't write that as her resume objective.

Elena is grateful to her aunt for giving her a job, but she would like to get a more interesting job. She is good at working with numbers and she likes working with people. She wants to practice her English on her job, if possible. She is capable of doing most office work except maybe answering telephones and taking messages. She is excited about finding and starting a new job.

Daisy has offered to help Elena write her resume. Daisy has written and rewritten her own resume many times. And she has been successful at creating good professional resumes for several of her friends. She is looking forward to sitting down with her new friend, Elena, and helping her write a nice, clear, professional resume. She has no doubt that Elena will find a job soon.

Listen *Listen to the conversations between Elena and her friends. Write sentences about Elena's friends using adjective + preposition combinations.*

1.
Elena: What's the matter ,Vicki? You look worried.
Vicki: I am worried. I have a typing test tomorrow and I don't know if I'm going to pass. I have to type sixty words per minute. I don't think I can type that fast.

2.
Elena: What are you so excited about, Daisy?
Daisy: I was just thinking about Andre. He's so good-looking and so smart. I really hope I'll see him again one of these days.
Elena: Don't worry. I'm sure you will.

3.
Elena: Hello, Andre. How are you?
Andre: I just wanted to thank you for inviting me to your party. I had a good time. You have some very . . . interesting friends.
Elena: It was my pleasure. Thank you for coming.

4.
Elena: What's the matter, Freddy? You look upset.
Freddy: I am upset. I lost my wallet with my identification and all my credit cards.
Elena: Oh, no. That's terrible.

5.
Elena: Hi, Alice. What's the matter?
Alice: I've been waiting and waiting and waiting to see an employment counselor. If they don't call my name soon, I'm going to just get up and leave.

6.
Elena: You look very happy today, Al. Do you have some good news?
Al: Yes, I do. I just got a new job—playing guitar and singing at the Coney Island café. I'll be singing there every Sunday and Monday night.
Elena: Wow. That's great.

Listen *Listen and write the objective you hear for each person. Don't write the person's long-term goal.*

1. Someday I would like to write children's books. But, for now, what I really need is a full-time teacher's assistant position in a preschool program.
2. I want to own my own business eventually. But, right now, I need a full-time mechanic position.
3. What I'd really like is to be a professional dancer, but I'm afraid that boat has left the dock. So, I'm looking for a medical billing position in a small medical office.
4. Well, I am a professional driver, but I'm tired of driving a cab. What I'd like is a job driving and providing security for a private individual. Working for a famous, beautiful movie star would be nice.
5. My field is accounting, but I'm going to need more training to be an accountant here. So, what I'd like right now is an entry-level position in a bank or accounting office. That would give me a chance to learn while I work.

Read and Listen *Read the story. Then listen to the story.*

A Big Mistake?

Daisy is thirty years old and has never been married. She has had two boyfriends. She used to have a boyfriend when she was in college in China. Then she dated a man in New York for about six months. The man who she dated in New York was Chinese-American. The man who she dated in China was Chinese. Now Daisy is interested in dating men who are not Chinese. She sometimes thinks about finding a nice, handsome man who speaks English perfectly and who can teach her everything about English and the United States that she doesn't know. But then she thinks about her parents and she gets nervous. Her parents think that marrying, or even dating, outside her culture is a big mistake. Accepting a non-Chinese husband would be very difficult for them.

Daisy used to agree with her parents. Living in New York, however, has changed her attitude. In New York, she has met people from different countries and cultures, and they all seem interesting and nice. The truth is that Daisy is excited about getting to know people who are not Chinese. She is grateful to her parents for raising her so well and for giving her love and an education, and she is worried about hurting them. But now she is a thirty-year-old adult. She is responsible for making her own decisions about her life. So, she plans on opening her heart, meeting different kinds of people, and letting her heart decide what is best for her. She hopes that isn't a big mistake.

Pronunciation *Linking*

We often link the consonant sound at the end of a word with a vowel sound at the beginning of the following word. Listen and repeat the linked two-word combinations.

1. dream about — I dream about taking a vacation.
2. talk about — Let's talk about the job.
3. think about — Let's think about going to the beach.
4. plan on — I plan on moving soon.
5. insist on — I insist on paying the bill.
6. afraid of — She's afraid of dogs.
7. good at — He's good at math.
8. succeed in — She'll succeed in finding a job.

Chapter 3:
Family Economics

Read and Listen *Read the story. Then listen to it.*

Bills

Elena is sitting in her dining room looking at her bills and trying to plan a monthly budget. She has been sitting there for an hour, but she has only paid two bills so far. She hasn't finished planning her budget, either. Mostly, she has been looking at coupons and ads and thinking about how to save money.

Elena has to make a budget now because the $3,000 she brought with her from Russia, her life savings, is shrinking fast. She doesn't make enough money to buy and do all the things she wants to every month. She has monthly bills for rent, gas, and electricity. She has bills for her English class, for Sasha's gym class, and for clothes. And, of course, she spends money on groceries, transportation, and restaurants. So, she needs to either make more or spend less money.

She has been considering applying for a credit card or a personal loan from a bank to help her pay her bills until she finds a better job. Of course, she wants to avoid borrowing too much money, but there are some things she can't help spending money on. Her gas and electric bills are high. English class costs $150 a month and Sasha's gym class costs $40 a week. Maybe she spends too much money on clothes, but she wants to look nice. Also, she likes to take Sasha to a restaurant once a week.

Hopefully, she will get a better job soon. But, in the meantime, she is thinking about the best way to budget the little money she has.

Listen *Listen to the conversation. Complete the bank account application for Elena.*

Clerk: The first step is to fill out a bank-account application form. Do you have a banking relationship with the Bank of Brooklyn right now?

Elena: You mean do I have a bank account? No, I don't. That's what I want to get today.

Clerk: OK. Let me ask you some questions, then, starting with personal information.

Elena: Can I just fill out the form myself? We don't have any paper forms anymore. All the forms are filled out on the computer. So, you can do it at home if you have a computer, or I can fill it out for you on my computer.

Elena: OK. Let's just go ahead and fill it out.

Clerk: So, what is your first name?

Elena: Elena.

Clerk: And middle initial?

Elena: I don't have a middle initial.

Clerk: And your last name?

Elena: Petrova. P-e-t-r-o-v-a.

Clerk: And your social security number?

Elena: I have to look at my card. Is it necessary to give a social security number?

Clerk: Yes, it is. That's how banks keep track of your records.

Elena: OK. Here it is. It's 123-45-6798.

Clerk: And your home phone number?

Elena: 718-555-5868.

Clerk: And what is your date of birth?

Elena: It's May five, nineteen seventy-six. I mean May fifth.

Clerk: And what is your address?

Elena: It's 1950 Ocean Avenue.

Clerk: Is it a house or an apartment?

Elena: It's an apartment. Apartment 303.

Clerk: In Brooklyn?

Elena: Yes. Brooklyn. New York. 11230.

Clerk: Do you have an e-mail address?

Elena: Yes, I do. It's EllaPet@coldmail.com.

Clerk: Do you own or rent your apartment, or live with someone else?

Elena: I rent.

Clerk: What is your monthly rent payment?

Elena: It's $850 a month.

Clerk: Now, I need to ask a few questions about your income and employer. First, what is the name of your current employer?

Elena: The business is called Moscow Direct.

Clerk: D-i-r-e-c-t?

Elena: Yes, that's right. It's owned by my aunt and uncle.

Clerk: And how much is your annual gross income from this job?

Elena: I have only been working there for a few months so I don't have an annual income yet. I'm not sure how to answer that.

Clerk: Well, you can take your monthly income and multiply it by 12. That will tell us approximately how much you will earn if you work there all year.

Elena: I think it would be about $25,000 for a year.

Clerk: May I ask for your work telephone number?

Elena: It's 718-555-2001.

Clerk: Do you have any income from any other sources?

Elena: No, I don't.

Clerk: All right. That's all the questions I have. Your application will go in right now and we can open an account for you in a few minutes.

Elena: Thank you.

Page 52 (Lesson 3, Activity 1)

Read and Listen *Read the story. Then listen to the story.*

Customer Service

Vicki works in the customer service department of the *Downtown Department Store*. That means that part of her job is to listen to customers' complaints. She doesn't mind hearing complaints as long as the customers are honest and the complaints are legitimate. But she can't help feeling annoyed with people who come to her with bogus complaints and tell her things that are not true.

Yesterday a woman came in to return an expensive dress. It was a yellow dress and it had a brown stain that looked like a coffee stain. "Did you wear the dress?" Vicki asked.

The woman denied wearing it. "The stain was there when I bought it," she said. Vicki knew that the woman had worn the dress. She knows that the *Downtown Department Store* doesn't sell dresses with big brown stains on them. But Vicki is supposed to avoid arguing with customers, so she just continued to smile.

Some people enjoy taking advantage of the store policy by returning things even after they've worn or used them. Vicki always recommends exchanging a stained or broken product for a new one. But sometimes the customer wants a refund rather than an exchange. The store doesn't like to return cash to people for broken or stained products unless there is a manufacturer's warranty that permits returning a damaged product for a full refund. But

the *Downtown Department Store* doesn't mind giving store credit to customers who have a legitimate complaint.

When Vicki encounters people who tell her bogus stories, she sometimes imagines arguing with them about it. But, of course, she never does because she would probably get fired. Her job is to listen to customers' complaints and report exactly what they say. So, she just listens and smiles and tries not to get upset.

Page 57 (Chapter 3 Review, Activity 1)

Read and Listen *Read the story. Then listen to the story.*

Making Ends Meet

Ever since she arrived in New York, Elena has been spending (1) several hundred dollars a month more than she earns. That means that she has been "living over her head." When she arrived from Russia, she had (2) almost $3,000, but now she has (3) less than $1,000 left. So, it's time for her to make some changes.

Now Elena is trying to spend less money. She is avoiding buying (4) unnecessary things. She has stopped buying (5) silly toys for Sasha. And the last time she bought new clothes was (6) about a month ago. She has also delayed buying some furniture she would like to get for her apartment. In fact, Elena hasn't bought anything new for her apartment in about a month.

But there are some things she hasn't stopped doing. She still has to pay her rent and utility bills. She hasn't stopped taking (7) English classes, and she hasn't stopped paying for Sasha's gym class (8) because she thinks it's important for him to exercise every day. And she wants him to be in a class with kids his own age who speak Russian. There are several Russian children in the class. She is still spending money on subway passes, but she isn't taking the bus to the beach anymore because she can walk there in about fifteen minutes, and she needs the exercise, too. She hasn't been exercising as much as she used to in Russia. She isn't taking Sasha (9) to eat in nice restaurants anymore. But sometimes she can't help buying (10) a slice of pizza when she gets off the subway after work. The pizza shop at the subway station has the best pizza in New York. When she buys pizza for herself, she sometimes brings home some for Sasha, too, and then she doesn't have to cook dinner. So, that is another way of making ends meet.

Page 59 (Chapter 3 Review)

Pronunciation *Rising intonation*

Yes/No *questions and clarification questions usually end with rising intonation.*

A. *Listen and repeat the following questions. Practice making your voice rise at the end of the sentences.*

1. May I help you?
2. Do you work here?
3. You want a house that has a *what*?
4. Is store credit okay?
5. Would you like to talk to the manager?
6. Do you have your receipt?

B. *Now ask a partner more* yes/no *and clarification questions. Practice using rising intonation.*

Chapter 4:
The Community

Page 62 (Chapter Opening, Activity 1)

Read and Listen *Read the story. Then listen to it.*

Diversity

Elena loves the diversity of her Brooklyn neighborhood. She likes to walk down the street and look into all the stores and shops. There is a pizza shop right next to the subway. She often stops there on her way home from work. She usually orders a slice of pizza and then stands for a few minutes in front of the store to eat it. It's interesting to watch all the people hurrying home from work.

There is a Chinese discount store where everything is always on sale. She likes to go in there to see what kind of bargains she can find. Sometimes she finds really nice things for very low prices. Across the street there is a Russian pharmacy where she goes to pick up medications and to get special Russian cosmetics that she likes. Around the corner there is a post office where she goes to buy stamps and to mail letters.

There are also several ethnic restaurants in the neighborhood. There is a Russian café that has good coffee and pastries. There is a Chinese seafood restaurant that she intends to visit for a nice shrimp dinner when she gets a new job. And there is a Japanese restaurant that has delicious sushi. Elena plans to try all the neighborhood restaurants when she gets a new job and has more money. But right now she is happy just to know that there are so many interesting places nearby.

Page 68 (Lesson 2, Activity 1)

Listen *Listen to the conversations. Write the numbers of the community service agencies below in the circles on the map.*

1.
A: Do you know where the Employment Development Office is?
B: Yes, I do. Just walk along West Houston to West Broadway. Turn left on West Broadway and you'll see it just south of West Houston.

2.
A: Can you tell me where the post office is?
B: Yes. Just walk straight down Broadway. Just after you cross Spring Street, you'll see it on the right side.

3.
A: Excuse me, Officer. I'm trying to find the Housing Authority Office.
B: OK. I can help you with that. It's on Spring Street just east of Broadway. So, if you walk south on Broadway and turn left on Spring Street, you can't miss it.

4.
A: I'm looking for the Sanitation Bureau. Is that near here?
B: Yes, it is. Just take West Houston to West Broadway and turn left. It's at the end of the block, before you get to Prince Street. It's just down the block from the Employment Development Office.

5.
A: Is the Animal Control Agency somewhere around here?
B: It's a few blocks east of here, on Bowery. If you take East Houston to Bowery and turn left, you'll see it before you get to East First Street.

6.
A: Is there a community health center around here somewhere?
B: Yes, there is. It's on East Third Street. From here you can walk east along East Houston to Bowery. Turn left on Bowery and go three blocks to East Third Street. Turn right on East Third and you'll see it.

7.
A: I'm trying to find the Senior Citizen Center.
B: Well, you're very close. It's on East Houston between Mott and Elizabeth.—just a block and a half east of here.

8.
A: Do you know where the public library is?
B: Well, there's one on Bleeker just east of Broadway. Walk north to Bleeker and turn right. It's right there.

9.
A: I'm trying to find the Neighborhood Legal Services Office. Do you happen to know where it is?
B: Actually I do. I'm a lawyer there. It's on Mercer between Bleeker and West Third. Take Broadway north to Bleeker. Turn left on Bleeker and right on Mercer. It's in the middle of the block.

10.
A: Where is the police station? I need to report a crime.
B: There's a police station on West Third just west of Mercer. Walk north on Broadway to West Third, and then turn left on West Third. It's just past Mercer.

Page 72 (Lesson 3, Activity 1)

Read and Listen *Read the story. Then listen to the story. Underline the infinitives.*

A Letter of Concern

Elena thought there was a problem in her neighborhood, so she invited several of her neighbors to come to her apartment to talk about it. After they discussed the problem, Elena asked her neighbors to help her do something about it. Vicki advised Elena to call the local police station and to talk to the police about the problem. But Elena wanted to do something more serious than just talk to someone. Finally, they decided to write a letter of concern. It took a little while, but Elena finally persuaded Daisy to write the letter because she had the best writing skills of their group. The others agreed to help. This is what they wrote:

Dear Captain Tasso:

We are a group of women who live in the neighborhood near your police station. We are writing to ask you to help us with a problem. The problem is that the area around our subway station isn't safe for women coming home alone at night. There are no bright lights outside the subway station and no police officers stationed there late at night. The street outside the station is so dark that you can't see if a dangerous person is standing in a doorway waiting to grab you as you walk past.

We would like you to put a police officer at this location from about 10:00 P.M. to about 3:00 in the morning. Also, we'd like you to please replace the broken streetlights and put even more lights on the street around the subway station for our safety.

Thank you for listening to our concern.

Sincerely,

Elena Petrova, *Daisy Yu, Vicki Martinez,* Alice Charles

Page 76 (Lesson 3, Activity 11)

Listen *Listen and help these concerned citizens write their letter by filling in the missing words.*

Dear Ms. Bernstein:

We are writing to you today (1)<u>to tell you about a problem</u> in our neighborhood. Every night there are stray dogs (2)<u>running around our neighborhood</u> without their owners and without any leashes. We believe that (3)<u>these dogs are dangerous</u> to our kids. Our children are (4)<u>too small to be on the street</u> when these dogs are nearby. We believe our children (5)<u>aren't safe enough</u> on the street when there are stray dogs around.

These dogs also push over our garbage cans and cause our street (6)<u>to look very dirty</u>. The dogs (7)<u>are too fast</u> and (8)<u>not friendly enough</u> for us to catch them. So, we are asking you (9)<u>to catch them and find homes</u> for them. Or, if they already have homes, (10)<u>please tell</u> their owners (11)<u>not to let them out</u> of their yards at night.

Thank you for your help with this problem.

Sincerely,
The Concerned Citizens of Downtown

Page 77 (Chapter 4 Review, Activity 1)

Read and Listen *Read the story. Then listen to the story.*

The Ocean Avenue Child-Care Co-op

Elena has learned that it is difficult to find good and inexpensive child care in her community. It is very important for a single parent to have a reliable child-care provider. There is a professional child-care center in her neighborhood, but it is too expensive for Elena to use. So, she has decided to start a child-care cooperative, or "co-op," in her neighborhood. Being part of a child-care co-op means that Elena will agree to take care of other people's children one night a week or a few hours on the weekend. In exchange, other parents will watch Sasha at another time of the week if Elena needs someone to watch him.

Elena put an ad in her school newsletter to advertise her idea. In the ad, she asked other parents with children between the ages of three and nine to call her for information about the new Ocean Avenue Child-Care Co-op. Four other parents called to say they were interested in her idea. Now Elena is planning to have a meeting to meet the parents and to set up a schedule. She thinks it is important for everyone to be comfortable with each other before they agree to leave their children in each other's care. Later on, they will organize a playdate at the park so the children can meet each other and all the parents.

Elena hopes that these parents are as nice as they sounded on the phone and that the co-op will work. It would be a good solution to her child-care problem. Of course, she would prefer to have her husband with her in New York. But at the moment that isn't possible. So, she is trying to do the best she can.

Page 79 (Chapter 4 Review)

Pronunciation *Rising and falling intonation*

Yes/No *questions and clarification questions usually end with rising intonation. Information questions usually end with falling intonation.*

Listen to the following questions and draw an up arrow ↑ for rising intonation and a down arrow ↓ for falling intonation. Then listen again and repeat with correct intonation.

1. Is he your son?
2. Where is the gas station?
3. Is it on the corner?
4. Where do you live?
5. Did you say the second floor?
6. Are you from Russia?

Chapter 5:
People and Places

Page 82 (Chapter Opening, Activity 1)

Read and Listen *Read the story. Then listen to it.*

A Night Out

Last week, Andre asked Daisy out. Daisy wanted to go out with him, but she was nervous. So, she asked Elena to go with them. "If the three of us go, it won't be so stressful," she told Elena. "In China, women often bring a friend along on a first date." Elena agreed to come.

They all got together at Elena's apartment. Elena had dropped Sasha off at the babysitter's home earlier. At the apartment, they looked through the entertainment section of the newspaper and tried to decide what to do. They wrote down a few possibilities, but couldn't agree on anything. Finally, Andre suggested that they get on the subway and go to the city. "We'll pick out something fun to do when we get there," he said.

They got off the subway in the middle of Manhattan. There were entertainment possibilities all around them. There was jazz music at a small club, but Daisy doesn't like jazz very much. "I would rather hear classical or rock-and-roll music," she said. There was a comedy club, but Elena thought that her English wasn't good enough to understand American comedy. "They talk so fast," she said, "and they use a lot of idioms." There was a dance club, but the style was salsa and none of them knew how to dance to salsa music. There was a karaoke bar, but Daisy and Elena both hate to sing in public. And there was a movie theater, but each of them wanted to see a different movie.

"There's a nice Italian restaurant," Elena said.

"I'm hungry," Daisy said. "But I'm not crazy about Italian food."

"Well," Andre said, "we need to make a decision."

The three of them stood looking at the bright neon lights blinking at them up the street as far as they could see.

Read and Listen *Read the story. Then listen to the story.*

The World of Work

Andre has learned that if you want to get ahead at work, you have to have "people skills," or be able to get along with people well. This is especially important if you work in sales, as Andre does. You have to be friendly with customers and, of course, you have to get along with your boss or, sooner or later, you could get fired.

There are many other things Andre has learned since he got hired at Best Electronics. He has learned that it is important to get up early and get in on time every day. Supervisors expect punctuality at U.S. businesses. They also expect you to be dependable. That means you shouldn't stay home every time you get a cold. If you work in sales, you have to be aggressive. When someone leaves you a message, you have to get back to him or her right away. You can't let a busy signal or answering machine stop you. Keep calling until you get through to your customer.

Managers also expect you to be responsible. If you make a mistake, don't try to get out of it. Just admit your mistake and apologize. Everyone will get over it quickly if you apologize. Managers also expect you to work well with others, to be a good team player. Andre has found that it helps to get together with his coworkers once in a while outside of work. That makes it easier to communicate when they are working together.

Right now, Andre is making enough money to get by. But he is getting better at his job every day. He may not get rich from his job at Best Electronics, but he thinks that he will make enough to live comfortably. Then he might think about getting married!

Listen *Listen to the conversations. Circle the communication strategies you hear in each conversation.*

Conversation 1
A: Jeff, have you got a minute?
B: Sure. What's up?
A: Could you give me a hand with this printer? I'm having a lot of trouble enlarging copies.
B: Why don't you read the instruction manual first? It's right there on the shelf. If you're still having trouble, I'll take a look at it with you after my break.
A: Great. That's a good idea.

Conversation 2
A: I'm sorry. I know you're the new cashier, but I didn't get your name.
B: It's Mahtab.
A: Did you say Mah-tab?
B: Yes, that's right. It means "full moon" in Farsi.
A: Well, Mahtab, how do you like it here so far?
B: Everybody I've talked to is really nice, so I guess I like it so far.

Conversation 3
A: That machine is really hard to operate, isn't it?
B: Oh, it's not that hard once you get used to it. It just takes some practice.
A: Well, I'm glad we have you to operate it. It's very helpful to have an operator who is confident and good at what he does.
B: Thank you. That's nice of you to say.

Listen *Listen to the story and check your answers.*

The Third Wheel

When Andre (1)<u>asked</u> Daisy out, Elena agreed to go with them on their first date so that Daisy would feel comfortable. Daisy had never (2)<u>gone</u> out with a Russian guy before so she was nervous about it. "Don't worry," Elena had said. "I'm sure you two will (3)<u>get along</u> fine." But Daisy had asked for her help, so Elena agreed to go with them.

They (4)<u>got on</u> the subway and took it over the bridge to the city. In the city they (5)<u>picked</u> out a nice café and went in. It was very romantic with candles on the tables and soft music playing. Earlier Daisy had (6)<u>written</u> down some information about things to do in the city. They sat for a while drinking coffee and (7)<u>talked</u> over the possibilities. There was a movie playing that (8)<u>was directed</u> by one of Elena's favorite directors. But Andre and Daisy didn't want to see a movie. They wanted to stay in the dark, romantic café. So, they ordered some food and sat listening to the music.

By the time they left the café, Andre and Daisy had gotten (9)<u>used</u> to each other's accents and really didn't need Elena at all. On the way back to the subway, they walked close together holding hands and Elena could feel herself (10)<u>getting</u> depressed. She was thinking about her husband, Alex. He (11)<u>had</u> sent her an e-mail a couple of days ago but she hadn't written (12)<u>back</u> yet. Now she suddenly couldn't wait to write to him.

Back in Brooklyn they stopped at the babysitter's and (13)<u>picked</u> up Sasha. Then Andre and Daisy (14)<u>dropped</u> Elena off at her apartment. As soon as she put Sasha to bed, Elena (15)<u>got</u> on her computer and began typing an e-mail. "Hello, Alex," she wrote in her native Russian language. "I miss you very much. . . ."

Pronunciation *Rising and falling intonation*

Listen and repeat the or *questions using rising and then falling intonation.*

1. Would you like coffee or tea?
2. Would you rather walk or drive?
3. Should we go on Saturday or Sunday?
4. Should we go alone or with the teacher?
5. Would you rather have soda or water?

Chapter 6:
Home and School

Page 102 (Chapter Opening, Activity 1)

Read and Listen *Read the story. Then listen to it.*

To Buy or Not to Buy

Al and Alice have saved almost $20,000 and they want to buy a house. They want to own a home because they think houses always go up in value if you keep them for a while. Unfortunately, they haven't found any homes in their price range that they really like. The homes they can afford seem to have a lot of problems.

Yesterday they were taken to see a "fixer-upper." (A fixer-upper is a house that has a lot of things that need to be fixed.) It was built in 1935 and Al liked it, but Alice didn't like it very much. Al liked the size of the house and the big window and fireplace in the living room. But Alice didn't like the age or condition of the house. She thought it needed a lot of work. Al liked the swimming pool and barbecue area in the back, but Alice didn't like the broken gate or holes in the concrete. Al liked the fruit trees and the front yard, but Alice didn't like the dog in the yard next door. Al liked the price of the house and the low down payment they would need, but Alice didn't like all the work it would take to make the house look really nice.

It isn't an easy decision because they both like the neighborhood where the house is located. And, according to their real estate agent, the most important thing when buying a home is location. So, they are going back with the agent again tomorrow to look at the house carefully one more time.

Page 106 (Lesson 1, Activity 5)

Listen *Listen to the conversations between a real estate agent and three callers. Take notes in the boxes below about the three properties.*

1.

A: Hello. I'm calling about the house for sale on East 42nd Street. Can you tell me a little about it?

B: Yes, of course. It's a very nice four-bedroom house with 2 bathrooms. It has about 2,100 square feet.

A: Do you know how old it is?

B: Yes, it was built in 1947.

A: How much is the asking price?

B: They're asking $419,500, but there might be a little flexibility in the price.

A: What is the neighborhood like around there?

B: It's a very convenient neighborhood—close to shopping, close to transportation. There are mostly older people on the block. And the house has a very nice backyard. There is a garden and several fruit trees. Would you like to take a look at it?

A: I'm not sure. I'll have to call you back about that.

B: OK. Thank you for calling. If you have any more questions, just call again.

2.

A: Bay Realty. Can I help you?

B: I'm calling about the condo on Ocean Parkway for sale or lease. Can you tell me if it's still available?

A: Yes, it is.

B: How big of a place is it?

A: It's a two-bedroom condo with one bath. A total of 900 square feet.

B: Do you know when it was built?

A: Yes. It was built in 1995. It has a modern kitchen and bathroom. It's a securie building two blocks from the beach.

B: That sounds good. Does it have parking?

A: Yes. There are two parking spaces in the back for each apartment.

B: Do you know how much they're asking for it?

A: The asking price to buy is $375,000. But it is also available for lease at $1,800 a month.

B: That sounds a little bit high. But I do love the location. I'll get back to you later. Thanks for your time.

A: You're welcome.

3.

A: Island Realty. What can I do for you?

B: I'd like to get some information on that cute starter home I saw on Mott Street.

A: All right. Let's see . . . it's a two-bedroom, one-bath home. Small, but cozy—about 1,100 square feet.

B: Can you tell me what the asking price is?

A: It's $310,000. Or you can rent it for $1,500 a month. It's available for sale or rent.

B: Do you happen to know when it was built?

A: It was built in 1965.

B: Do you know if it's been remodeled?

A: No. Everything is original.

B: Can you tell me about the neighborhood?

A: Yes. It's very nice. It's a safe, quiet, friendly neighborhood.

B: What else can you tell me about the house?

A: Well, it has a two-car garage, a pool, a jacuzzi, and a very large yard. Do you want to take a look at it?

B: I'm not sure yet. I'll have to get back to you in a couple of days.

A: All right. Thank you for calling.

Page 112 (Lesson 2, Activity 7)

Listen *Listen and write the missing information on the rental agreement.*

1. All rent <u>must be paid</u> in full on the first of the month. If rent is more than three days late, a $500 late fee <u>will be</u> charged.
2. All dogs and cats <u>must be kept</u> on leashes when on the apartment grounds.
3. Landlord <u>doesn't have to</u> supply heat or hot water to tenants.
4. Guests and visitors <u>are not allowed</u> in apartments after midnight.
5. All TVs and loud music must be <u>turned off</u> by 10:00 P.M.
6. Any leaks or plumbing problems <u>must be repaired</u> and paid for by the tenant.
7. All furniture <u>must be seen</u> and approved by the landlord. Ugly furniture will not <u>be permitted</u> in apartments.
8. Children under 18 are not allowed in the pool area, or any other place on apartment grounds, <u>without a parent</u>.
9. Only church music <u>may be played</u> in apartments on Sundays.
10. Landlord <u>may enter</u> apartment at any time without permission of tenant.

Page 113 (Lesson 3, Activity 1)

Read and Listen *Read the story. Then listen to the story.*

Vocational Education

In Russia, vocational education is very important. In Russian secondary schools, many students take classes that prepare them to get a special type of job when they graduate. In the U.S., there aren't as many vocational classes available to high school students. But there are a lot of programs and classes available for adults who want to learn skills to get a job. Some vocational classes like nursing and accounting are taught in community colleges. Training for jobs like auto repair and cosmetology is offered at public adult schools. Some job-training programs for fields, such as X-ray technology, are available at hospitals or other community organizations.

Many of Elena's friends have enrolled in vocational training programs in the U.S. Alice studied nursing in Haiti, but she also received an LVN (Licensed Vocational Nurse) degree from a community college that helped her get a job at the hospital. Her husband, Al, received a certificate in culinary arts that helped him get a job as a chef. Vicki is studying cosmetology in a private trade school so she can get a cosmetology license in New York. Andre took several computer classes at Downtown Adult School that helped him get his current job. And Daisy received an Associate of Arts degree from a local community college that was required for her teaching assistant position.

There are other kinds of jobs that you can get with an on-the-job training program, called an apprenticeship. These are usually available in trades, like carpentry or construction. An apprentice usually works for a small amount of pay while learning job skills from an experienced professional. There are also some jobs that let you start as a volunteer to allow you to "get your foot in the door." These are sometimes called internships. Interns usually work without pay in order to gain experience and get a paying job in the same field or business later.

Elena can't afford to work as a volunteer. And she doesn't want to be an apprentice. But she would like to find a vocational training program that would give her the skills or certificate she needs to get a higher paying job. She is thinking about a certificate program in tax preparation or banking. She is also interested in learning about real estate. She can take real estate classes at the local community college, but she will have to pass a state exam in order to become a real estate agent. So, Elena is going to wait until her English is better before she makes a firm decision about her career. She will continue to study English because she knows she will need it for any job she gets.

Page 116 (Lesson 3, Activity 5)

Listen *Read the questions below. Then listen to Elena's telephone conversation. Listen for the information you need to answer the questions. Take notes if necessary. Then write the answers to the questions.*

Elena: I'm interested in taking some classes next semester. Can you tell me what I have to do to register?

Clerk: Yes. You have never attended classes here. Is that right?

Elena: Yes.

Clerk: Then the first thing you will have to do is fill out a college application. You can get one here at the school registration office, or you can fill it out online if you prefer.

Elena: And then what?

Clerk: After that, you will need to show proof of citizenship.

Elena: I'm not a citizen, but I am a permanent resident. Do you know if that's OK?

Clerk: Yes, that's fine. Just bring proof of your immigration status when you come in to register.

Elena: Can you tell me what time the registration office is open?

Clerk: It's open from 8:00 A.M. to 5:00 P.M. on weekdays—Monday to Friday.

Elena: Can I register for English class when I come in to fill out the registration?

Clerk: No, not right then. Before you can register for any English class, you will have to take an assessment test. This is mandatory. When we see the results of your English assessment test, we will be able to tell you what level of English class you need.

Elena: Do you know if there is a charge for the assessment test?

Clerk: No, it's free.

Elena: And the classes? How much do they cost?

Clerk: Right now it's $26 per unit. So, a five-unit English class will cost $130. Then there are a couple of other small registration fees. All fees must be paid prior to the first day of class or you will be dropped.

Elena: OK. I understand. Thank you very much.

Clerk: My pleasure.

Page 117 (Chapter Review, Activity 1)

Read and Listen *Read the story. Then listen to the story.*

Buying a Home

Al and Alice went to a real estate agent (1) a couple of months ago (2) to get some help and advice about buying a home. The first question the real estate agent asked was, "How much do you have for a down payment?" They told her that they had about $20,000. She seemed happy about that. "The next step," she said, "is to go to a bank or a mortgage broker to get prequalified. It's important to get prequalified (3) so you will know how expensive a house you will be able to buy."

After they were prequalified, (4) they were taken around the city by the agent to look at homes in their price range. They looked at (5) about twenty different places. Then finally they found a house that they both liked. It was not too small, not too old, and in a good neighborhood. They talked it over with their agent. Then they made an offer for the house that was $10,000 below the asking price. Their first offer wasn't accepted. They were both really depressed that night. But then, (6) the next day, they received a counter offer from the seller. This counter offer was (7) $5,000 below the original asking price.

Al and Alice had another meeting with their agent to discuss the counter offer. Then Al called (8) his father for some last-minute advice. His father told him that they should buy it if they really liked it. So, the next day they decided to accept the counter offer. They gave the seller a deposit of 2% of the asking price. Then they had the house inspected (9) to make sure there weren't any problems that the seller hadn't told them about.

The inspector didn't find any big problems, so six weeks later they moved in. Pretty soon they will be able (10) to invite all their friends to a party at their very own home. The thought of that makes both of them very happy.

Page 119 (Chapter Review)

Pronunciation *Word stress: can/can't*

It is not only the contracted sound of "t" that distinguishes the pronunciation of the two modals can *and* can't. *English speakers rely on stress.* Can *is **not** stressed in normal conversation.* Can't ***is** stressed. Listen and repeat the sentences with* can *and* can't.

1. I can **have** a pet here. Pets are allowed.
   I **can't** pay that much rent. It's too expensive.

2. You can **park** over there, at the meter.
   You **can't** park there. You'll get a ticket.

3. I can **call** you tomorrow.
   I **can't** call you tomorrow. I'm working.

Chapter 7:
Health and Safety

Page 122 (Chapter Opening, Activity 1)

Listen and Read *Read the story. Then listen to it.*

The Flu

Sasha has the flu. It started with a headache and a sore throat. At first, Elena thought that he just had a cold. Kids get colds all the time. But he was coughing too, and he couldn't get out of bed. Elena gave him some over-the-counter cough medicine, but it didn't work. Finally, she called the doctor. When she called the doctor's office, the nurse told her to take Sasha's temperature. His temperature was 103 degrees. He also had chills and body aches. The nurse asked her to bring him in to see the doctor.

At the doctor's office, Elena filled out a Medical History form for Sasha. Then the doctor took him to the examination room and checked him over. "He has the flu," the doctor said. He told Elena to give Sasha plenty of liquids and to make sure he got a lot of rest. He told her to keep him home from school for at least a week. Sasha didn't seem too unhappy about that. But Elena felt terrible.

"I should have gotten him a flu shot," she told Daisy on the phone later. "They were giving free flu shots at the clinic last month."

"Maybe we all should have gotten flu shots!" Daisy said.

Elena thought for a minute about trying to get a flu shot for herself. But she was already getting a headache and a sore throat, so it was probably too late. She told herself she'd be sure to get a flu shot next year!

Page 126 (Lesson 1, Activity 5)

Listen *Listen to the conversation between Lucy and her doctor. Take notes on the healthy things he tells her to do and the unhealthy things he tells her not to do.*

Lucy: I've been having problems with stress and feeling tired all the time. I would really like to have a healthier lifestyle, but I'm not sure where to begin.

Doctor: Well, the first thing is to look at your current health habits. For example, do you get enough sleep? People who live stressful lives often don't get enough sleep.

Lucy: I guess that's true. I usually sleep about five to six hours a night.

Doctor: That's not enough. So, the first thing I'd advise you to do is to get at least seven hours of sleep a night. Can you do that?

Female: Sure. I can try.

Doctor: Next, we should look at your diet. How is your diet?

Lucy: I guess it's not so good. I eat a lot of fast food, and I love desserts. And I like to have a donut with my coffee each morning.

Doctor: I would like you to cut down on donuts, desserts, and any food that has a very high sugar content. I want you to cut down on sugar.

Lucy: OK.

Doctor: And you should eat a lot less fast food. Instead, eat more fruit and vegetables; doctors recommend at least five a day, you know. Now, how about coffee? How many cups a day do you drink?

Lucy: Five, maybe six.

Doctor: That's too many. That could be one reason why you are feeling stressed. Coffee will do that to you. My suggestion is to limit yourself to two cups a day. Does that sound reasonable?

Lucy: Yes, I guess so.

Doctor: How about alcohol and tobacco? Do you drink or smoke?

Lucy: Um, yes, I do both.

Doctor: Well, my advice on that is to stop smoking *as soon as possible!* And as far as alcohol is concerned, the key is moderation. It's OK to have a glass or two of wine, but don't have more than that.

Lucy: I don't usually have more than one or two except if I go to a party or something like that.

Doctor: Now, let me get to what I think is the most important thing for you. You need to get some regular exercise. It could be jogging, or swimming, or even dancing, but it should be done on a regular schedule—at least three times a week. That will keep your stress level down even if you don't do any of the other things I told you to do. So, can you start a regular exercise program this week, and try to stick to it?

Lucy: Sure. I'll start tomorrow. Thank you, doctor.

Page 130 (Lesson 2, Activity 3).

Listen *Listen to the pharmacist and complete the information on the medicine label.*

Patient: Is there anything important I should know about this medication?

Pharmacist: You should take one capsule every four hours.

Patient: Yes, I know that.

Pharmacist: You should take it with food. It's better not to take these on an empty stomach.

Patient: OK.

Pharmacist: And be sure to keep it refrigerated. It says that on the label. Also, don't stop taking it until it's finished. Make sure you take all the capsules, even if you feel better right away.

Patient: OK, thanks. Anything else?

Pharmacist: You can not drink alcohol while you are taking this medication. It doesn't mix with alcohol.

Page 131 (Lesson 2, Activity 6)

Listen *Listen and check your answers to Activities 4 and 5.*

First, in the waiting room, the receptionist asked Elena for her medical insurance card. She made a copy of the card. Then the nurse took Elena's into the doctor's office. In the office, the nurse told Elena to stand up straight on the scale. She checked Elena's height and weight. Then she took Elena into the examination room. Elena sat on the examining table, and the nurse put a thermometer in her mouth. She told her to hold it under her tongue and to roll up her sleeve. Then the nurse took her temperature and her blood pressure. After that, she told her to hold out her arm and make a fist. She took some blood from Elena's arm. Then the doctor came into the room. He told her to open wide and say "Aaaaaahhh," and he looked down her throat. After that, he told her to take a deep breath. And he told her to exhale while he listened to her heart and lungs. Fortunately for Elena, everything was fine. It was a very normal checkup.

Page 133 (Lesson 3, Activity 1)

Read and Listen *Read the story. Then listen to the story.*

Emergencies

In the last few months, several of Elena's friends have experienced emergencies on their jobs. Some of them were prepared and knew what to do, but some did not. Elena decided that everyone should know more about safety, so she asked Al and Alice, along with several other friends, to come to her house for dinner. Al, who is a chef, and Alice, who is a nurse, agreed to give everyone some information about safety and about what to do in an emergency.

First, Al talked about an emergency that happened at his job. There was a fire in the kitchen. Al was in the office talking to the restaurant manager when the fire started. A kitchen helper left a pot holder on the stove and it caught on fire. The fire spread to some grease, and the helper tried to put it out by throwing water on it. "You never throw water on a grease fire," Al said. "He should have used baking soda to put out a grease fire." And, of course, he shouldn't have left the pot holder so close to the burner."

Another emergency happened on the street in front of Andre while he was walking to work. There was a car accident and a man was seriously hurt. Andre tried to help. He pulled the man out of his car. "My leg!" the man screamed. Andre tried to move his leg to see how serious the injury was, but the man screamed even louder. Andre didn't know where the nearest emergency room was, so he left the man on the street and ran into his manager's office and called 911.

"Andre," Alice said, "you shouldn't have moved his leg. Actually, you probably shouldn't have even pulled him out of the car unless there was some danger of another car hitting him. And you should always know where the nearest emergency room is. But it was good that you called 911."

The third emergency happened at Daisy's school. An eight-year-old boy was walking too fast in the cafeteria with food in his mouth. He tripped and fell, and then started to choke on a piece of meat. By the time Daisy got to him, he couldn't talk or breathe. Daisy didn't know who to call or what to do. Finally, another teacher heard Daisy calling for help. She ran over and put her arms around the boy from behind. She held her hands together and pushed up and in on the top part of the boy's stomach. The piece of meat popped out of his mouth.

"First of all," Alice said, "the boy shouldn't have been running with food in his mouth. But, Daisy, you should have known how to do the Heimlich maneuver, which is what the counselor did to save the boy. Would you like to learn how to do it?" Alice went around the room and taught everyone how to do the Heimlich maneuver.

Page 137 (Chapter 7 Review, Activity 1)

Read and Listen *Read the story. Then listen to the story.*

Help!

One of the members of Elena's child-care co-op had an emergency at her home last Saturday. Irina was babysitting for three children along with her own two kids. Maybe that was too many children for one parent to handle. She left a four-year-old boy named Rudy alone in her bathroom for a few minutes. She was supervising the other children playing a board game and trying to cook dinner at the same time. Then suddenly she heard Rudy screaming.

Irina dropped everything and ran into the bathroom. Little Rudy was sitting on the floor next to the toilet rubbing his eyes and crying. There was a spray-top bottle of household cleaner on the floor next to him. Irina could see blue liquid from the bottle on the floor and on Rudy's face and hair. When she saw the blue liquid on Rudy's face, Irina panicked and screamed. Her own two children heard her and started to cry, too.

Irina picked Rudy up, but he just kept crying. She didn't know what to do. She had left the cleaner in the cabinet under the sink, but there wasn't a lock on the cabinet. She didn't think anyone would open it and try to play with anything inside. Her children had never done that. And she never thought a child would squirt himself in the eyes with a cleaning bottle! Irina didn't know if she should take him to an emergency room, try to call a doctor, or do something to try to help him. She didn't have a car and she hadn't written down an emergency-room or hospital phone number. She did have Alice's number, and Alice was a nurse, so she ran to the phone and called Alice.

Rudy was still crying as Irina told Alice what had happened. "Look at the bottle," Alice said. "And read the label. What does it say?"

"It says, 'Keep away from children' and 'Harmful if swallowed'."

"Read more. What does it say about eyes?"

Irina found it. "In case of eye contact, immediately flush with water and continue flushing for fifteen minutes. Get medical attention right away!"

"OK," Alice said. "Start flushing his eyes with water. Use slightly warm water. I'll be there in a few minutes."

Page 138 (Chapter 7 Review, Activity 4)

Listen *Listen to the conversations. Write what the doctor tells, advises, or asks each patient to do.*

1.
A: I have a high fever and I feel awful.
B: Why don't you come into the office and we'll take a look at you.

2.
A: I really don't want to get the flu this year. Last year I got really sick. I was out of work for a week!
B: I suggest that you get a flu shot. That will most likely prevent you from getting it.

3.
A: I don't have any energy. I'm tired all the time.
B: Do you get any exercise? Why don't you start an exercise program?

4.
A: I've gained fifteen pounds and I'd like to lose it. Should I try a diet?
B: I don't really believe in diets. You just have to stop eating junk food and fatty desserts.

5.
A: My cough seems to be getting worse all the time.
B: There's only one thing I can say—the same thing I've been telling you for years—quit smoking!

Page 139 (Chapter 7 Review)

Pronunciation *Shoulda, coulda, woulda*

The contracted forms of past modals are often pronounced with strong reductions:

should've = shoulda
could've = coulda
would've = woulda

Listen and repeat the sentences with the reduced pronunciation.

1. You *shoulda* quit smoking years ago.
2. She *shoulda* called first.
3. He *woulda* gone with you.
4. They *coulda* gotten lost.

Chapter 8:
Work: Getting a Job

Page 142 (Chapter Opening, Activity 1)

Read and Listen *Read the story. Then listen to it.*

A Great Job?

"Elena," Daisy said excitedly, "I think I've found a great job for you."

Elena listened closely and agreed that it did sound like a great job for her. It was a job as an administrative assistant in a small law office. The boss, Mr. Christov, was the father of one of Daisy's students. He wanted to hire someone who spoke Russian, was organized, and knew about accounting and record keeping. The pay was $20 an hour.

Elena was very interested. The next day she called Mr. Christov. They spoke in Russian and in English for twenty minutes. He asked her to send him a resume and a cover letter that included her job skills and her personal strengths. He also told her to go online to fill out an application on his law office Web site. Then he made an appointment for her to come in for an interview.

Elena was nervous. She sat down and made a list of things she needed to do to get ready. She had to look at, and probably rewrite, her resume. She had to write a cover letter to send with her resume. She wanted to ask her aunt for a letter of recommendation that she could bring with her to the interview. And then she wanted to think about questions Mr. Christov could ask her at the interview and how she would answer them. Finally, she had to decide what to wear to the interview because she wanted to look good. She wanted to look organized and professional—like someone Mr. Christov would want to represent his business.

This job interview could be a real opportunity for her in the "land of opportunity," and she wanted to be prepared for it.

Page 148 (Lesson 1, Activity 8)

Listen *Listen and check your answers to Activity 7.*

March 14, 2007

Dear Mr. Christov:

I am enclosing my (1)<u>resume</u> for the (2)<u>administrative assistant</u> position that was advertised in *The Brooklyn News* on March 9. I am an administrative assistant in my current job, so I believe that my background, (3)<u>skills</u>, and personality match what you are looking for.

I have a degree in accounting from a major Russian university, so my (4)<u>oral</u> and (5)<u>writing</u> skills in Russian are very strong. I am friendly and I enjoy meeting and talking to people, so I believe that I have good (6)<u>people skills</u>. I also have the kind of experience you are looking for because on my last job I used my computer skills to (7)<u>organize</u> and (8)<u>maintain</u> the company's business records.

Thank you for taking the time to consider me for this position. I look forward to meeting with you soon.

Sincerely,
Elena Petrova

Page 154 (Lesson 3, Activity 1)

Read and Listen *Read the story. Then listen to the story.*

Benefits

Elena got the job!

Elena was very excited because getting a new job is always exciting. She was pleased with the amount of money she was going to make and thrilled about the benefits of the job. She was also interested in getting to know the people at her new job because they all seemed to be smart and interesting. So, there was a lot to be happy about after Mr. Christov told her the good news.

The benefits Mr. Christov offered were excellent for a small business. First of all, he told her they would provide medical and dental insurance for her and Sasha. She would get eight paid holidays—days when the office would be closed—and two weeks paid vacation after one year. She would get one paid sick day, or personal necessity day, for every two months that she worked. Also, she could have a flexible schedule on days when they didn't have any clients coming in for a meeting.

Mr. Christov told her that they expected her to look professional every day because she would often be meeting with clients in addition to answering phones and keeping business records. Most of their clients were Russian and part of Elena's job would be to speak with them in their own language and to make them feel relaxed and comfortable. "One of the reasons we chose you for this job is because we thought you would make the best impression on our Russian clients," Mr. Christov said.

Elena found it amusing that it wasn't her accounting or computer skills that had helped her get the job. It was her ability to speak Russian and to make people feel comfortable that had gotten her first real job in the United States.

Page 156 (Lesson 3, Activity 5)

Listen *Listen to the conversation. Write a participial adjective that describes how each person felt.*

1. I really thought he would call me. He seemed so nice. He said he would call, but then . . . nothing.
2. I thought I was doing great. I was up in front of the room, in front of the whole group, and then I called her by the wrong name.
3. **A:** We thought we knew where we were going, but it seemed like we were going around in circles. He kept looking at the map . . .
4. I was looking at the numbers coming up on the screen. I had the first one and then the second and the third. When the fourth one came in, I just screamed. I couldn't believe it. I had never won anything in my whole life.
5. She just kept talking, on and on, about her job, about what she had for dinner, the kind of food she usually eats for dinner . . . then her previous job . . . it was awful.

Page 157 (Chapter 8 Review, Activity 1)

Read and Listen *Read the story. Then listen to the story.*

I Got a Job!

Finding a job can be a long and difficult process. Elena realizes that she was lucky. She found a job through word of mouth—by networking. And she got the first job she interviewed for. Most people don't get the first job they apply for. But, on the other hand, she had been looking for a long time before she found something she wanted to apply for.

Mr. Christov wants her to start on Monday, so now she is getting ready for her first day. First, she is going to buy some new clothes because she wants to look professional. Next, she is going to study a list of legal vocabulary words that Mr. Christov gave her because part of her job will be to interview Russian-speaking clients and translate for them, if necessary. She hopes it won't be necessary in the first few days at least. She has been studying English since she arrived in the U.S., but there are still a lot of English words and idioms she doesn't know. It takes a long time to speak another language really well.

The night after her job interview, Elena called Alex in Russia. "I got a job!" she said. "The pay is $20 an hour," she said. "And I will have medical insurance for Sasha and me." Alex sounded happy. The salary was a lot more money than she had ever made in Russia. She told Alex a little about her job duties and a little about Mr. Christov. "He speaks Russian," she said, "but not very well. That's what he needs me for." She told him how nice Mr. Christov was and how much she was going to learn on this job. Alex was quiet for a moment.

"Elena," he asked, "is Mr. Christov married?"

"Yes, Alex," she said, "he's married. And so am I." She hesitated for a moment. "I haven't forgotten that," she said. "Have you?"

"No, Elena," Alex said. "I haven't forgotten either."

Page 159 (Chapter 8 Review)

Pronunciation *Sentence stress*

Negative words are usually stressed in a sentence, but sometimes we don't want to stress the negative. Listen and repeat the negative sentences, and the "No, but . . ." sentences.

1. I <u>don't</u> have a resume.
   I don't have a <u>resume</u>, but I brought an <u>application</u>.

2. I <u>don't</u> have a car.
   I don't have a <u>car</u>, but I have a <u>motorcycle</u>.

3. I <u>haven't</u> worked in <u>sales</u>.
   I haven't worked in <u>sales</u>, but I'm <u>sure</u> I'd be <u>good</u> at it.

Chapter 9:
Work: On the Job

Page 162 (Chapter Opening, Activity 1)

Read and Listen *Read the story. Then listen to it.*

Work

Elena likes her new office a lot. It is a nice, big office with a lot of new modern equipment. She sometimes shares it with Amy, who is a legal secretary and the person Elena relies on to teach her all the new things she has to learn. Amy has her own office, too. She told Elena that she would only come in when Elena needed help with something or someone.

On her desk, Elena has a large, modern, flat-screen computer monitor. When he hired her, Mr. Christov told Elena that he would

get her a new computer with a large, flat-screen monitor because she would be spending a lot of her time typing or doing Internet research. Mr. Christov kept his word.

There are a lot of things Elena has to learn. There is a new filing system, as well as a fax machine, a copy machine, a fancy printer, and even a paper shredder that she has to learn how to use. There are new accounting programs she has to operate. And she has to learn how to research many new Internet Web sites. But, with Amy to help her, she is pretty sure she will be able to learn all that sooner or later. The thing she worries most about is her English. Part of her job is to answer the phone and take messages. Another part is to help translate things for Russian clients if necessary. So, she is still working hard to improve her English as much as she can. Elena doesn't know what she will be doing a year from now, but for now she is very happy with her new job.

Page 166 (Lesson 1, Activity 5)

Listen *Listen to the conversations and take down the messages.*

1.

Mr. Brown: This is Mr. Brown. I'm calling for Mr. Christov.
Elena: He isn't in right now. Can I take a message?
Mr. Brown: Yes. Tell him I need some help with my taxes this year. Can I come in tomorrow?
Elena: OK. I'll ask him. Should he call you back?
Mr. Brown: Yes, please have him call me.

2.

Judy: Is Amy in the office? This is an old friend of hers.
Elena: No, she's in a meeting for the next couple of hours. Can I take a message for her?
Judy: Yes. Tell her that Judy called. Tell her I'll be in the neighborhood. Ask her if I can drop by to talk. I'll call back this afternoon.
Elena: OK. I'll give her the message.

3.

Sid: This is Sid Kane, calling for Mr. Christov. Is he in?
Elena: No, he's in court today. Can I take a message?
Sid: Sure. Tell him Sid called . . .
Elena: S-I-D?
Sid: Yes, Sid Kane. K-a-n-e. Tell him I'll accept his last offer. He'll know what it's about.
Elena: OK. I'll tell him.

Page 170 (Lesson 2, Activity 3)

Listen *Listen to the conversation between Elena and Mr. Christov. Help Elena fill in the information on the travel Web site.*

Elena: Mr. Christov, I'm on the travel Web site right now. I need to ask you a couple of questions so I can start the search.
Mr. Christov: OK. Go ahead.
Elena: Do you want to look for a hotel room with the flight?
Mr. Christov: Why not? Let's just see what kind of price they offer.
Elena: I know you're going from New York to L.A. and the departure date is April seventeenth, but I wasn't sure of the return date.
Mr. Christov: I think I'd like to return on Sunday, the twenty-second.
Elena: Do you want to travel on those exact dates? Or should I look for a lower price within one to three days of the date?

Mr. Christov: Why don't you look for a lower price. I guess I am a little bit flexible. I could stay a day or two longer if the price is much lower.

Elena: And is it for one adult only?

Mr. Christov: No, it will be two adults.

Elena: OK. I'll get you the information in a few minutes.

Page 173 (Lesson 3, Activity 1)

Read and Listen *Read the story. Then listen to the story.*

Following Directions

One of the hardest things about starting a new job is learning the rules and expectations of the job. There are a lot of things Elena has to learn about her new job. There are a lot of new directions she has to follow. Fortunately, she has a boss who is very patient.

The first thing she had to learn was how to answer the phone properly. She is supposed to say, "Christov Associates, how may I help you?" That isn't a sentence she hears in her everyday life. It is more formal English that is appropriate for a law office.

Elena also has to learn about the rules of the office. One way to learn is to read memos and the employee handbook. But, fortunately, she has her coworker Amy, who is willing to help her. On the second day of her job, Elena brought a cup of coffee from lunch back to the office. "If I were you," Amy said, "I wouldn't drink coffee in the office." "If I were you, I wouldn't . . ." is Amy's favorite expression. That is how she warns Elena whenever she does something wrong.

"If you spill coffee on any of Mr. Christov's legal papers,'" she said, "he'll hand you your walking papers." She explained that that meant she would be fired. Idioms are another thing that Amy is helping Elena with.

Elena has to learn how to operate several new machines. She has to learn how to access several important Web sites. She has to learn a lot of legal vocabulary and terminology. She has to learn several organizational charts. But she realizes that if she were Daisy, she would have to learn rules about the school district. If she were Vicki, she would have to learn rules about customer service. If she were Alice, she would have to learn a lot of medical vocabulary and terminology. So, everybody has to learn the rules of his or her job. Elena's plan is to learn it all as quickly as she can.

Page 177 (Chapter Review, Activity 1)

Read and Listen *Read the story. Then listen to the story.*

Changes

Having a new full-time job has made Elena's life better in some ways, but more challenging in other ways. A full-time job takes time. It requires not just eight hours a day on the job, but also time to learn the new things that she needs to know to do her job well. Mr. Christov told her at her job interview that he wanted a dedicated, hard worker for the position. Of course, nobody asked her if she had any children because that is an illegal question to ask at a job interview. But Elena has a child. If she didn't have Sasha, it would be a lot easier to work long hours. But her child needs time, too.

After she got her new job, Elena had to explain to Sasha that she wouldn't be able to pick him up from school anymore. She told him that his grandma would be picking him up and he would be staying at Grandma's house for a while after school every day. He looked very sad, and asked if Grandma would help him with his homework after school like Elena always did. "Honey," she told him, "you know your grandma doesn't speak English very well."

Elena's friends were sympathetic about her problem. Daisy told her that it was going to be difficult to get used to the new schedule, but she eventually would. Alice told her that she would just have to make the best of it.

After her first week of full-time work, Elena was feeling depressed. She decided to call Alex in Russia. When he answered the phone, he sounded excited. "Did you get my message?" he asked. She told him that she hadn't gotten any message. She started to talk about the problems with her new schedule, but he stopped her. "Elena," he said, "it was approved."

For a moment, she didn't know what he was talking about.

"Elena," he said, "my application was approved! I'm coming to New York."

"You're coming to New York?"

"Yes," he said. "Soon. As soon as possible."

"Is it true?" she said. "I can't believe it!"

She had never felt so happy in her whole life.

Page 181 (Chapter 9 Review)

Pronunciation *Sentence rhythm and stress*

In most English sentences, only the important words are stressed. If we stress every word equally, the speaker sounds angry. Listen to the sentences with equal stress.

1. **I won't be attending the meeting.**
2. **I am ready to leave now.**
3. **Can I please have a check?**

Now listen and repeat the same sentences with normal stress.

1. I **won't** be **attend**ing the **meet**ing.
2. I'm **ready** to **leave** now.
3. Can I **please** have a **check**?

Chapter 10:
Government and the Law

Page 182 (Chapter Opening, Activity 1)

Read and Listen *Read the story. Then listen to it.*

The Law

Now that Elena works in a law office, she has been thinking a lot about the law. She is now aware of how many people break the law every day. Today she took a walk on Ocean Avenue and counted all the illegal activities she saw along the way. She saw a motorcycle rider, not wearing a helmet, speed through a red light. She saw numerous people cross streets in the middle of a block or at a red light. Although it is against the law to write on someone's property, she saw graffiti on several walls that she passed. Hitchhiking is illegal in New York, but she saw a teenage girl doing just that.

The law says that all dogs must be licensed and on leashes, but she saw several people walking dogs without leashes. Although it's against the law to sleep on the street, she saw two homeless men sleeping in alleys. The law prohibits littering, but she saw plenty of trash on the street. The law says you are not allowed to sell or give cigarettes to minors, but she saw several teenagers smoking anyway. She even saw two guys who were probably selling and buying stolen watches.

She also saw people breaking traffic laws: people not wearing seat belts, making illegal turns, double parking, and speeding. And what about the violations she couldn't see? How many people were driving without insurance or without a license? How many people didn't file their tax returns? How many young men hadn't registered with the selective service? There are so many laws to keep track of, Elena thought, and so many people who are breaking them. Maybe that's why there are so many lawyers!

Listen *Listen and fill in the missing words in the story.*

Taxes

Vicki didn't file her tax return on time this year. She knew she (1)<u>was supposed to</u> file her return by April 15th, but she was going on vacation and just didn't want to think about taxes. "It's OK," Elena told her, "you (2)<u>can</u> file a Form 4868 instead. Form 4868," Elena explained, "is a request for an automatic four-month extension. When you file Form 4868, you (3)<u>don't have to</u> file your return until (4)<u>August 15th</u>." "The bad news," Elena said, "is that you still (5)<u>have to pay</u> all your taxes by the normal tax deadline. And if you owe money and you don't pay by the deadline, you will have to pay penalties and interest, too."

Vicki didn't like that idea at all. But, Elena cheered her up again. "Actually, you (6)<u>shouldn't have</u> a problem. You don't have a very high income so you (7)<u>can't</u> owe very much. In fact, you (8)<u>might not</u> owe any taxes at all. If your employer withheld the right amount from your paychecks, you (9)<u>shouldn't</u> owe anything. You will probably get a refund. And if the government owes you money, you are (10)<u>allowed to</u> wait as long as you want to file your tax return."

Now it is August and Vicki has decided that she (11)<u>had better not</u> wait any longer. She got her W2 form and a 1040 EZ form and copied the information from her W2 to the (12)<u>tax return</u>. She put in her exemptions and standard deduction. When she subtracted that from her gross income, she saw that she didn't owe any money! Then she signed the form. She wasn't filing a joint return so she (13)<u>didn't have to</u> have anyone else sign it. Then she went to the post office and sent it by certified mail. There are two addresses where all returns (14)<u>are supposed</u> to be sent. She sent hers to the one for people who are getting a refund. Now she just (15)<u>has to</u> decide what she is going to do with the money!

Listen *Listen and check your answers to Activity 1.*

Citizenship

Elena has now been living in (1)<u>the</u> United States for more than six years and has decided to become (2)<u>a</u> naturalized citizen. After you have been (3)<u>a</u> resident for at least five years, you are eligible to apply for U.S. citizenship, if you are (4)<u>a</u> person of "good moral character." Elena hasn't been convicted of any felonies, so she filled out (5)<u>an</u> application and sent it in. Now she is waiting for (6)<u>an</u> appointment for her interview.

At (7)<u>the</u> interview they will ask her questions about U.S. history and government. And they will ask her to write (8)<u>a</u> sentence or two in English. You are supposed to be able to speak, read, and write English, and you are supposed to know (9)<u>a</u> little about U.S. history and government in order to pass (10)<u>the</u> interview test.

Elena has worked in (11)<u>a</u> law office for more than five years, so she doesn't think she will have any trouble passing (12)<u>the</u> test. But, just to be sure, she has been studying information about U.S. history and government. Some of (13)<u>the</u> questions they might ask are easy. You are supposed to know that (14)<u>the</u> stars on the flag represent (15)<u>the</u> fifty states in (16)<u>the</u> union, and that (17)<u>the</u> stripes represent (18)<u>the</u> thirteen original colonies. You are supposed to know a little bit about (19)<u>the</u> Constitution. They expect you to know about (20)<u>the</u> three branches of government: (21)<u>the</u> executive, (22)<u>the</u> legislative, and (23)<u>the</u> judicial. And you are expected to know that there are 100 senators in (24)<u>the</u> Senate and 435 congressmen in (25)<u>the</u> House of Representatives.

Elena knows all of that, so she doesn't think she will have any trouble. But, she is studying anyway because she really wants to become (26)<u>a</u> United States citizen.

Listen *Listen to the conversations about three U.S. presidents. Take notes about each president. Write the most important things you hear.*

1.
A: What do you know about George Washington?
B: I know quite a bit about him, don't you?
A: Well, I know they call him the father of our country, and I know that he was the first president. But, did he really have wooden teeth?
B: I'm not sure if he had wooden teeth, but I don't think that's very important. Do you know that he was the leader of the Revolutionary Army that won the war of Independence from England? Without Washington there probably wouldn't be a United States of America.
A: I guess that's why his face is on the dollar bill.
B: And on the quarter.

2.
A: What do you know about Thomas Jefferson?
B: He was a great man. He was one of the most important founding fathers of the country.
A: He was the third president, wasn't he?
B: Yes, he was. And he wrote the Declaration of Independence. Along with the Constitution, the Declaration of Independence is the most important statement of what our country is supposed to be about.
A: So, he wrote the Declaration of Independence, and he was the third president.
B: And his face is on one of our bills.
A: Which one?
B: The two-dollar bill, of course. Not to mention the nickel

3.
A: What do you know about Abraham Lincoln? Was he one of the founding fathers?
B: No, he was the sixteenth president actually. That was almost a hundred years after the founding fathers.
A: So, why is he so famous?
B: Well, he was president during the Civil War. So, he was responsible for keeping the country together when the South wanted to leave the union.
A: And he ended slavery, didn't he?
B: Well, that was part of the reason for the Civil War, I guess.
A: He's on the five-dollar bill, isn't he?
B: Not only that, he's also on the penny.

Listen *Listen and take notes about the three branches of government.*

1.
A: What do you know about the three branches of government?
B: I know that the president is the head of the executive branch.
A: What else do you know about the executive branch?
B: Umm. The vice president and the cabinet are part of the executive branch, too. Their main duty is to enforce the laws. What else do you want to know?
A: How long is the president elected for?
B: The president's term is four years, and he can be re-elected once, but only once.

A: What happens if he dies in office?

B: The vice president becomes president. And then he appoints another vice president. And speaking of appointing—the president also appoints the Supreme Court justices when there is a vacancy on the court. That's an important part of his job. And, I almost forgot, he's also the commander-in-chief of the army.

2.

A: What do you know about the legislative branch of the government?

B: Quite a lot, actually. The legislative branch makes the laws. The two houses of Congress make up the legislative branch: The Senate and the House of Representatives.

A: How long are they elected for?

B: The term of a senator is six years. Representatives are elected every two years. There's no limit to how many times either one can be re-elected.

A: Which one is more important—the Senate or the House of Representatives?

B: Both houses are equally important. But since there are only 100 senators and there are 435 representatives, I guess an individual senator is more important. Also, their term is a lot longer.

3.

A: So, what do you know about the judicial branch of government?

B: The judicial branch consists of the Supreme Court and the other federal courts. The Supreme Court has nine justices.

A: Who are appointed by the president.

B: Right. And they are appointed for life. They can serve until they die or until they decide to retire.

A: Is that a good idea?

B: Yes, I think so.

A: OK, Mr. Smart Guy, who is the Chief Justice of the court right now?

B: Umm.

A: That would be John Roberts, wouldn't it?

Page 197 (Chapter 10 Review, Activity 1)

Read and Listen *Read the story. Then listen to the story.*

Congratulations

On a rainy Monday, Elena went to an office in downtown Brooklyn for her citizenship interview. She was nervous even though she had studied everything she needed to know. "All you have to do is be polite," Mr. Christov told her, "and answer any questions they ask you. You are the smartest young lady they will see all month."

The first thing Elena had to do was sit down and be patient because the interviewer was running behind schedule. When she finally went into the office, she smiled and shook the interviewer's hand. He invited her to sit down. Then he asked her a few questions from her application form. After that, he asked her about her job. And then he asked her a few questions about U.S. history and government. He asked her what the colors of the American flag were. Elena smiled because the flag was right behind him in his office. He asked her if she knew who wrote the Declaration of Independence. "That beautiful document was written by Thomas Jefferson," she said, "wasn't it?"

"Yes," he said, "that's right."

He asked her about the three branches of government, and she described them for him. Then he asked her who the Chief Justice of the Supreme Court was. That was a hard one and her mind went blank for a minute. "The Chief Justice," she finally said, "is John Roberts, isn't it?"

The interview looked surprised and then he smiled for the first time. "Yes," he said, "it certainly is."

When she left the building, Alex and Sasha were outside waiting for her. "What happened?" Alex asked. "Was it hard?"

"No," she said, "it wasn't hard at all."

"Congratulations, Mom," Sasha said. "I'm proud of you."

Elena put her arms around her husband and her son and hugged them both tight.

Page 199 (Chapter 10 Review)

Pronunciation *Tag questions*

When we think we know something but aren't sure, a tag question can be used for confirmation. In this case, a tag question has rising intonation like a yes/no question. Listen and practice saying the tag questions with rising intonation.

1. You passed the test, didn't you?
2. You have a license, don't you?
3. You aren't a citizen, are you?
4. She isn't your sister, is she?

Sometimes tag questions are used just to make conversation and we don't really want an answer. In this case, we use falling intonation.

1. Nice day, isn't it?
2. Terrible storm last night, wasn't it?

INDEX

ACADEMIC SKILLS

CULTURE TIPS

DOWNTOWN JOURNAL

GAME TIME

INTERNET IDEAS

NOTES

TOPICS